D1288721

THE PATIENT
AND THE ANALYST

THE PATIENT
AND THE ANALYST
The Basis of
the Psychoanalytic Process

Joseph Sandler
Christopher Dare
Alex Holder

Second Edition

Revised and expanded by
Joseph Sandler and Anna Ursula Dreher

INTERNATIONAL UNIVERSITIES PRESS, INC.
Madison · Connecticut

First published in 1973 by International Universities press, Inc.

Revised and enlarged edition published in 1992 by
International Universities press, Inc.
59 Boston Post Road
Madison, Connecticut 06443-1524

Library of Congress Cataloging-in-Publication Data
Sandler, Joseph.
   The patient and the analyst; the basis of the psychoanalytic
   process/Joseph Sandler, Christopher Dare, Alex Holder, —2nd ed.
   /rev. and expanded by Joseph Sandler and Anna Ursula Dreher.
      p. cm.
   Includes bibliographical references and index.
   ISBN 0-8236-4031-0
   1. Psychoanalysis. 2. Psychotherapist and patient. I. Dare,
   Christopher. II. Holder, Alex. III. Title.
      (DNLM: 1. Professional–Patient Relations. 2. Psychoanalysis—
      history. 3. Transference (Psychology). WM 11 S217p)
   RC506.S24 1992
   616.89'17—dc20
   DNLM/DLC
   for Library of Congress   92-1427
                                                                CIP

Manufactured in Great Britain

CONTENTS

PREFACE TO THE FIRST EDITION

Some three years ago we began an intensive research study on basic psychoanalytic concepts. This was felt to be necessary because of the difficulties we had encountered in teaching psychoanalytic theory to intelligent postgraduate students of psychiatry—a difficulty that, we had realized, was due in no small part to a lack of clarity in the concepts themselves. Fortunately, the clarification of certain basic ideas was a research task appropriate to our role in the Institute of Psychiatry. This book presents the results of our work in a form which we hope will make the basic clinical concepts of psychoanalysis clearer in their meaning and development. We also believe that it may provide the basis for the adequate and appropriate extension of psychoanalytic concepts to related fields, such as those of psycho-analytically orientated psychotherapy and casework. We hope that this book can help to dispel some of the mystique still surrounding psychoanalytic ideas. As students and teachers of psychoanalysis we found, in the course of this work, that our own thinking in this area had been substantially clarified and in many respects modified. It is our hope that this book will be of particular value to those training and teaching in psychoanalytic training institutes.

We are indebted to Sir Denis Hill, Professor of Psychiatry at the Institute of Psychiatry, for the special efforts which he made to provide us with the opportunity and facilities to carry out our work, and for his continued encouragement. Dr Eliot Slater risked his reputation as Editor-in-Chief of *The British Journal of Psychiatry* in accepting a series of ten papers (Sandler, Dare, & Holder, 1970a, b, c, d, 1971; Sandler, Holder, & Dare, 1970a, b, c, d, e; some additional material has been drawn from two other papers: Sandler, 1968, 1969) containing much of the work included in this book after seeing only the first two, and we are grateful to him for this, as for his tolerant and good-humoured support.

A number of colleagues—in particular Dr Max Hernandez, Dr Robert L. Tyson, and Mrs Anne-Marie Sandler—read drafts at various stages and helped us with their comments. Financial support was provided by the Bethlem Royal Hospital and the Maudsley Hospital Research Fund as well as the Foundation for Research in Psychoanalysis, Los Angeles. We valued in particular the personal interest shown by Mrs Lita Hazen and Dr Ralph R. Greenson of the latter foundation. We gratefully acknowledge the permission given to us by Sigmund Freud Copyrights Ltd, The Institute of Psycho-Analysis, Mrs Alix Strachey, and The Hogarth Press Ltd, for permission to quote from *The Standard Edition of the Complete Psychological Works of Sigmund Freud*, revised and edited by James Strachey.

London,
March, 1971

PREFACE TO THE SECOND EDITION

More than twenty years have passed since the papers that were drawn together to form *The Patient and the Analyst* were first published. Since then there have been a number of very significant developments in psychoanalytic thought, a consequence in part of the awareness of the 'widening scope of psychoanalysis' which began in the 1950s. In particular, attention has been paid in recent years to the involvement of the analyst as a partner in the analytic situation, and a move has been made away from the classical metaphor of the analyst-as-mirror. A greater understanding of the dimensions of transference and countertransference has been reached, and indeed each of the concepts treated in this book has undergone significant extension of meaning over the past two decades.

As a consequence, a second edition of this book was more than warranted, and we are grateful to the original authors for allowing us to revise and extend a work that has become a classic in its own right. The original text has been brought up to date, and substantial additions have been made. A new chapter has been added, and there are some 250 additional references to the literature, resulting in a new text that is half as long again as the first edition. It has, of course, not been our purpose to include all the existing literature on the clinical concepts of psychoanalysis— that would be an impossible task. However, we have tried to give an overview of the field and to give specific references where possible, so that the interested reader may find his own way further in the jungle of current psychoanalytic writings.

In the quotations from the published literature cited in the text we have taken the liberty of adhering as far as possible to a consistent spelling. As a consequence, some authors may be startled to find that their 's's have turned to 'z's, and vice versa, and cherished hyphens may have disappeared. While generally the spelling of 'fantasy' with an 'f' is used, it is written as 'phantasy' in extracts from Freud and from Kleinian authors. We hope that our colleagues will forgive us for this literary licence.

Special thanks are due to Jane Pettit for her careful editorial help and meticulous proofreading, to Paula Shop who carefully scanned and word-processed the text, as well as to Victoria Hamilton and Bruna Seu, who helped in researching some of the literature. Klara King, who translated the book into print, did a splendid job which we very much appreciated. We are indebted also to The Edith Ludowyk-Gyomroi Trust, London, and The Sigmund Freud Foundation, Frankfurt, for financial assistance towards the expenses involved in the preparation of this second edition. Finally, we want to thank Alex Holder for numerous useful suggestions.

J. S. and A. U. D.
London and Frankfurt
August, 1991

THE PATIENT
AND THE ANALYST

CHAPTER ONE

Introduction

This book is about basic psychoanalytic clinical concepts and their meanings. Many concepts that have developed within psychoanalysis, in particular those dealt with in this book, have been extended in their meaning, and it is one of the purposes of this work to examine some fundamental concepts from the point of view of the changes in meaning and usage that have occurred over time. The book is not, however, intended to be a sort of dictionary or glossary, although we believe that our discussion of basic psychoanalytic clinical concepts will lead to a better understanding of the role they play in present-day psychoanalysis.

The first two chapters introduce the discussion of specific terms. The philosophical implications of change of meaning when concepts are transferred from their original context have been discussed by a number of writers (e.g. Kaplan, 1964; Sandler, 1983; Schafer, 1976; Schon, 1963), and in this connection psychoanalytic theory presents special problems of its own. It is often regarded as being a completely integrated and consistent system

1

of thought, but this is far from being the case. Psychoanalytic concepts are not all well defined, and changes in their meanings have occurred as psychoanalysis has developed and aspects of its theory have changed. Moreover, in some cases a given term has been used with different meanings even at the same point in the historical development of psychoanalysis. Prime examples of this are the multiple meanings of such terms as *ego* (Hartmann, 1956), and of *identification* and *introjection* (Sandler, 1960b). It will be seen how strikingly the problems engendered by this enter into the concepts considered in this book. We find a situation within psychoanalysis in which the meaning of a concept is only fully discernible from an examination of the context in which it is used. The situation is complicated further by the fact that different schools of psychodynamic thought have inherited, and then modified for their own use, much of the same basic terminology (for example, the meanings given to *ego, self,* and *libido* in Jungian psychology are different from those in the Freudian literature). The overall purpose of the present work can be regarded as an attempt to facilitate communication, not only within the realm of clinical psychoanalysis itself, but also where situations other than the classical psychoanalytic treatment situation (such as psychotherapy and some forms of casework) need to be conceptualized in appropriate psychodynamic terms (see Sandler, 1969). This need is all the greater in view of the emphasis placed on training in psychotherapy as part of general psychiatric education.

In this context it is worth remembering that psychoanalysis refers not only to a specific treatment method but also to a body of theory which aspires to be a general psychology. Some of its concepts can be regarded as predominantly technical or clinical and do not form part of the general psychological model of psychoanalysis; it is these with which we are concerned in this book. Clinical concepts of this sort include, for example, *resistance*, a concept that refers to a set of clinical phenomena but can also be seen as a specific manifestation of the operation of the mechanisms of defence (part of general psychoanalytic psychology and regarded as existing in 'normal' as well as in disturbed persons). The distinction between clinical psychoanalytic concepts and those of general psychoanalytic psychology ('metapsychology') is important to bear in mind.

While the clinical concepts of psychoanalysis can be extended outside the psychoanalytic consulting room and may be capable of application in some degree to any therapeutic situation, such use may necessitate some re-evaluation and possible redefinition of the concepts. Thus, if we refer again to resistance, which was first defined in psychoanalysis as resistance to free association, there is no doubt that essentially the same phenomenon may show itself even in pharmacotherapy in the form of a patient's failure to take helpful medication. While this may reflect a process of resistance similar to that seen by the psychoanalyst, its definition in terms of free association cannot be sustained. All psychiatrists and social caseworkers are familiar with the phenomenon of resistance, even though forms of communication other than free association are involved.

The wish to give a precise definition of a concept, particularly a clinical one, cannot be entirely fulfilled if it is to be used in a variety of situations. The attempt to formulate precise definitions has led to difficulties and inconsistencies in the presentation of psychoanalytic concepts in the increasingly available psychoanalytic glossaries and dictionaries (e.g. Eidelberg, 1968; Hinshelwood, 1989; Laplanche & Pontalis, 1973; Moore & Fine, 1967, 1990; Rycroft, 1968). It is clear from both the virtues and the shortcomings of all these dictionaries that a historical approach is a *sine qua non* for the understanding of any psychoanalytic concept. For this reason, therefore, we will proceed more or less chronologically.

Psychoanalysis developed to a very great extent in and through the work of Freud, but during the course of its evolution Freud himself modified his formulations many times, revising concepts and adding new dimensions to technical procedures. This has also been true of psychoanalysis after Freud. Thus when one talks of one or other aspect of psychoanalysis, one has to stamp it with a date and also, for convenience, to divide the history of psychoanalysis into a number of phases (after Rapaport, 1959), beginning with Freud's early work.

After qualifying in medicine in Vienna in 1881 and working for a while as a physiologist in Meynert's laboratory, Freud journeyed to France to study with the eminent neurologist, Charcot. There he was impressed by the parallel drawn by Charcot between the phenomenon of mental dissociation that could be induced by hypnosis and the dissociation between a conscious and an unconscious part of the mind that appeared to occur in patients with gross hysterical symptoms. This dissociation was regarded by Charcot and by other French psychiatrists, notably Janet, as being due to some acquired or inherited fault in the nervous system, which also prevented the mind being held together in one piece, so to speak. On returning to Vienna, Freud began his collaboration with Josef Breuer, a physician who some years previously had found that a patient (the famous Anna O) suffering from hysterical symptoms experienced relief if allowed to talk freely under hypnosis. During and following his work with Breuer, Freud became convinced that the process of dissociation into conscious and unconscious regions of the mind was not specific to the psychoneuroses, but occurred in everyone. The appearance of neurotic symptoms was regarded as being due to the breaking through of pent-up unconscious forces that could not find adequate expression in some other way. He now saw this dissociation as *active,* as a process of defence whereby consciousness was protected from being overwhelmed by feelings and memories that were unpleasant or threatening. This belief in a process of active dissociation is one that has remained, in one form or another, as a central viewpoint in psychoanalytic writings, although at different times Freud and others have emphasized different aspects of the content of the dissociated and unconscious part of the mind. Initially, particularly during the course of his early work with Breuer, the unconscious content which was being defended against was regarded as consisting of emotionally charged memories of a real traumatic event. In the book which they published jointly, the well-known *Studies on Hysteria* (1895), *real* traumatic events were thought to lie behind the symptoms of the neurotic patient. Such traumatic experiences were postulated as having given rise to a 'charge of affect'. This, together with the memories of the traumatic event, was actively dissociated from consciousness and could find expression by being converted into symptoms. Based on this view, treatment consisted of a variety of attempts to force the forgotten memories into consciousness, thus simultaneously bringing about a discharge of affect in the form of 'catharsis' or 'abreaction'.

The *first phase* of psychoanalysis can be taken to include Freud's work with Breuer and lasted till 1897, when Freud discovered that many of the 'memories' of traumatic experiences, especially seductions, given to him by his hysterical patients were not in fact memories of real events at all, but rather accounts of fantasies (Freud, 1950a [1887–1902]).

The *second phase* can be regarded as having lasted from the point at which Freud rejected the trauma theory of neurosis until the early 1920s, when he introduced the so-called structural model of psychoanalysis (Freud, 1923). The second phase reflected a change from the early emphasis on external events (the traumatic situation) to an emphasis on unconscious wishes, promptings, and drives, and to the way in which these impulses manifested themselves on the surface. At this time the unconscious wishes came to be seen as largely sexual in nature. It was the phase in which attention was shifted predominantly to what came from within, to the way in which childhood reactions were repeated over and over again in the present. Attention was also directed to the study of what we might call the analyst's translation of the patient's conscious productions into their unconscious meaning. Indeed, the aim of psychoanalysis was seen by Freud as being 'to make what is unconscious conscious'. In this phase, as we might expect when we consider the inevitable to and fro of theory development, there was a radical swing from the consideration of the person's relation to external reality to the study of his relation to his unconscious wishes and impulses. Most of the clinical concepts that we consider in detail in this book had, as we shall see, their original elaborations in the second phase of psychoanalysis.

In 1900 Freud published *The Interpretation of Dreams* (1900a). His study of dreams provided an example of the way in which unconscious wishes were thought to find their way to the surface. The urge for direct expression of these wishes created a situation of conflict with the individual's assessment of reality and with his ideals. This conflict, between instinctual forces on the one hand and repressive or defensive forces on the other, resulted in the construction of compromise formations which represented attempts at obtaining fulfilment of the unconscious wishes in disguised form. Thus the *manifest dream content* could be considered to be a 'censored' or disguised fulfilment of an unconscious wish. Similarly, the free associations of the patient in analysis were also regarded as disguised derivatives of unconscious wishes.

In the second phase, as in the first, Freud assumed that there was a part of the mind or 'mental apparatus' which was conscious and a further, substantial, unconscious part. In this connection, Freud distinguished between two sorts of unconsciousness. One, represented by a 'system', the *Unconscious,* contained instinctual drives and wishes, which, if they were to be allowed to emerge into consciousness, would constitute a threat and would give rise to anxiety or other unpleasant feelings. The strivings in the Unconscious were seen as being constantly propelled towards discharge, but they could only be allowed expression in a distorted or censored form. The other sort of unconsciousness was that attributed to the *Preconscious* system, which contained knowledge and thoughts that were outside consciousness but not held back by the counterforces of repression, as were contents relegated to the Unconscious. Preconscious mental content could enter into consciousness at the appropriate time and could not only be utilized by the individual for rational tasks but could also be seized upon by wishes from the Unconscious in their attempts to force a passage through to consciousness—i.e. they could be used to represent these wishes. The model of the mental apparatus in the second phase is generally known as the 'topographical' model, and in it the Preconscious system was thought of as lying between the Unconscious and consciousness (the latter being the quality of the system *Conscious).*

Freud saw the instinctual drives as 'energies' which could be invested in different mental contents. (In English translations of Freud, the German word for 'investment' [*Besetzung*] has been rendered, in our view unfortunately, as 'cathexis'.) He made use of the term *libido* for the sexual energy of the instinctual drives, but, although aggression was later given a status equal in importance to sexuality, he coined no corresponding term for 'aggressive energy'. In the Unconscious these drive energies were regarded as being freely displaceable from one content to another and functioned according to the so-called *primary process.* Logical and formal relations between the elements in the Unconscious were regarded as absent: there was no awareness of time, and only simple and primitive rules of association applied. Drives and wishes in the Unconscious functioned according to the 'pleasure-principle', i.e. they were regarded as seeking discharge, gratification, and relief of painful tension at all costs. The systems Preconscious and Conscious could be considered as being in direct opposition to this. In them, logic, reason (*secondary process*), and the knowledge of external reality and of ideals and standards of conduct predominate. Unlike the Unconscious, the Preconscious and Conscious systems take (or attempt to take) external reality into account, to follow what Freud called the 'reality-principle'. Thus situations of conflict, for example between sexual wishes of a primitive sort which had been repressed into the Unconscious and the person's moral and ethical standards, must inevitably arise and some sort of solution sought which would take the opposing forces into account.

Thus far we have referred to the instinctual drives and instinctual wishes as if they were regarded as existing somewhat in isolation. In Freud's view this was far from being the case, as from early in the child's development the instinctual urges were seen as having become attached to important figures in the child's world, or objects, to use the unfortunately impersonal term employed by psychoanalysts to describe these emotionally significant figures. Every unconscious wish was regarded as having an object, and the same object could be the recipient of quite opposing wishes manifested typically in feelings of both love and hate for the same person. This *ambivalence* is in itself a most potent source of mental conflict. Freud took the view that people, in their adult relationships to others, repeated (often in a very disguised way) their infantile attachments and conflicts, and that this tendency to repetition was often at the root of a great many of the difficulties that his patients brought.

Among the early conflicts of the child reconstructed through analysis, one constellation—the Oedipus complex, in which the child, at about the age of four or five, has to deal with a conflict of the most intense sort in regard to his wishes and object relationships—was thought to be universal. Essentially Freud regarded it as the wish of the little boy to have intercourse with his mother, to possess her completely, and to get rid of father in some way, not the most uncommon being to have him die. These wishes were seen by Freud as being in conflict with the little boy's love for his father, and also with his fear of rejection or bodily damage at his hands, in particular the fear of father's retaliatory damage to his genitals, the so-called 'castration anxiety'. The picture in regard to the little girl is somewhat similar, the roles of the parents being reversed, although in both boys and girls the two opposing constellations are also thought to exist. Thus we find in the boy a wish to be possessed by the father and to be rid of mother, a consequence of the innate bisexuality in everyone, male or female.

These views of mental functioning and infantile sexuality were the product of the second phase, a period of intense study of the vicissitudes of unconscious instinctual drives, particularly sexual drives (Freud, 1905d), and their derivatives. It has been described here at some length because of its importance for the more detailed consideration of the clinical concepts discussed in the chapters that follow. In the context of the psychological model of the second phase, these concepts can be regarded as relatively simple and straightforward. However, as we shall show, developments in Freud's thinking caused complications to appear.

The *third phase* can be dated from 1923, when a decisive change occurred in Freud's conceptualization of mental functioning. Freud had been deeply impressed by the operation in his patients of what he could only conceive of as an unconscious sense of guilt. In addition, a number of inconsistencies and contradictions were emerging in the detailed application of the 'topographical' division of the mental apparatus into the systems Unconscious, Preconscious and Conscious, and this led Freud to put forward a revised theoretical model. Perhaps it would be more appropriate to say that he introduced a further point of view, for his new formulations did not entirely replace the former ones but rather existed alongside them. It was such a situation we had in mind when we referred earlier to the fact that psychoanalysis, as a developing body of thought, does not have a fully consistent and integrated theoretical model. In 1923 Freud formulated, in *The Ego and the Id* (1923b), the 'structural' model, or what has been called the 'second topography'—the three-fold division of the mental apparatus into what he referred to as *id*, *ego*, and *superego*.

The *id* was seen as corresponding roughly to much of what had been encompassed by the concept of the Unconscious. It can be regarded as that area of the mind containing the primitive instinctual drives, with all their hereditary and constitutional elements. It is dominated by the pleasure principle, and it functions according to the primary process. During maturation and development and as a consequence of the interaction with the external world, a portion of the id undergoes modification to become the *ego*. The primary function of the ego was seen as the task of self-preservation and the acquisition of means whereby a simultaneous adaptation to the pressures of the id and the demands of reality can be brought about. It gains the capacity to delay instinctual discharge, or to control it by means of a variety of mechanisms, including the mechanisms of defence. The third agency, the *superego,* was seen as developing as a sort of internal precipitate or residue of the child's early conflicts, particularly in relation to his parents or other figures of authority and his identifications with them. The superego is the vehicle of the conscience, including that part of the conscience which is regarded as unconscious; for large parts of the superego, as well as of the ego, and all of the id, were seen as functioning outside consciousness.

It is worth mentioning that in this 'structural' theory there is again a change of emphasis from that which dominated the previous phase. The ego's role was seen to be that of a mediator, a problem-solver, having at each and every moment to meet the demands arising from the id, from the superego, and from the external world. In order to resolve these often conflicting demands, the ego has at times to create the most complicated compromises, and in the last resort these compromises may result in the symptoms which, although painful and distressing to the individual who experiences them, represent the best possible adaptation that he can bring about in the particular circumstances. Such compromises are regarded as entering into the formation of character and personality, into choice of career and love-objects, and into all those things which go into making any one person a unique individual.

This particular phase in the development of psychoanalysis lasted till Freud's death in 1939. This is a rather arbitrary dating, for what we can refer to as the *fourth phase* represents the contributions of psychoanalysts other than Freud. Thus there were important additions to theory and practice from the time that colleagues first came to be associated with Freud in his work and identified themselves with his point of view.

An important line of development in the fourth phase of psychoanalytic theory, although already evident in Freud's work, was given a strong impetus by the publication in 1936 of Anna Freud's *The Ego and the Mechanisms of Defence* and in 1939 by Hartmann's *Ego Psychology and the Problem of Adaptation*. Anna Freud drew attention to the role of defence mechanisms in normal mental functioning and extended the concept of defence to include defence against dangers arising both from the external world and from internal instinctual impulses. Hartmann placed special emphasis on the innate development of what he called the 'conflict-free sphere' of the ego. Whereas Freud had orientated himself constantly towards clinical phenomena and to the way in which special skills and capacities can develop in the individual as means of resolving conflict, Hartmann maintained that there are many areas of normal functioning that follow a relatively autonomous course of development and are not the product of mental conflict. What was called 'ego psychology' represented the special interests of many psychoanalysts who placed normal as well as abnormal ego functioning at the centre of their attention. However, the relevant contributions of psychoanalysts other than Freud will be discussed throughout this book where appropriate, and there is no need to mention them in any detail here. It is, nevertheless, necessary to point out that much of current psychoanalytic thinking, particularly that part relating to the clinical situation, is still firmly rooted in the second phase of psychoanalysis. In describing their patients, psychoanalysts make use of topographical (i.e. second phase) concepts alongside those of the structural theory of the third phase, although heroic efforts have been made by certain psychoanalysts (e.g. Arlow & Brenner, 1964) to write psychoanalytic theory entirely in terms of the concepts of the structural theory.

From the 1960s, ego psychology in the United States began, to a certain degree, to give way to a number of new developments, which are considered in the chapters that follow. These include, among others, the 'self psychology' of Heinz Kohut and the 'object relations' approach of Edith Jacobson, Hans Loewald, and Otto Kernberg. Kernberg's views can be seen as a development from both ego psychology and the views of Melanie Klein. In Britain the Kleinian school has been extremely influential, as has the work of the British object relations theorists Ronald Fairbairn, Michael Balint, and Donald Winnicott. In recent years the writings of Wilfred Bion have been regarded as important, and the controversial views of Jacques Lacan have played a significant role in the consideration of psychoanalysis in certain intellectual circles. The work of developmental psychoanalysts, beginning with Margaret Mahler and continuing with the so-called 'baby watchers' such as Daniel Stern and Robert Emde, has been regarded by many psychoanalysts as being of the utmost relevance for the psychoanalytic understanding of human development.

The psychoanalytic theory of the mind has undergone substantial elaboration since Freud, and the gap between psychoanalytic theories and their application has steadily widened. Accordingly, it has become all the more important to consider and reconsider the clinical concepts of psychoanalysis.

CHAPTER TWO

The analytic situation

The clinical concepts used to describe, understand, and explain the psychoanalytic treatment process have arisen at different points in the history of psychoanalysis. Terms that derived their original meaning in the context of one phase have been carried over into later phases, with the sort of repercussions we have alluded to earlier and shall discuss later. In this chapter we shall try to describe the development of the psychoanalytic treatment setting in relation to the different phases of psychoanalysis (see chapter one).

The first phase (which was essentially pre-psychoanalytic) lasted until 1897 and was principally characterized by the application of the hypnotic method to hysterical patients. With the inclusion of patients suffering from other disturbances (e.g. obsessional disorders), Freud saw his methods as being appropriate to the treatment of the 'neuropsychoses' (which would now be called the neuroses). The setting in the first phase was the usual one in use at the time for inducing hypnosis in the consulting

room. It was conducted in privacy, as opposed to the public dem-
onstrations of such workers as Charcot, and the patient lay on a
couch while the therapist, sitting behind him, induced a state of
hypnosis. Freud was disappointed with the results obtained by
hypnosis (he also confessed that he was not very good at it), and
he later tried to encourage the recall of forgotten events by a
variety of other methods. One of these was to apply pressure with
his hand to the patient's forehead with the suggestion that this
would bring thoughts to mind, as described in the case of Frau
P. J. (1950a [1887–1902]). While such techniques were later to be
replaced by 'free association' on the part of the patient, the structure of the treatment situation of the first phase persisted. As
Freud put it later (1925d):

> My patients, I reflected, must in fact 'know' all the things which
> had hitherto only been made accessible to them in hypnosis;
> and assurances and encouragement on my part . . . would, I
> thought, have the power of forcing the forgotten facts and con-
> nections into consciousness. No doubt this seemed a more labo-
> rious process than putting the patients into hypnosis, but it
> might prove highly instructive. So I abandoned hypnosis, only
> retaining my practice of requiring the patient to lie upon a sofa
> while I sat behind him, seeing him, but not seen myself.

In chapter one we described Freud's change of view in 1897
from the traumatogenic theory of neurosis to one in which the role
of conflict over the expression of unconscious instinctual
wishes was seen to be of paramount importance. This change of
view coincided, more or less, with the technical emphasis on un-
ravelling the meaning of the patient's conscious productions, in
particular dreams which, in the early years of the second phase,
were regarded as being the most important part of the patient's
material and are still regarded as the most important source of
unconscious material by many psychoanalysts. They certainly
have a special significance for all analysts. Much of Freud's analytic work was initially directed towards the painstaking analysis
of dreams, the analyst being assisted by the patient's associations
to the various parts of the remembered dream. Dream analysis
provided the basis for Freud's understanding of mental processes
in general, although as the second phase progressed, the under-

standing of the unconscious meaning of the patient's productions was extended to his free associations, and analysis of transference, especially of transference resistances, came to play a major role in psychoanalytic technique. During the second phase, which lasted until 1923, the basic psychoanalytic treatment setting, and the clinical concepts related to it, were developed. Although major theoretical changes occurred during the later phases of psychoanalysis, the 'classical' psychoanalytic treatment situation has remained essentially that of the second phase. By the time Freud came to write his 'technical' papers on psychoanalysis (1911e, 1912b, 1912e, 1913c, 1914g, 1915a), the technique had been formalized. It is worth noting, however, that at that time the patient was expected to attend six days a week, for sessions of an hour each.

Some years later in *An Autobiographical Study* (1925d) Freud commented that:

It may seem surprising that this method of free association, carried out subject to the observation of the *fundamental rule of psycho-analysis*, should have achieved what was expected of it, namely the bringing into consciousness of the repressed material which was held back by resistances. We must, however, bear in mind that free association is not really free. The patient remains under the influence of the analytic situation even though he is not directing his mental activities on to a particular subject. We shall be justified in assuming that nothing will occur to him that has not some reference to that situation. His resistance against reproducing the repressed material will now be expressed in two ways. Firstly it will be shown by critical objections; and it was to deal with these that the fundamental rule of psychoanalysis was invented. But if the patient observes that rule and so overcomes his reticences, the resistance will find another means of expression. It will so arrange it that the repressed material itself will never occur to the patient but only something which approximates to it in an allusive way; and the greater the resistance, the more remote from the actual idea that the analyst is in search of will be the substitutive association that the patient has to report. The analyst, who listens composedly but without any constrained effort to the stream of associations and who, from his experience, has a general notion of what to expect, can make use of the material brought to light by the patient according to two possibilities. If the resistance is slight he will be able from the patient's allusions to infer the unconscious material itself; or if the resistance is stronger he will be able to recognize its character from the associations, as they seem to become more remote from the topic in hand, and will explain it to the patient. Uncovering the resistance, however, is the first step towards overcoming it.

The 'basic model of psychoanalysis' (Eissler, 1953) can be described as follows. The patient is, as a rule, in possession of relatively few personal facts about the psychoanalyst. The analyst attempts to maintain this area of relative ignorance on the patient's part, but encourages him to talk as freely as possible (free association) about his thoughts as they come into his mind during the daily sessions, however illogical they may be or apparently disconnected with what has been expressed before. Stone (1961) has given an excellent and detailed account of the psychoanalytic situation.

The analyst also applies as far as possible 'the rule of abstinence', according to which:

> the analytic treatment should be so organised as to ensure that the patient finds as few substitutive satisfactions for his symptoms as possible. The implication for the analyst is that he should refuse on principle to satisfy the patient's demands and to fulfil the roles which the patient tends to impose upon him. In certain cases, and at certain moments during the treatment, the rule of abstinence may be given explicit expression in the form of advice about the patient's repetitive behaviour which is hindering the work of recollection and the working out. [Laplanche & Pontalis, 1973]

The psychoanalytic session is normally of 50 minutes' duration, four or five times a week. The psychoanalyst's contributions will tend to be limited to questions to elucidate the material and to *interpretations, confrontations*, and *reconstructions* (chapter ten) which represent the major therapeutic interventions. In the course of his associations the patient will begin to evade certain topics and to show signs of *resistance* (chapter seven) to expressing certain thoughts and to the psychoanalytic procedure, although he may not know he is doing this. The psychoanalyst expects that the material produced by the patient will, sooner or later, contain overt or covert references to thoughts and feelings about the psychoanalyst which will have that quality of distortion of reality which is referred to as *transference* (chapters four and five). These distortions are the result of the modification of the patient's present perceptions and thoughts by the addition of specific components derived from past wishes, experiences, and relationships. A distinction is often made between such transference phenomena and the working relationship that develops between patient and psychoanalyst, based, among other things, on the patient's wish to recover and to co-operate in treatment. This working relationship, the *treatment alliance* (chapter three) is regarded as including, as an essential part, the patient's motivation for continuing in analysis in the face of his resistances. At times the patient will not bring emergent past and present feelings verbally but rather in the form of behaviour and acts which may also be expressed in a displaced form outside the consulting room. The latter is often referred to as an aspect of *acting out* (chapter nine).

The demands of the psychoanalytic procedure on the analyst naturally include his conscious attempts to understand the patient's material in order to make his interventions. In addition to this, he is faced with the necessity to scan his reactions to the patient in an attempt to determine his own blocks in appreciating the meaning of the patient's communications. Such scanning of his own feelings and reactions also enables the analyst to obtain further insight into what is going on in the patient through his appreciation of his own emotional responses to the patient. These aspects of the analyst's reactions are conceptualized as *countertransference* (see chapter six). If the patient is able to gain and to retain an understanding of links between his conscious and unconscious tendencies, and between the present and the past, he is said to have acquired a degree of *insight* (see chapter eleven).

Interpretations given by the analyst, even if they seem to increase the patient's insight, are not always immediately effective in producing a significant change in the patient. A period of time has to be allowed for *working through* (chapter twelve) during which time the ramifications both of interpretations and the material encompassed by them are explored and extended. At times, when the patient appears to have made significant progress, he may have what appears to be a paradoxical relapse. This may be a manifestation of a *negative therapeutic reaction* (chapter eight), initially attributed to the workings of an unconscious sense of guilt (Freud, 1923b) related to the significance to the patient of a perceived improvement.

It is obvious that the 'model situation' as described here does not apply to every psychoanalytic treatment, and that from time to time special alterations of the technical procedure have to be introduced. These have been referred to as 'parameters of technique' (Eissler, 1953), but the introduction of such 'parameters' (e.g. sitting up rather than lying on the couch, changing the frequency of the sessions) is regarded, from the point of view of the basic model of psychoanalysis, as a temporary expedient. In this respect, the methods of psychoanalysis have been contrasted with some other forms of psychotherapy in which the so-called 'parameters' have been extensively and regularly employed. Adaptations of psychoanalytic technique to make it suitable for special classes of disturbances have been increasingly prominent during the fourth phase of psychoanalysis.

The bald and simplified account given in this chapter and the previous one is intended to serve as an introduction to the more detailed examination of some of the clinical psychoanalytic concepts to which we have referred. In the chapters that follow we discuss the historical vicissitudes of each concept within the clinical framework of psychoanalysis. We also examine the multiplicities and ambiguities of meanings within that framework and explore the degree to which such concepts are available for application in situations other than that of classical psychoanalytic treatment.

A feature of the psychoanalytic process that deserves special mention is the occurrence of the phenomenon of *regression*. While the term has been used in a number of senses in psychoanalytic theory, we are concerned in this book with one specific meaning of regression, i.e. the emergence of past, often infantile, trends that are thought to represent the reappearance of modes of functioning that had been abandoned or modified. Regression of this sort appears as a characteristic part of the psychoanalytic process, but the same phenomenon can also be seen outside analysis. We need only note the way in which a toddler may relinquish bowel control in the period of stress following the birth of a sibling, or the way in which a child (or adult) may become clinging and demanding when ill. Such regressions, which may affect any part of personality functioning, may be temporary or more permanent, slight or severe. Regressions of this sort are to be expected at critical phases in the individual's development and, unless unusually prolonged or severe, may be regarded as normal (A. Freud, 1965).

In psychoanalytic treatment one of the functions of the analytic situation is to permit or to facilitate regression within the analytic setting. Regressive trends are seen most clearly in analysis as transference phenomena develop, and appear in the re-emergence of childhood wishes, feelings, modes of relating, fantasies, and in behaviour towards the analyst. However, as well as being an essential vehicle whereby important data and ways of functioning are brought from the past in a convincing and meaningful way, regression may at times also have a more obstructive and damaging aspect. This is particularly so when it becomes intense or prolonged in patients who have a tendency to regress, and who may then experience difficulty in regaining that capacity for self-observation and insight which is a necessary part of the analytic treatment alliance (chapters three and eleven). It appears to be likely that different psychoanalysts vary in the degree to which they (consciously or unconsciously) encourage regressive trends in their patients.

As a consequence of the normal analytic regression, it is quite common that the patient may become, at some stage in the course of the analysis, increasingly demanding of love, affection, and tokens of esteem from the analyst; hostile feelings towards the analyst may also develop. The way in which such feelings and attitudes develop can be an important source of understanding of the early relationship between the patient and, for instance, a mother who was experienced as depriving or withdrawn, loving or indulgent. Such information may constitute essential material for understanding the patient's current difficulties and problems. However, if demandingness or hostility become the main point of the patient's communications to the analyst and the analyst is unable to reverse this trend through appropriate interpretations or other interventions, the capacity to pursue the analytic work may be impaired or even lost. This is evident in certain special varieties of transference (chapter five).

A number of authors have pointed out the value of the ability to regress inside and outside the psychoanalytic situation. For example, Kris (1952) has discussed the role of the capacity for controlled and temporary regression in the realm of artistic creativity. Balint (1934, 1949, 1965, 1968) and Winnicott (1954) have stressed the importance of the patient's regression as a means of obtaining access to material that would not otherwise be available. Winnicott's concept of a 'holding environment' and his discussion of transitional phenomena (1951) have led a number of authors to elaborate on the idea that the analytic situation can provide a 'transitional space' in which the patient, in his safe relationship to the analyst, can regress, experiment with new ideas, and try out resolutions of internal problems (see Adler, 1989; Giovacchini, 1987a). Balint has called this 'regression in the service of progression'. It should be noted that although the term 'regression' had a number of meanings in Freud's writings, we are concerned in this chapter with what he called *formal* regression, 'where primitive methods of expression and representation take the place of the usual ones', and *temporal* regression, i.e. 'a harking back to older psychical structures' (Freud, in a passage added in 1914 to *The Interpretation of Dreams*, 1900a). However, regression need not necessarily be seen as a 'going back to the past'; it can also be viewed as a sort of 'release' phenomenon in which current unconscious tendencies become manifest in the special circumstances of the analytic situation. These include various forms of 'externalization' of internal processes and relationships which are based on projection and projective identifications (see chapters four, five, and six).

Regression may well be the path to the development of useful and appropriate analytic material that can be dealt with in the analysis, but reliance should not be placed on it as a therapeutic agent in its own right, nor on the idea that regression can bring to the surface aspects of the very early mother–child relationship which might not otherwise be available to the analyst. In Balint's view regression is thought to facilitate the development of a 'new beginning', but many analysts take the view that the role of regression as a therapeutic agent in itself has been overvalued (see, for instance, Anna Freud, 1969). Modell (1989) puts it well when he says: 'I do not question the validity of the clinical observations offered by Balint and Winnicott. The fact that aspects of an early mother–child relationship can be recreated in the transference cannot be doubted. What is at fault here is the use of regression as an explanation for the therapeutic action of the analytic setting.'

In chapter three the role of the treatment alliance in analysis is discussed, and some aspects of the contribution of the analyst to the analytic procedure are considered. Among these we have to include the 'holding' function of the analyst and of the analytic situation, i.e. the function of providing an atmosphere in which the patient can feel safe and 'contained' even when severe regression has occurred (e.g. Balint, 1968; Khan, 1972; Modell, 1984; Spitz, 1956; Winnicott, 1954, 1965, 1971).

The description of the analytic situation given thus far has emphasized what is required of the patient, and the role of the analyst has been seen as being that of one who attempts to understand the unconscious processes occurring in the patient and to convey this understanding to him. However, the view that the interpersonal aspects of the analytic process are of paramount importance has been receiving increasing attention in recent years (for example, Bleger, 1967, 1981; Kohut, 1977; McLaughlin, 1983; Modell, 1988, 1989; Spruiell, 1983), with emphasis being placed on the analytic *relationship*. Consequently, the notion of the analyst's 'neutrality' in the analytic situation has been increasingly questioned (see Leider, 1984). In this regard Modell (1988) says that 'we need to recognize that the process of defence and resistance occurs not only intrapsychically but also in the context of a two person relationship. For this reason attention must be paid to the process of communication and the process of relatedness.'

The provision of an appropriate atmosphere by the analyst is extremely important. Psychoanalytic treatment is not simply a process of making the unconscious conscious or of giving increased strength and autonomy to the patient's ego. It is vital that the analyst provide a setting in which the analytic process can occur and connections with split-off aspects of the self, which have been defended against, can be set up again. Rycroft (1985) has underlined the fact that the ability of the analyst to provide such a setting depends not only on his skill in making 'correct' interpretations but also on the analyst's capacity to maintain a sustained interest in, and relationship with, his patients.

CHAPTER THREE

The treatment alliance

A s we noted in chapter two, much attention has been paid in recent years to the relationship between patient and doctor. Psychoanalytic concepts have been applied in order to formulate various aspects of this relationship, and one of those most commonly taken from its original context and applied outside it is that of *transference*, now often loosely used in a variety of senses—even as a synonym for 'relationship' in general. We will discuss the concept in greater detail in chapters four and five.

A distinction has always been made within clinical psychoanalysis between 'transference proper' and another aspect of the patient's relation to the doctor which has been variously referred to as the 'therapeutic alliance', 'working alliance', or 'treatment alliance'—i.e. an alliance between patient and analyst necessary for the successful carrying out of the therapeutic work (e.g. Curtis, 1979; Eagle & Wolitzky, 1989; Friedman, 1969; Gitelson, 1962; Greenson, 1965a, 1967; Gutheil & Havens, 1979; Kanzer, 1981; Loewald, 1960; Stone, 1961, 1967; Tarachow, 1963; Zetzel, 1956). Terms other than 'alliance' have also been used. Fenichel

(1941), for example, writes of 'rational transference', Stone (1961) of 'mature transference', and Greenacre (1968) of 'basic transference'; Kohut (1971) refers to 'the realistic bond' between analyst and analysand. Zetzel (1958) puts it as follows: 'It is also generally recognized that, over and above the transference neurosis, successful analysis demands at its nucleus a consistent, stable relationship which will enable the patient to maintain an essentially positive attitude towards the analytic task when the conflicts revived in the transference neurosis bring disturbing wishes and fantasies close to the surface of consciousness.'

The concept has been used in reference to aspects of what is familiar to many as the 'therapeutic contract' (Menninger, 1958) between the patient and his therapist. It is related to what has been defined as 'the non-neurotic, rational, reasonable rapport which the patient has with his analyst and which enables him to work purposefully in the analytic situation' (Greenson & Wexler, 1969). The notion of the treatment alliance, as it has developed, is not simply the patient's conscious wish to get better, and is not to be equated with it. We shall return to this point later. In regard to the psychoanalytic situation, the recognition of the difference between 'treatment alliance' and other aspects of the patient–analyst interaction (such as transference) leads to an increased understanding of the processes that occur in that situation and, in particular, of those that enter into therapeutic success and failure. For psychoanalysis, and other methods of treatment as well, the assessment of the capacity to develop a treatment alliance is important when a decision has to be made about the appropriate form of treatment.

Although the treatment alliance was never designated by Freud as a distinctive concept, the idea can be traced back to his early work (1895d) in which he says, 'We make the patient a collaborator'. There are similar references to such collaboration at many points in his writings, and as late as 1937 he commented that 'the analytic situation consists in our allying ourselves with the ego of the person under treatment' (1937c). He went on to speak of the 'pact' between the analyst and the patient. Finally, in his very last work (1940a [1938]), Freud commented:

> The analytic physician and the patient's weakened ego, basing
> themselves on the real external world, have to band themselves

together into a party against the enemies, against the instinctual demands of the id and the conscientious demands of the superego. We form a pact with each other . . . to give his ego back its mastery over lost provinces of his mental life. This pact constitutes the analytic situation.

In contrast to the idea of a therapeutic 'pact' between patient and analyst, what we now call 'treatment alliance' was originally encompassed by Freud within the general concept of transference, and was not well differentiated from other transference elements. In his early writings on technique, Freud had divided transference into transference of positive feelings on the one hand and negative transferences on the other (Freud, 1912b, 1912e). Positive transferences, in turn, were seen as divisible into transference of friendly or affectionate feelings (of which the patient was aware) and those transferences that represented the return, possibly in a distorted form, of childhood erotic relationships. The latter were not normally remembered but rather *re-experienced* by the patient towards the analyst. Such positive transferences, together with negative ones, could develop into resistance to treatment. The friendly and affectionate component of the positive transference was described as representing 'the vehicle of success in psychoanalysis, exactly as it is in other methods of treatment' (Freud, 1912b).

Shortly afterwards Freud (1913c) made reference to the need to establish an 'effective transference' before the full work of psychoanalysis could begin. He maintained that it was necessary to wait 'until an effective transference has been established in the patient, a proper *rapport* with him. It remains the first aim of the treatment to attach him to it and to the person of the doctor.' The essential distinction was between the patient's capacity to establish a friendly rapport and attachment to the doctor on the one hand, and the emergence, within the framework of the treatment, of revived feelings and attitudes that could become an obstacle to therapeutic progress. The fact that Freud used the term 'transference' for the 'friendly rapport' as well as for transference has led to some confusion in the subsequent literature, with some authors still using the term 'positive transference' incorrectly to designate the treatment alliance. Warm and affectionate feelings towards the analyst do not always indicate the presence of a treatment alliance.

We can probably link the crystallization of a concept of treatment alliance as something other than a special aspect of transference with the development of psychoanalytic 'ego psychology'. This aspect of psychoanalytic thinking developed after the formulation of the 'structural' model of the mental apparatus (Freud, 1923b, 1926d), in which the concept of the ego, as an organized part of the personality having to cope with the outside world and the conscience (superego), as well as with the instinctual drives (id), was elaborated. Psychoanalytic writers (e.g. Hartmann, 1939, 1964; Anna Freud, 1965) have developed the notion of ego functions and attributes that are relatively independent of the drives ('autonomous' ego functions), and much of what has been written about treatment alliance in its various forms implies that it makes use of such autonomous functions and attitudes.

The development of the idea of a treatment alliance among writers other than Freud can be seen in two papers by Sterba (1934, 1940), who emphasizes the need for the psychoanalyst to bring about a separation within the patient of those elements that are focused on reality from those that are not. He refers to this as a 'therapeutic split in the ego' (1934). The reality-focused elements in the ego allow the patient to identify with the aims of the therapy, a process which Sterba regards as an essential condition for successful psychoanalytic work. Sterba's view is consistent with a reference by Freud (1933a) to the necessity, in successful treatment, for the patient to utilize his capacity to observe himself as if he were another person. In this context, Fenichel (1941) writes of a 'reasonable' aspect of the patient, and of what he calls a 'rational transference'. In tracing this concept through the psychoanalytic literature, it has become evident that the 'friendly transference', 'effective transference', 'reality-focused elements', 'rational transference', and self-observing and self-critical capacities are often treated as if they were equivalent, whereas these capacities can more usefully be seen as separate elements that can be brought under the general heading of the capacity for forming a treatment alliance. Useful discussions of the elements that enter into the broad 'alliance' concept may be found in papers by Friedman (1969), Dickes (1975), Gutheil and Havens (1979), and Thomä and Kächele (1987).

Beginning with an important paper on the topic by Elizabeth Zetzel (1956), psychoanalytic writers have been increasingly concerned with differentiating the treatment alliance from transference 'proper'. A trend in subsequent publications, reflected in the work of Greenson (1965a, 1967) and Greenson and Wexler (1969), is to regard the core of the treatment alliance as being anchored in the 'real' or 'non-transference' relationship which the patient establishes with the doctor. Yet the nature of this 'real' relationship is not entirely clear. Schowalter (1976) remarks that while 'there is general agreement that for the analytic situation with adults to survive the buffeting of resistances engendered by the transference . . . part of the analysand–analyst relationship must be relatively non-neurotic and recurrently focused on the continuation and completion of the treatment. Agreement as to how separate . . . this part of the object ties from the rest of the transference is less clear.'

In recent years a number of analysts, in particular Brenner (1976, 1979), have challenged the validity of the notion of the treatment alliance, maintaining that the concept cannot in fact be distinguished from that of transference. Fonagy (1990) points out that over-emphasis on the transference aspects of the analyst–patient relationship may lead to its reification and place it beyond analytic scrutiny. As a result we may 'inadvertently deprive ourselves of the opportunity to understand its basis in unconscious intrapsychic conflict'. While the complete rejection of the concept is unconvincing, attention has been drawn by Curtis (1979) to 'the danger of a shift of focus away from the nuclear analytic concepts of unconscious intrapsychic conflict, free association, and interpretation of transference and resistance'. He goes on to say, 'This danger lies especially in the tendency to see the therapeutic alliance as an end in itself—to provide a new and corrective object relationship—rather than a means to the end of analysing resistance and transference'.

Although the concept of treatment alliance appeared to be relatively simple in the various forms in which it was originally introduced, we need to take into account the fact that, however we look at it, it has both conscious and unconscious aspects (see Evans, 1976). Thus a patient may appear hostile to treatment, showing a strong resistance to the analytic work (see chapter seven), yet have an underlying unconscious wish to undertake that work. In contrast, there may be what Sodré (1990) refers to as an unconscious anti-therapeutic alliance, in which 'the unconscious need to repeat, or to hold on to an infantile phantasy, may be perpetuated, due not only to the severity of the patient's psychopathology, but also to an unconscious alliance between the patient who wishes for an idealized interminable analysis and something in the analyst which identifies with [the patient's] . . . terrible fear of change and therefore unconsciously avoids facing some aspect of the analytic relationship'.

Novick (1970) has a similar danger in mind when he suggests that the use of the term 'treatment alliance' draws too much attention to the rational as opposed to the irrational aspects of analysis. A similar point has been made by Eagle and Wolitzky (1989), who are concerned that emphasis on the alliance may impede the resolution of the transference on the basis of interpretation and insight. They also argue that such emphasis may lead the analyst to give undue weight to the role of non-interpretative factors in analytic treatment, and as a consequence he might be less sensitive to transference manifestations. It is certainly true that giving undue importance to the fostering of a treatment alliance may result in collusion with the patient to prevent the emergence of hostile transference.

In the techniques advocated by Melanie Klein and her followers (Joseph, 1985; Meltzer, 1967; Segal, 1964), all communications by and behaviour of the patient in treatment tend to be conceived of and interpreted as transference of infantile attitudes and feelings, or as the outcome of the patient's externalization of internal object relationships. This view is not held by all members of the Kleinian school. Bion has referred to 'task-relatedness' in groups (1961), and this may be taken to imply an aspect of what we have been discussing under the heading of 'treatment alliance'. Spillius (1983) has drawn attention to the changes in Kleinian technique in recent years, changes which in our view bring it closer to psychoanalytic techniques that have developed within the more 'classical' tradition.

In spite of the fact that the 'alliance' is difficult to define precisely, there appears to be a strong case for distinguishing it from other aspects of the patient's relationship to his doctor, which are not in themselves sufficient to form a successful basis for psychoanalytic treatment (see, e.g., Adler, 1980). These latter transference aspects include the revival of loving or sexual feelings originally directed towards an important figure of the patient's past, showing themselves in extreme form by the patient falling in love with the therapist. They also include idealization of the therapist in which he is seen as perfect or supremely capable—an idealization that can defensively disguise and deny unconscious hostile feelings. The idealization may break down (often quite dramatically) if the patient feels disappointed or if the underlying hostility becomes too strong. The ability to develop a treatment alliance can be thought to draw on qualities that have become a relatively stable part of the individual. While it is true that these qualities may be related in their development to successful aspects of the child's early relationships, they are to an important degree independent of those feelings and attitudes that can be conceptualized as 'transference'. Thus the treatment alliance can be regarded as

> being based on the patient's conscious or unconscious wish to co-operate, and his readiness to accept the therapist's aid in overcoming internal difficulties. This is not the same as attending treatment simply on the basis of getting pleasure or some other form of gratification. In the treatment alliance there is an *acceptance* [by the patient] of the need to deal with internal problems, and to do analytic work in the face of internal or (particularly with children) external (e.g. family) resistance. [Sandler et al., 1969]

It is certain that the concept must also draw upon what Erikson has called 'basic trust' (1950), an attitude to people and the world in general which is based on the infant's experiences of security in the first months of life. This is probably linked with the internalization of a developmentally early 'alliance' between the infant and its primary object (see Stern, 1985). The absence of the quality of 'basic trust' is thought to account for the absence of a fully functioning treatment alliance in certain psychotics and in others who have experienced severe emotional deprivation as children. Erikson (1950) puts it thus: 'In psychopathology the

absence of basic trust can best be studied in infantile schizophrenia, while weakness of such trust is apparent in adult personalities of schizoid and depressive character. The re-establishment of
a state of trust has been found to be the basic requirement for
therapy in these cases.' (It should be pointed out that the term
'infantile schizophrenia' as used by Erikson is not current. We
would probably refer today to 'infantile psychosis' or 'autism', and
to the severe personality problems of the multiply deprived child.
Moreover, Erikson's comments about adult personalities of 'schizoid' character would apply to what later came to be known as
'borderline' states.)

One thing is clear: the treatment alliance should not simply be
equated with the patient's wish to get better. While such a wish
certainly contributes to the treatment alliance, it may also carry
with it unreal and even magical expectations from treatment—
unreliable allies in the therapeutic task. The inadequacy of the
wish for recovery as the sole basis of a treatment alliance is evident in those cases who break off treatment as soon as they experience a degree of symptomatic relief. Such patients lose any
desire to explore the factors leading to their illness once the symptoms have lessened or disappeared. Recovery may also represent
a 'flight into health', and if the treatment alliance in such cases is
based only on the wish for relief of symptoms, no adequate basis
for the continuation of psychoanalytic treatment remains, even
though the patient may know from his own history that his relief
from suffering is likely to be only temporary. We can conclude
that most of the elements mentioned by the psychoanalytic
writers on the topic (the ability to regard oneself as one might
regard another, the capacity to tolerate a certain amount of frustration, the existence of a degree of 'basic trust', identification
with the aims of treatment, etc.) are, to some degree, essential.

It may be difficult, especially at the beginning of treatment, to
distinguish the patient's *capacity* for establishing and maintaining a treatment alliance from the positive feelings towards the
therapist and treatment that stem from other sources. As we have
indicated, apparent regard or even affection for the therapist and
initial willingness to attend do not necessarily indicate that the
patient is ready to continue to work in therapy. This is high-
lighted in those cases where the patient asks for help in order to

appease a relative or even his general practitioner, and in some people undergoing psychoanalysis as a required part of a psychoanalytic or psychotherapeutic training (Gitelson, 1954). In general it is essential at the outset to determine (a) whether the patient has the *capacity* for forming an alliance, and (b) whether he can develop sufficient appropriate motivation to build an alliance during the course of the analysis to enable him to weather the stresses and strains of treatment.

The importance of assessing a patient's capacity to form a treatment alliance is emphasized by such writers as Gerstley et al. (1989), who consider that the assessment of the capacity for a treatment alliance is an important prognostic indicator for patients with antisocial personality disorder.

Nevertheless, the evaluation of the probable treatment alliance is clearly an important prognostic factor in all cases considered for psychoanalytic treatment. So most psychoanalysts would not normally take a grossly psychotic patient into analysis, because it is likely that the patient does not, at the time, possess the capacity to work analytically and constructively with the therapist. Some analysts also have reservations about working with so-called borderline patients. The vicissitudes of the treatment alliance in borderline states have been discussed by Shapiro, Shapiro, Zinner, and Berkowitz (1977) and by Gabbard et al. (1988). However, treatment may be directed towards the development of this ability.

In the past, analysts often made use of a 'trial period' of analysis, after which a joint decision about continuation could be made. This decision was based, in part, on what would nowadays be known as the patient's capacity for a treatment alliance as revealed during the trial period. Similarly, Anna Freud, in her early work (1928), advocated an 'introductory phase' in child analysis, during which the child was introduced to the idea of treatment and established a bond with the analyst. She later dropped the recommendation of a specific pre-analytic introductory phase. Hoffer (personal communication to J. S.) has spoken of 'seducing the patient into treatment'. Morgenthaler (1978) makes essentially the same point.

Occasionally, irrational motives may assist the development of a treatment alliance. An example might be a patient who has very strong sibling rivalry and works hard at his analysis in order to be more successful than a rival colleague, also in analysis. Here the patient's rivalry, while constituting analytic material to be understood, may for a while help the progress of the analytic work.

Treatment may gratify concealed wishes in the patient (e.g. for dependence, for attention and love, and even for masochistic suffering). A consequence of this is that he may continue in psychoanalytic treatment for many years, showing no inclination to leave, yet making no significant improvement. On the other hand, there are also those people who have strong paranoid trends in their personalities, who are supremely 'untrusting', and who are still able to establish some sort of treatment alliance with the therapist. In some way they appear to recognize their need for help and to make an 'exception' of the therapist.

Although treatment can be begun without a strong treatment alliance, some form of therapeutic 'contract' is usually necessary at the outset of treatment. A treatment alliance may, and ideally should, develop during the course of treatment, and it is a major part of the work of the psychoanalyst to assist in its development. Such assistance can take the form of providing a constant and regular setting for the patient's communications. It also includes the analyst's interpretation of the patient's resistances to the development of an adequate treatment alliance. An example of the latter would be the analyst's interpretation of how a patient, because of his fear of passive submission, does not allow himself to co-operate fully in the analytic work. Although this resistance may have many sources, it manifests itself, in effect, as a resistance to the alliance, even though we could also see it as a resistance to, say, a developing sexual transference. A further example of a resistance to the development of an adequate treatment alliance is the case of the patient who is very afraid of the invitation to regression posed by the analytic situation. While most patients can tolerate their regressive tendencies in the analytic situation to some degree, some are afraid that if they 'let go' they will become completely infantilized and lose control over their thoughts and actions. Interpretation of the patient's fears may help him to deal with this and thus allow for the further development of an appropriate treatment alliance.

The treatment alliance is not only a function of the patient, as the skill of the individual analyst must play an important role in its development (see Schowalter, 1976). The more the analyst can convey, in an emotionally meaningful way, his tolerance of those aspects of the patient's unconscious strivings which are being defended against, and the more he can show his respect for the patient's defensive activities, the greater the reinforcement of the treatment alliance. As a result the patient may internalize the analyst's tolerant attitude so that he can develop a greater tolerance towards previously unacceptable aspects of himself (Sandler & Sandler, 1984).

In this connection there is increasing recognition of what Stone (1961) considers to be the need 'for a basically friendly or "human" quality in the analyst' and of what Schafer (1983) calls 'an atmosphere of safety'. Rothstein (reported in Auchincloss, 1989) comments: 'It is the analyst's attitude toward the patient's behaviour rather than any specific routine parameters of the analytic situation which is important in the introductory phase.' He goes on to say, 'Flexibility in the introductory phase that allows for modifications to accommodate character resistances may facilitate some patients' induction into an analytic experience. Many patients are lost as potential analysands if the analyst insists that the patient begins analysis in a particular manner.'

The treatment alliance should not be regarded as a constant throughout psychoanalytic treatment, because, apart from the fact that it has to be established as the analysis proceeds, it is also frequently diminished by the patient's resistances and augmented by the development of positive feelings. It may be completely disrupted by gross regressive manifestations during treatment (Dickes, 1967) and may also diminish or even disappear if an 'erotized' transference develops (chapter five).

Offenkrantz and Tobin (1978) point to the role of the loss of self-esteem and shame in preventing a treatment alliance: '. . . patients experience shame about needing help from another person. The way in which they deal with this shame is a crucial element in their readiness or lack of it to accept a dependent relationship with the analyst.'

Langs (1976) has introduced the concept of the 'therapeutic misalliance', defined as conscious or unconscious interactions within the therapeutic relationship aimed at undermining the goals of psychoanalysis or psychotherapy, or at achieving symptom modification rather than insight and constructive inner change. In this connection, Novick (1980) describes a 'negative therapeutic alliance' in which the motivation 'is an unconscious wish to go into analysis or therapy in order to make the analyst fail . . . in order to maintain an idealized image of a loving, loved and omnipotent mother. This is maintained by the externalization and displacement of negatively cathected parts of self and object onto the analyst.'

This view can be regarded as allied to the unconscious motivation for certain forms of the negative therapeutic reaction (chapter eight). It is worth commenting that 'negative therapeutic alliance' is an unsatisfactory term, because the alliance is either present to some degree or absent. What Novick is referring to can be regarded as a 'pseudo-alliance' obscuring unconscious resistance to analytic work. Such a pseudo-alliance can only be present if the analyst colludes with it (Davies, 1990; Sodré, 1990).

Based on experience in the analysis of children, Sandler, Kennedy, and Tyson (1980) comment that there are at least two ways in which the definition of treatment alliance can be approached. The first is to treat the alliance as a broad descriptive umbrella concept, a composite of all those factors that keep the patient in treatment and enable him to remain there during phases of resistance and hostile transference. The second approach is to see the alliance as a narrower concept, relating specifically to the patient's awareness of illness and to his conscious and unconscious feeling of a need to do something about it; this is linked with the presence in the patient of a capacity to tolerate the effort and pain of facing internal conflict. In line with the wider definition, the therapeutic relationship can—but only for a time—be maintained predominantly on the basis of gratifications containing instinctual elements, such as love for the analyst or object hunger. Such aspects can be regarded as the instinctual or id elements in the treatment alliance. However, the treatment relationship needs also to be based on the ego elements included in the narrower definition. Ideally, the therapist should be sensitive to the different ingredients of the treatment alliance as they exist in the 'here and now' of the analysis, and the way in which the different components vary as the alliance fluctuates in strength, composition, and stability.

The concept of the treatment alliance appears to be readily capable of being extended outside psychoanalysis without substantial modification, although it is true that different clinical 'contracts' (to use Menninger's term) exist in different clinical situations. A treatment alliance would not be required in the emergency medical treatment of an unconscious patient. At the other extreme, it is essential for the success of a prolonged course of rehabilitation. In many treatment situations it may be useful to extend the concept to include the capacities and attitudes of the patient's family or of other environmental agencies. In the same way as a treatment alliance is necessary between patient and analyst, it appears to be equally necessary in those situations where the patient cannot carry the burden of treatment on his own. This is particularly the case in the treatment of children, where a treatment alliance with the child's parents is absolutely necessary. It is also necessary to have such an 'extended' alliance in the case of the out-patient treatment of psychotic patients. This is so no matter what the form of treatment is, as the co-operation of the patient's family may be necessary in order to ensure that he attends at all.

Changes in attitudes to mental health, and the acceptance of the voluntary principle, must inevitably place weight on the assessment, not only of the patient's insight into his illness, but also of his capacity to form a treatment alliance with his therapist. This applies particularly to psychotic patients and to those patients who have, in the past, been labelled as 'psychopathic' or suffering from 'severe personality disorder' or 'character disorder'. The assessment, during an initial period of doctor–patient interaction, of the patient's capacity for forming a treatment alliance must have diagnostic significance in regard to the severity of the disorder, and prognostic significance where the prognosis is related to the method of treatment. In those cases where psychotherapy is judged to be indicated, the clinical assessment of the patient's ability to tolerate and to co-operate with the therapist in a prolonged, time-consuming, and often painful process seems crucial, and the concept of treatment alliance, or of potential for treatment alliance, has value. It is useful for the referring physician to come to some decision about the patient's capacity and motivation for developing an enduring treatment alliance which could support the treatment process. But even in situations where there is no question of psychotherapy, the concept of treatment alliance is useful in considering the nature of the patient's involvement in the treatment situation and the nature of his relationship with the therapeutic figures in that situation. Certainly in casework, the social worker implicitly assesses the state of the treatment alliance between the client (or the client and his family) and himself. Naturally, the treatment alliance is affected by the requirements of the treatment situation and by the style of work of the particular agency involved. For example, some clients may be able to sustain a relationship with an agency so long as regular appointments are provided, but would not be able to maintain a treatment alliance if the initiative for contact were left to them. Special and interesting problems arise in the case of persons on probation, who are required to see the probation officer regularly. While compulsory attendance may aid the treatment alliance in some cases, it may produce a 'pseudo-alliance' in others.

CHAPTER FOUR

Transference

A spects of the therapist–patient relationship were discussed in chapter three, where it was pointed out that the concept of the treatment alliance included some features that have also been referred to as 'transference'. The purpose of the present chapter is to consider the meanings of the latter term. The transference concept, too, can only be fully appreciated in terms of its historical development, and different schools within psychoanalysis at present tend to emphasize different aspects of what is understood by the term. The analysis of transference phenomena is regarded by psychoanalysts as being at the very centre of their therapeutic technique, and the concept is widely applied outside psychoanalysis in the attempt to understand human relationships in general. A dissection of the various meanings attributed to the term seems necessary in order to consider its current and potential applications.

Freud first made use of the term 'transference' when he was reporting on his attempts to elicit verbal associations from his patients (Freud, 1895d). The aim of the method of treatment was for the patient to discover, primarily through his associations and emotional responses, the link between his *present* symptoms and feelings on the one hand and his *past* experiences on the other. Freud assumed that the 'dissociation' of the past experiences (and the feelings connected with them) from consciousness was a major factor in the genesis of the neurosis. He noted that changes developed during the course of treatment in the patient's attitude to the physician, and that these changes, involving strong emotional components, could cause an interruption to the process of verbal association, often resulting in substantial obstacles to treatment. He commented (1895) that 'the patient is frightened at finding that she is transferring on to the figure of the physician the distressing ideas which arise from the content of the analysis. This is a frequent, and indeed in some analyses a regular, occurrence.' These feelings were regarded as 'transference', coming about as a consequence of what Freud called a 'false connection' between a person who was the object of earlier (usually sexual) wishes and the doctor. Feelings connected with past wishes (which had been excluded from consciousness) emerge and become experienced in the present as a consequence of this 'false connection'. In this context Freud remarked on the propensity of patients to develop neurotic attachments to their doctors.

In a paper published ten years later (Freud, 1905e [1901]), the term 'transference' was once again used in the context of the psychoanalytic treatment situation. Freud put the question:

What are transferences? They are new editions or facsimiles of the impulses and phantasies which are aroused during the progress of the analysis; but they have this peculiarity, which is characteristic for their species, that they replace some earlier person by the person of the physician. To put it another way: a whole series of psychological experiences are revived, not as belonging to the past, but as applying to the person of the physician at the present moment. Some of these transferences have a content which differs from that of their model in no respect whatever except for the substitution. These then—to keep to the same metaphor—are merely new impressions or reprints. Others are more ingeniously constructed; their content has been subjected to a moderating influence ... by cleverly taking advantage of some real peculiarity in the physician's person or circumstances and attaching themselves to that. These, then, will no longer be new impressions, but revised editions.

Thus far transference had been seen as a clinical phenomenon which could act as an obstacle or 'resistance' (chapter seven) to the analytic work, but a few years later (1909d) Freud remarked that transference was not always an obstacle to analysis but may also play 'a decisive part in bringing conviction not only to the patient but also to the physician'. This is the first mention of transference as a therapeutic agent. It should be noted that Freud consistently distinguished the analysis of transference as a technical measure from the so-called 'transference-cure', in which the patient appears to lose all his symptoms as a consequence of feelings of love for and a wish to please the analyst (1915a). In this context it should be mentioned that the 'transference-cure' can be distinguished from a 'flight into health', a somewhat different form of resistance in which the patient's symptoms disappear (at least temporarily) in the service of resistance, enabling the patient to declare that treatment is unnecessary because he has been cured. The relation of transference to resistance is dealt with in chapter seven.

Freud (1916–17) pointed out that 'a transference is present in the patient from the beginning of the treatment and for a while is the most powerful motive in its advance'. By now it would appear that Freud was using the term to include a number of rather different phenomena, although they all had the quality of being seen as a repetition of past feelings and attitudes in the present. In 1912 Freud had spoken of 'positive' transferences as opposed to 'negative' ones, and had further subdivided positive transferences into those that helped the therapeutic work and those that hindered it. Negative transferences were regarded as the transference of hostile feelings on to the therapist, the extreme form being manifested in paranoia, though in a milder form negative feelings could be seen to co-exist with positive transference in all patients. This co-existence enabled the patient to use one aspect of his transference to protect himself against the disturbing emergence of the other. Thus a patient might use the hostility that he has transferred to the analyst as a means of keeping positive feelings at bay. Here the patient employs the hostile side of his ambivalence to protect himself against emerging and threatening positive (usually erotic) wishes directed towards the analyst. Moreover, that aspect of the positive transference which 'is present . . . from the beginning of treatment' is different in quality from the erotic transferences that arise during the course of treatment (1912b). The former can be regarded as a component of the treatment alliance, previously discussed (chapter three).

Freud suggested that the particular characteristics of a patient's transference stem from the specific features of that patient's neurosis; they are not simply an outcome of the analytic process. This phenomenon is common to all patients (1912b). The specific qualities of a patient's transference were given a further meaning when the concept of 'transference neurosis' was introduced (Freud, 1914g). This emphasized the way in which the earlier relationships, which were major components of the neurosis, also mould the dominating pattern of the patient's feelings towards the psychoanalyst. Freud said (1914g) that,

> Provided only that the patient shows compliance enough to respect the necessary conditions of the analysis, we regularly succeed in giving all the symptoms of the illness a new transference meaning and in replacing his ordinary neurosis by a 'transference neurosis' of which he can be cured by the therapeutic work. The transference thus creates an intermediate region between illness and real life through which the transition from the one to the other is made. The new condition has taken over all the features of the illness; but it represents an artificial illness which is at every point accessible to our intervention. It is a piece of real experience, but one which has been made possible by especially favourable conditions, and it is of a provisional nature.

The concept of the 'transference neurosis' was amplified by Freud (1920g) when he commented that the patient in analysis is

> obliged to *repeat* the repressed material as a contemporary experience instead of, as the physician would prefer to see, *remembering* it as something belonging to the past. These reproductions which emerge with such unwished-for exactitude,

always have as their subject some portion of infantile sexual life ... and they are invariably acted out in the sphere of the transference, of the patient's relation to the physician. When things have reached this stage, it may be said that the earlier neurosis has now been replaced by a fresh, 'transference neurosis'.

It is extremely unfortunate that the term 'transference neurosis' as used by Freud is so close to the label which he applied to a whole class of psychiatric *disorders*—the so-called 'transference neuroses', i.e. those disorders in which transference phenomena could be observed. In his earlier writings he showed his belief that these could be distinguished from the 'narcissistic neuroses', in which transference phenomena were not thought to develop readily. However, most psychoanalysts now accept that transference phenomena occur in patients belonging to *both* groups.

The repetition of the past in the form of contemporary transferences was seen by Freud as a consequence of the so-called 'repetition compulsion'. The repetition compulsion is inappropriately named in that it implies an explanation for the observation that people tend to repeat earlier (usually childhood) patterns over and over again. This is an instance of the way psychoanalysts have tended to elevate descriptive concepts to the status of explanatory principles. Moreover, the tendency to repeat is not a 'compulsion' in the psychiatric sense of the term; nor is it a 'drive' to repeat, in the sense in which Freud spoke of instinctual drive [*Trieb*]. It might be more appropriate to speak of a 'pressure to repeat'.

In order to put later developments into perspective, it is necessary to point out that the concept of transference was elaborated by Freud during the years in which mental functioning was largely thought of by him and by his colleagues in terms of the vicissitudes of the instinctual drives and of the energies that were thought to propel them. Freud conceived of sexual wishes towards an important figure of the past as an investment ('cathexis') of sexual drive energy ('libido') in the image of the person (the 'libidinal object') concerned. Transference, a process of which the patient was unaware, was thought of as the displacement of libido from the memory of the original object to the analyst, who became the new object of the patient's sexual wishes.

The increasing emphasis on the analysis of transference, to-gether with developments in ego psychology, have led to an exten-sion of the meaning of transference, and psychoanalytic writers have attempted to refine and expand the concept in order to achieve a clearer understanding of clinical phenomena and to integrate the concept of transference with other developments in psychoanalytic theory. The history of the expansion of the trans-ference concept is a prime example of the problems that are engendered when a concept, developed during an early phase of psychoanalysis, is maintained in its original form even when newer theoretical formulations have been made.

Anna Freud, in her book *The Ego and the Mechanisms of Defence* (1936), proposed a differentiation of transference phe-nomena according to their degree of complexity. She distin-guished between (1) *transference of libidinal impulses*, in which instinctual wishes attached to infantile objects break through towards the person of the analyst, and (2) *transference of defence,* in which former defensive measures against the drives are repeated (see Sandler et al., 1969). An example of the second category would be the development, during the course of a patient's analysis, of an attitude of belligerent rejection of the analyst, transferring an attitude that he had taken up in child-hood in order to protect himself against feelings of love and affec-tion which he feared would lead him into danger. Such a formulation extends the earlier and simpler view of Freud in which the 'defensive' hostility would have been seen, not as a repetition of a defensive measure of childhood, a repetition of a mode of ego functioning, but rather as the employment of current hostile feelings to protect the individual against the consequences of his emerging positive transference.

Anna Freud also wrote of *acting in the transference*, in which the transference intensified and spilled over into the patient's daily life. Thus feelings and wishes towards the analyst, aroused during the course of treatment, might be enacted towards other people in the patient's current environment. 'Acting in the trans-ference' is close to the concept of *acting out* (chapter nine). At the same time, Anna Freud added a further category which she re-garded as a sub-species of transference, and which she at the time believed should be kept separate from transference proper. She referred here to *externalizations,* exemplified by the patient who feels guilty and, instead of experiencing the pangs of conscience, expects the analyst's reproaches. This externalization of structured aspects of the personality (e.g. the superego) was thought to be different from the repetition in the transference of the patient's childhood relationships towards, for example, a punitive father. A further example of externalization would be that of the patient who develops the belief (or fear) that the analyst wishes to seduce him, such a belief being based upon the externalization, or in this case the particular form of externalization usually known as 'projection', onto the analyst of the patient's own sexual feelings towards him. What is 'externalized' is the patient's current unconscious sexual wish, in a sense an aspect of the patient's 'id', and this externalization need not necessarily be regarded as the repetition of an infantile libidinal impulse nor the repetition of a childhood defensive manoeuvre. It is of interest that both Alexander (1925) and Freud (1940a [1938]) referred to the psychoanalyst 'taking over' the role of the patient's conscience (or superego), and saw this as being an important part of the therapeutic process.

The later distinction between externalization of structure parts of the personality and transference 'proper' made by Anna Freud has not been systematically pursued by later writers, and indeed 'externalizations' of various sorts have tended to be absorbed into the general concept of transference, as will be seen later in this chapter.

We have indicated that there has been a strong tendency within psychoanalysis towards a widening of the transference concept. This can be traced in part to two trends in psychoanalysis which found their expression in the so-called 'English school' of psychoanalysis. The first of these developed from James Strachey's (1934) suggestion that the only effective interpretations in psychoanalytic treatment were transference interpretations. It was thought that these needed to be related to processes of projection onto the analyst of the 'primitive introjected imagos' which were regarded as forming a significant part of the patient's superego. As a consequence of the emphasis on transference interpretations analysts who were influenced by Strachey's views chose to formulate as many of their interpretations as possible in transference terms in order to increase the effectiveness of their interventions. Strachey comments that if the patient projects his primitive introjected imagos onto the analyst, the analyst becomes like anyone else that he meets in real life—a 'fantasy object'. By 'primitive introjected imagos' Strachey refers to primitive images of the parents which are set up in the mind as part of normal development, and which remain as active constituents of unconscious mental life.

The second trend is represented by the theoretical formulations of Melanie Klein (1932) who, as a consequence of her analytic work with children, came to view all later behaviour as being very largely a repetition of relationships which she considered to obtain in the first year of life. The combination of these two trends resulted in a tendency for some analysts to regard all communications brought by the patient as indicating the transference of very early infantile relationships, and to refrain from comments that did not refer to the transference. This phenomenon has been fully discussed by Zetzel (1956).

Many other analysts have contributed to the development of new perspectives on the transference concept. For example, Edward Glover (1937) emphasized that 'an adequate conception of transference must reflect the *totality* of the individual's development . . . he displaces on to the analyst not merely affects and ideas but *all* he has ever learnt or forgotten throughout his mental development'. While some authorities in this early period extended the transference concept within the psychoanalytic situation, others (while not accepting that all aspects of the patient's relationship to his analyst should be regarded as transference) have taken the view, in line with Freud's comment on the ubiquity of transference (1910a [1909]), that transference should be regarded as a general psychological phenomenon. Thus Greenson (1965a) writes:

> Transference is the experiencing of feelings, drives, attitudes, fantasies and defences towards a person in the present which are inappropriate to that person and are a repetition, a displacement of reactions originating in regard to significant persons of early childhood . . . for a reaction to be considered transference it must have two characteristics: it must be a repetition of the past and it must be inappropriate to the present.

Such a definition appears to include more than Freud had originally intended. For example, it would include habitual types of reacting to other persons which have become part of the patient's character (e.g. a tendency to be afraid of authority), and which might be regarded as inappropriate to the present. This phenomenon of 'character transference' (Sandler et al., 1969) is then different from the conception of transference as the emergence, during the process of the psychoanalytic work, of feelings and fantasies about the analyst which were not apparent at the beginning of treatment, and which emerged as a consequence of the conditions of treatment.

Because of the belief that the widening and extension of the transference concept must lead to less rather than greater clarity, a return to a more limited view has been advocated by a number of psychoanalysts. Thus Waelder (1956) suggests that the transference should be restricted to occurrences within the classical psychoanalytic situation. He says, 'Transference may be said to be an attempt of the patient to revive and re-enact, in the analytic situation and in relation to the analyst, situations and fantasies of his childhood. Hence transference is a regressive process. . . . Transference develops in consequence of the conditions of the analytic experiment, viz., of the analytic situation and the analytic technique.' Somewhat later, in a very full discussion of the divergent trends in regard to the transference concept, Loewenstein (1969) similarly concludes that 'transference outside of analysis ob-viously cannot be described in identical terms with the transferences which appear during and due to the analytic process.' Loewenstein arrived at this view because of his conviction that the two aspects of transference seen in analysis, i.e. transference as resistance and transference as the vehicle for discovery and cure, exist exclusively in the analytic situation and can never be observed outside it. Nowadays, most psychoanalysts do not accept the restricted view of transference advocated by Waelder and Loewenstein. The argument that the concept of transference should be limited to the psychoanalytic situation alone is unconvincing, although it is possible to understand the motive that prompts such a limitation, i.e. concern about the increasing tendency to wide and indiscriminate application of the term. It is clear that the same phenomena which occur in psychoanalytic treatment can occur outside it. Indeed, Freud (1912b) had said, 'It is not a fact that transference emerges with greater intensity during psychoanalysis than outside it. In institutions in which nerve patients are treated non-analytically, we can observe transference occurring with the greatest intensity'. However, the classical analytical situation does appear to provide conditions that foster the development of transferences and enable the phenomena to be examined in relatively uncontaminated forms (Stone, 1961).

There is no doubt that socio-cultural factors enter into the way in which the transference develops. For example, the gender of the analyst is certainly significant in determining, at the very least, the sequence in which the transference elements emerge. The issue of gender has been examined intensively in recent years, possibly due to the influence of the feminist movement (see, for example, Lasky, 1989; Lester, 1985; Person, 1983; Wrye & Welles, 1989). Similarly, interracial analyses have also been discussed. Fischer (1971) comments that racial difference between analyst and analysand involves issues of unconscious meaning at many levels, and that 'there are serious hazards in either overestimating or in ignoring the interracial factor'. The school of ethno-psychoanalysis has had much to contribute in this area.

In recent years there have been a number of significant developments in regard to the concept of transference. In particular, the original idea of transference as a repetition of the past has been challenged. Cooper (1987a) comments that 'historical, relatively simple, concepts of the transference as the reproduction in the present of significant relationships from the past do not adequately meet current clinical and theoretical demands', and distinguishes between what he calls the 'historical' and 'modernist' views of transference. The historical view is, he points out, that 'the transference is an enactment of an earlier relationship and the task of transference interpretation is to gain insight into the ways that the early infantile relationships are distorting or disturbing the relationship to the analyst, a relationship which is, in turn, a model for the patient's life relationships.' In contrast, the modernist conception sees the transference 'as a new experience rather than an enactment of an old one. The purpose of transference interpretation is to bring to consciousness all aspects of this new experience including its colourings from the past.'

Taking Cooper's distinction between the historical and modernist points of view, it is appropriate to consider the transition from the one to the other under a number of different headings: *The controversy over the transference neurosis*, *The Kleinian theory of transference*, *Transference and externalization*, and *Developmental considerations in relation to transference*.

The controversy over the transference neurosis

Earlier in this chapter we referred to Freud's introduction of the concept of the transference neurosis (1914g), regarded as an 'artificial illness' in the analysis which replaces the 'ordinary neurosis'. The patient's current neurosis was seen by Freud as a new version of the so-called 'infantile neurosis', and consequently the transference neurosis could be regarded as a revival of the infantile neurosis, within the analysis, involving the person of the analyst. Kepecs (1966) has shown that much confusion attaches to the term 'transference neurosis' and subsequently a number of authors (e.g. Cooper, 1987b; Harley, 1971; Jacobs, 1987; London, 1987; Reed, 1987, 1990) have discussed both the difficulties inherent in the concept and the idea that it is a *sine qua non* of psychoanalytic treatment. Among those who have argued for the retention of the concept, the view has emerged that transference as a general psychic phenomenon is to be distinguished from the specific clinical entity of transference neurosis. Blum (1971) comments that with the arrival of the structural theory 'complex ego and superego aspects of transference were gradually recognized. Transference in the analytic situation was seen to involve the transfer of defences, affects, and integrated fantasies, and attitudes related to infantile object relations.' It is fairly generally accepted that the concept of the infantile neurosis has two main meanings. The first is 'the prototypical source of intrapsychic conflict during the Oedipus complex', and the second a 'metapsychological construct referring to the inner structure and organization of the infantile personality as a result of such conflict' (Moore & Fine, 1990). The concept of the infantile neurosis has become increasingly controversial (see, for example, Calogeras & Alston, 1985; A. Freud, 1971; Loewald, 1974).

In sharp contrast, Brenner (1982), normally regarded as a conservative theoretician, states quite emphatically that

the term transference neurosis is a tautology. The concept is an anachronism. Analysts define neurosis as a symptom, or a group of symptoms, which are compromise formations arising out of conflicts . . . transference manifestations are also compromise formations arising from conflicts . . . A transference manifestation is dynamically indistinguishable from a neurotic symptom. To call it neurotic, or to call the totality of the transference a neurosis is to add a word without adding meaning. Transference is enough. Nothing is gained by expanding the term to transference neurosis . . . 'True transference neurosis', it has often seemed to me, is customarily used as a synonym for 'analysable transference'.

We are entirely in agreement with Brenner's statement and would suggest that the concept of transference neurosis has outlived its usefulness, particularly because it is often used as a synonym for transference in general, and this leads to confusion. Nevertheless , it is important to be aware that the range of transference manifestations is great, varying from so-called 'character transference' to such an intense preoccupation with the analyst that the thoughts and feelings about the analyst's person occupy a major part of the patient's mental life. It is of interest that Moore and Fine, in their first edition of the *Glossary of Psychoanalytic Terms and Concepts* (1968), define transference neurosis as 'the new "version" of the neurosis which develops in the course of psychoanalytic treatment', while in their later *Psychoanalytic Terms and Concepts* (1990) the transference neurosis does not merit a separate entry and is given only a passing mention in the entry on 'Transference'.

The Kleinian theory of transference

From the outset, the analytic technique introduced by Melanie Klein has emphasized the centrality of transference interpretation. Transference was seen as a reflection of the unconscious fantasies of the patient and, in this connection, Segal (1981) has remarked that

> in the phantasy world of the analysand, the most important
> figure is the person of the analyst. To say that all communica-
> tions are seen as communications about the patient's phantasy
> as well as current external life is equivalent to saying that all
> communications contain something relevant to the transfer-
> ence situation. In Kleinian technique the interpretation of the
> transference is often more central than in the classical tech-
> nique.

Spillius (1988), herself a Kleinian analyst, notes, in a careful
review of Kleinian clinical papers, the changes that have occurred
in Kleinian technique since the late 1940s. She points out that in
general the Kleinian view of transference is that it is

> the expression in the analytic situation of the forces and rela-
> tionships of the internal world. The internal world itself is
> regarded as the result of an ongoing process of development,
> the product of continuing interaction between unconscious
> phantasy, defences, and experiences with external reality both
> in the past and in the present. The emphasis of Klein and her
> successors on the pervasiveness of transference is derived from
> Klein's use of the concept of unconscious phantasy, which
> is conceived as underlying all thought, rational as well as
> irrational, rather than there being a special category of thought
> and feeling which is rational and appropriate and therefore
> does not need analysing and a second kind of thought and
> feeling which is irrational and unreasonable and therefore ex-
> presses transference and needs analysing.

However, Spillius points out that most of the Kleinian papers
written in the 1950s and 1960s tended 'to emphasize the patient's
destructiveness in a way that we would now assume might have
felt persecuting to the patient. A second feature of these early
papers is that unconscious phantasies were evidently interpreted
to the patient immediately and very directly in part-object language (breast, nipple, penis, etc.).'

Spillius remarks that changes in Kleinian interpretative technique have gradually occurred. There was less emphasis on
destructiveness and less use of part-object language, and the con-

cept of projective identification (introduced by Melanie Klein in 1946) began to be used more explicitly in transference interpretation. Increased emphasis was put on living out experiences in the transference, rather than thinking and talking about them, and more stress was laid on the unconscious pressure put by the patient to force the analyst to join in. There has also been increased interest in the role of the past as it appears in the present patient–analyst relationship. Spillius notes that interpretations that had been formulated in terms of verbal and behavioural content 'seen in a rigidly symbolic form now seems likely to have been detrimental to the recognition of alive moments of emotional contact. Such interpretations are based not on the analyst's receptiveness to the patient but on the analyst's wish to find in the patient's material evidence for the analyst's already formed conceptions.'

A major extension of the Kleinian theory of transference is contained in a paper by Joseph (1985) on 'Transference: The Total Situation'. She enlarges the conception of transference by regarding it as 'a framework, in which something is always going on, where there is always movement and activity'. Not only is what occurs in the transference the repetition of the past, but on the contrary whatever occurs in the analysis *is* transference. To illustrate this, Joseph describes how a colleague experienced confusion about her work with an extremely difficult patient. The analyst was dissatisfied with the way she was conducting the analysis, and the problem was brought for discussion to a seminar. Those present experienced difficulty in understanding what was going on, until it dawned on them that the problem in the seminar probably reflected the analyst's difficulty in the transference. The conclusion was reached that the analyst was experiencing confusion as a result of the patient's projection of her own confused inner world into the analyst, and that the analyst's unsuccessful attempts to interpret the meaning of the patient's associations reflected the patient's own defensive system, 'making pseudo-sense of the incomprehensible'. Joseph comments that 'If we work only with the part that is verbalized, we do not really take into account the object relationships being acted out in the transference.' A fundamental element in all of this is the externalization of internal object relationships through the mechanism of projective identification (Klein, 1946). From this it follows that great technical importance is attached to the capacity of the analyst to contain and become aware of the patient's projections, to experience these in the countertransference (chapter six), and to return them to the patient in the form of appropriate interpretations. It is worth noting that whereas for Klein introjective identification was a process of taking an external object into the ego or self, projective identification was seen as the converse process of putting some aspect of the self into an object, i.e. making the object contain an aspect of one's own self (see Sandler, 1987, for a full discussion of the subject).

With this technical approach the analyst's attention is directed primarily towards making emotional contact with the patient in the 'here and now' of the analysis. It seems to us, however, that the temptation to regard everything that occurs in the analysis as transference, and to understand this transference on the basis of countertransference feelings and fantasies, can lead to a form of 'wild countertransference analysis'. Spillius (1988) shows her awareness of this danger when she remarks that there may be a tendency, especially for inexperienced analysts, 'to become overpreoccupied with monitoring their own feelings as their primary clue to what is going on in the session, to the detriment of their direct contact with their patient's material.'

In contrast to the position taken by Kleinian authors, many analysts—including ourselves—consider that not everything brought by the patient to the analysis should be regarded as transference. Anna Freud (1968), for example, has criticised the indiscriminate application of the transference concept, and a useful review of the controversy over this issue is to be found in 'Transference Interpretations Only?' by Leites (1977).

It is a misconception and a simplification to imagine that all the patient's material is transference. It would seem that the point of view that 'it is all transference' has arisen precisely because many analysts on principle focus on the transference aspects of the patient's material at the expense of non-transferential ones. It is the transference aspects which can usually be examined and interpreted more directly and effectively than any others; as a consequence the centrality of transference is to some extent a technical artefact deriving from the view that only interpretations of the transference bring about psychic change.

The analyst is not simply a passive partner in the transference relationship. While this aspect will be discussed in greater detail later (chapter six), it should be emphasized that the analyst's personality plays an important role in determining the nature of the patient's transference. Thus those who maintain that 'all is transference' tend to neglect the function of the analyst as a real person engaged in a collaborative task with the patient and place stress instead on the transference distortions of the patient's perception of and fantasies about the analyst (Escoll, 1983; Thomä, 1984). Greenson distinguishes transference from the 'working alliance' (1965a) and from the 'real' relationship of the patient to his analyst (Greenson & Wexler, 1969). Szasz (1963) attempts to discuss the difficulties that arise in the distinction between transference and 'reality', as do Laplanche and Pontalis (1973).

Although the formulation of transference purely in terms of one or other form of externalization of internal object relationships, as advocated by some Kleinian analysts, is certainly too sweeping a view, there can be little doubt nowadays that such processes play a major role in our present conceptions of transference. This will be discussed further below.

Transference and externalization

The discussion of the extension of the transference concept in this chapter has shown that the term has come to mean more than the simple repetition of significant childhood relationships. A major factor in the widening of the concept has been the increasing importance attached to the role of so-called internal object relationships in mental life. The elaboration of theoretical ideas relating to internal objects led to a view of transference in which the 'projection' or 'externalization' of internal object relationships played a major part. Kernberg (1987) puts it thus:

> Transference analysis consists in the analysis of the reactivation in the here-and-now of past internalized object relations. The analysis of past internalized object relations in the transference constitutes, at the same time, the analysis of the con-

stituent structures of ego, superego, and id and their intra- and interstructural conflicts.

He adds:

> I conceive of internalized object relations as not reflecting actual object relations from the past. Rather, they reflect a combination of realistic and fantasied—and often highly distorted—internalizations of such past object relations and defences against them under the effects of activation and projection of instinctual drive derivatives. In other words, there is a dynamic tension between the here-and-now, which reflects intrapsychic structure, and the there-and-then unconscious genetic determinants derived from the 'actual' past, the patient's developmental history.

Loewald (in a Panel reported by Valenstein, 1974), has commented in this connection that 'when we speak of experiences we do not speak of "objective facts". We speak of experiences a child has on various levels of his development in its interaction with the external world, with objects. These experiences may be repeated in the transference and one may say these are fantasies, . . . not facts as observed by an objective observer but elaborations that the patient in childhood had contributed to what "actually happened".' In our view it is precisely because the internal representation of the object as well as the representation of the self are highly modified during development by defensive processes such as projection, identification, and displacement, that we should rather speak of 'internal' rather than of 'internalized' ones.

Schafer (1977) makes a number of important points about our understanding of internal objects. After giving an account of the analysis of a male patient, he says,

> First, when I say 'his father', I am referring to the father imago, which I take to have been only partly faithful to the father more objectively considered. It was an imago maintained mostly unconsciously and built up during different phases of psychosexual development. Second, this imago had been defined principally through close inspection of his various father-transferences and my countertransference reactions to them. Third, it had been possible to define these transferences at all clearly

only by sorting them out from an array of mother-transfer-ences, each with its own developmental and attitudinal complexities. Fourth, the relevant analytical data included the usual wide range of phenomena: they extended from bodily fantasies and enactments, such as constipation, masturbation, and archaic ideas of retribution and damage, to sober attempts to remember, reconstruct, and organize just how events, long remembered in a neurotic way, had actually transpired.

As we have seen, the Kleinian approach to the transference as externalization tends to be formulated in concrete terms, involving such statements as 'putting split-off parts of the self or parts of an internal object into the analyst' or the conception of the analyst as a 'container' (Bion, 1962). On the other hand, non-Kleinian writers (e.g. Bollas, 1987) tend to speak more in terms of the externalization of an internal object relationship than in terms of projective identification (see Berg, 1977). Sandler (1983) remarks that

It may be relevant to our understanding of transference if we consider that introjects are constantly being externalized, in a sense being *actualized* so that they can be related to as external objects rather than as internal ones. Such a tendency to externalize one's introjects is probably a fairly general one. . . . It is a tendency which can be observed particularly well in the psychoanalytic situation and we regularly see attempts to force, manipulate or seduce the analyst into taking over the role of one or other introject so that an internal fantasy scenario involving a dialogue between self and introject can be enacted. This externalization is as much what we mean by transference as anything else and it is certainly a major error to consider the externalization of internal object relationships as simply the direct or indirect fulfilment of unconscious wishes, previously attached to a figure of the past and transferred in disguised form to the analyst in the present.

Developmental considerations in relation to transference

One of the reasons for the criticisms of the transference neurosis concept is the awareness that transference cannot be linked as wholly with oedipal experiences and conflicts as it was in the past. The earlier tendency had been to think of any transference manifestation showing pre-oedipal features as a regressive retreat from intolerable oedipal conflict. Because pre-oedipal conflicts have increasingly come to be seen as existing in their own right, attention has been directed towards the developmental aspects of transference (see Escoll, 1983). Arlow (reported by Valenstein, 1974) says,

> Developments in child analysis and the direct observation of children, as well as a widened scope of psychoanalytic interest and experience with the analysis of character disorders, perversions, borderline patients and narcissistic personality disorders, have increasingly underscored the importance of early object relations for the form of the ego as it develops, either normatively or defectively out of the early mother–child relationship.

Settlage (reported by Escoll, 1983) comments,

> With arrest or failure of developmental process, there is a continuing need for its reinstatement . . . in the analytic relationship . . . transference interpretation frees up developmental process by distinguishing the pathology-related transference object of the past from the analyst as a new, neutral, and actual object in the present. . . . In clinical work with children and adults, it has become possible, more so than in the past, to discern the representation in the transference of the pathological structures and conflicts of earliest development, and to decipher their interrelations with the structures and conflicts of later development.

Post-oedipal developmental processes, including those occurring in adult life, are also significant in personality and pathology. Colarusso (in Escoll, 1983), reporting previous work (Colarusso & Nemiroff, 1979), points out that

> development in adulthood is an ongoing dynamic process . . . adult development is concerned with the continuing evolution of existing psychic structure and with its use . . . the developmental processes in adulthood are influenced by the adult past as well as the childhood past. Within such a conceptual framework, the adult past may become an important source of transference . . . fundamental developmental issues of child-

hood continue as central aspects of adult life, but in altered form.

He adds,

> The adult presentation of the neurosis is the result of the infantile predisposition, subsequent elaboration, and current developmental experience, all condensed into the symptom picture forged by the psychic apparatus of the present . . . the adult developmental framework adds a new and complementary dimension to transference. By shedding light on the developmental processes in the adult and relating these to childhood experience, the adult developmental framework influences the analyst's attitude toward his adult patient and increases his understanding of transference material from all phases.

It may be useful to conclude this chapter by summing up and commenting on the various senses in which the term 'transference' is used:

1. to include what we have discussed as the treatment alliance (chapter three);

2. to denote the emergence of infantile feelings and attitudes in a new form, essentially a disguised repetition of the past, now directed towards the analyst, as described by Freud;

3. to include 'transference of defence' and 'externalizations' of psychic agencies as described by Anna Freud;

4. to encompass all 'inappropriate' thoughts, attitudes, fantasies and emotions which are revivals of the past and which the patient may display (whether he is conscious of them or not) in relation to the analyst; this would include such things as the patient's initial 'irrational' anxieties about coming to treatment and particular attitudes towards people which form part of his personality structure, and which also show themselves towards the analyst;

5. to refer to the externalization of current internal object relationships so that they affect the patient's perception of the analyst. This includes the variety of mechanisms subsumed under 'projective identification';

6. to include *all* aspects of the patient's relationship to his analyst: this view of transference sees every aspect of the patient's
involvement with the analyst as being a repetition of past
(usually very early) relationships; indeed, every verbal and
non-verbal communication or expression by the patient during the course of his analysis may be regarded as transference;
analysts who take this view of transference regard all the
patient's associations as referring to some thought or feeling
about the analyst.

The widest use of the concept, in which all communications and
behaviour within the psychoanalytic setting are regarded as
transference, removes all value from the concept if it is to be
extended outside psychoanalytic treatment, for it would then follow that all behaviour and all relationships could be described as
transference and understood as the repetition of past relationships. While it is true that aspects of past reactions and even
infantile experiences will tend to be repeated in the present in all
sorts of situations and relationships, and that present reality will
always tend to be perceived to some extent in terms of the past,
there are also factors that oppose this distortion. For example, in
ordinary human relationships, the person towards whom a transference is made often acts in such a way as to correct the distorted
transference perception that has arisen: he may or may not allow
himself to accept the transference role that has been thrust upon
him (chapter six). However, it seems likely that the relative lack
of opportunity to 'test' reality in the psychoanalytic treatment
situation allows transference distortions to develop readily and to
be seen most clearly. The analyst provides both an opportunity
for transference distortions by the patient by not 'feeding back'
reality in order to correct the patient's misperception, at the same
time not accepting the role enjoined upon him by the patient's
transference, enabling the irrational determinants of the transference to be explored.

On the basis of an examination of child psychoanalytic material, Sandler et al. (1969) reject the notion that all the material
of the analytic patient can be regarded as transference; they
stress, instead, that the very concept of transference as a unitary
or 'unidimensional' phenomenon may impede the understanding

of what is happening in the relationship between the patient and his analyst. They suggest that the analyst should not think solely in terms of what is transference and what is not, but should rather understand the many different aspects of relationships as they arise within the analysis, particularly those that are directed towards the analyst. The point is made that if the clinical concept of transference is to be understood, relationships in general have to be studied. Transference is a special clinical manifestation of the many different components of normal relationships. The authors stress that the special features of the psychoanalytic situation may facilitate the emergence of particular aspects of relationships, especially of past relationships, but also that it is technically of the greatest importance to distinguish between these various elements rather than regarding *all* aspects of the patient's relationship to the analyst as being repetitions of past relationships to important figures.

It is essential to distinguish between the general tendency to repeat past relationships in the present (e.g. as can be observed in persisting character traits such as 'demandingness', 'provocativeness', 'intolerance of authority', and the like) and a *process* characterized by the development of feelings and attitudes towards another person (or an institution) which represent a concentration of attitudes or feelings, inappropriate to the present, and directed *quite specifically* towards the other person or institution. From this point of view, the anxieties which a patient might have on entering treatment need not be regarded as transference, even though they may be a repetition of some earlier and important experience. On the other hand, a patient who has been in treatment for some time may develop fears about coming to treatment—fears that are now believed and felt by the patient to be a function of the specific qualities of the therapist, even though there may be little foundation in reality for such transference beliefs and feelings. In this sense, transference can be regarded as *a specific illusion* which develops in regard to the other person, one which, unbeknown to the subject, represents, in some of its features, a repetition of a relationship towards an important figure in the person's past or an externalization of an internal object relationship. It should be emphasized that this is felt by the subject as strictly appropriate to the present and to the particular person involved.

Schafer (1977) has made an interesting comment on the relation of past to present in the transference. He says:

> The transference phenomena that finally constitute the transference neurosis are to be taken as regressive in only some of their aspects. This is so because, viewed as achievements of the analysis, they have never existed before as such; rather, they constitute a creation achieved through a novel relationship into which one has entered by conscious and rational design. . . . It seems a more adequate or balanced view of transference phenomena to regard them as multidirectional in meaning rather than as simply regressive or repetitive. This would be to look at them in a way that is analogous to the way we look at creative works of art. We would see the transferences as creating the past in the present, in a special analytic way and under favourable conditions. Essentially, they represent movement forward, not backward.

It must be added that transference need not be restricted to the illusory apperception of another person, but can be taken to include the unconscious (and often subtle) attempts to manipulate or to provoke situations with others which are a concealed repetition of earlier experiences and relationships, or the externalization of an internal object relationship. It has been pointed out previously that when such transference manipulations or provocations occur in ordinary life, the person towards whom they are directed may either show that he does not accept the role, or may, if he is disposed in that direction, in fact accept it, and act accordingly. It is likely that such acceptance or rejection of a role is not normally based on a conscious awareness of what is happening, but, rather, on unconscious cues. Transference elements enter to a varying degree into all relationships, and these (e.g. choice of spouse or of employer) are often determined by some characteristic of the other person who represents some attribute of an important figure of the past.

It is useful to differentiate transference from non-transference elements, rather than labelling all elements in the relationship (arising from the side of the patient) as transference. This may lead to greater precision in defining the clinically important elements in a whole variety of situations, helping to elucidate the relative roles of the many factors that enter into the interaction between patient and therapist.

CHAPTER FIVE

Further varieties of transference

The concept of transference, as developed by Freud, arose within the context of the psychoanalytic treatment of neurotic patients. The extension of the techniques of psychoanalysis to a wider range of patients, including psychotics, has led to the introduction of a number of terms to describe special and additional forms of transference. This chapter is concerned with aspects of the relationship between patient and doctor which are discussed in the literature under such headings as 'erotic transference', 'erotized transference', 'transference psychosis', 'delusional transference', 'narcissistic transference', and 'transference in borderline states'.

In chapter four we were concerned with transference in the forms in which it normally develops. Following a review of the main trends in the literature it was seen that the concept was understood and applied in a number of different ways. We concluded that a useful statement of the transference concept would be to regard it as '*a specific illusion* which develops in regard to

61

the other person, one which, unbeknown to the subject, represents, in some of its features, a repetition of a relationship towards an important figure in the person's past or an externalization of an internal object relationship. It should be emphasized that this is felt by the subject as strictly appropriate to the present and to the particular person involved . . . [and] that transference need not be restricted to the illusory apperception of another person, but can be taken to include the unconscious (and often subtle) attempts to manipulate or to provoke situations with others which are a concealed repetition of earlier experiences and relationships, or the externalization of an internal object relationship.'

The literature that has evolved around the special forms of transference discussed in this chapter implies, fairly consistently, that the phenomena described are some form of repetition of past psychological situations or relationships, occurring in the course of psychoanalysis or psychoanalytically orientated psychotherapy, and can consequently be regarded as transference. However, they have qualities that warrant special designation. Authors writing on these topics usually regard these 'special' transference phenomena as consequences of a regressive revival of primitive relationships, thought to occur either as a consequence of the patient's psychopathology or because the regression is fostered by the particular characteristics of the psychoanalytic treatment situation (or as a consequence of both). However, as we noted in chapter four, increasing emphasis has been placed in recent years on the externalization of internal object relationships as an integral aspect of transference, and this extension of the transference concept is as relevant to the 'special' transference phenomena described in this chapter as it is to so-called 'ordinary' transferences.

It is generally accepted that psychoanalytic treatment normally creates suitable conditions for regression. Some analysts (e.g. Waelder, 1956) link the normal development of transference with regression in the analytic situation, and the extent of the regression, together with the form it takes in certain types of patient, is regarded as leading to special forms of transference. Many psychoanalysts subscribe to the view that severe psychiatric disturbances, in particular the psychoses, can be seen as regressively revived repetitions of earlier, infantile states. By some (e.g. Klein, 1948), these early states are regarded as being 'psychotic'. Other psychoanalysts (e.g. Arlow & Brenner, 1964, 1969) consider that the major role of regressive processes in producing psychotic states is not explained by the reproduction of childhood states, but rather by their effect on the more organized parts of the personality, i.e. on the ego and superego. They do not accept the notion of infantile psychotic states. Arlow and Brenner (1964) put it as follows:

> The great majority of the alterations in the ego and superego functions which characterize the psychoses are part of the individual's defensive efforts in situations of inner conflict and are motivated by a need to avoid the emergence of anxiety, just as is the case in normal and in neurotic conflicts. In the psychoses the defensive alterations in ego functions are often so extensive as to disrupt the patient's relationship with the world about him to a serious degree.

Erotized (or eroticized) transference

In 1915 Freud described certain cases of 'transference love' in which the patient undergoing psychoanalytic treatment declared herself to be 'in love' with the analyst (1915a). While the 'ordinary' erotic transference may be a normal and manageable occurrence in the course of analysis, some patients may experience it to such a degree that they refuse to carry on the usual work of treatment, may reject interpretations relating the present feelings to the past, and seek no further enlightenment as to the meaning and cause of the symptoms of which they had previously complained. The analytic sessions are used for the expression of love, for gratification through the presence of the beloved, and these patients beseech the analyst for a return of their love. Although Freud did not necessarily regard such patients as suffering from unusually severe neurotic disturbances and did not see the emergence of this form of transference as an inevitable contraindication to psychoanalytic therapy, he suggested that sometimes a change to another analyst might be necessary. He spoke of such patients as possessing 'an elemental passionateness', as being 'children of nature'.

When the 'passionate' transference occurs to the extent that there is an intense demand for gratification, and productive analytic work ceases, then serious psychopathology is thought to be present. (The term 'sexualized' transference is sometimes used, but as it covers a much wider range of phenomena than the erotized transference, its use as a synonym for 'erotized' transference should be avoided—see Coen, 1981. The term 'erotic transference' should be reserved for positive transferences accompanied by sexual fantasies that are known by the patient to be unrealistic.) Alexander (1950) has drawn attention to the problem of the dependent patient, who both demands love and wishes to give it. Blitzsten (whose unpublished remarks are quoted by Rappaport, 1956, and Greenson, 1967) is regarded as the first to have linked a highly erotic transference attitude with serious pathology. Rappaport (1956), in an extensive discussion of the subject, comments that 'Blitzsten noted that in a transference situation the analyst is seen "as if" he were the parent, while in erotization of the transference "he is" the parent (a form of over-statement not uncommon in psychoanalytic writings; this statement probably reflects the analyst's feeling that he is treated very much like a parent might be, without the quality of "as if" existing to the same degree as with his other patients). The patient does not even acknowledge the "as if".' The difficulties inherent in such a formulation are obvious, and we shall return to this point later.

Rappaport states that patients who show such an intense erotic component in the transference 'insist unequivocally, from the very beginning, that they want the analyst to behave toward them as the parent [had done]'. The patients are not embarrassed or ashamed by such wishes. They express their anger openly when the analyst does not comply with their demands. Rappaport correlates such intensely sexual demanding reactions in analysis with the severity of the patient's pathology. 'Such an erotization of transference corresponding to a severe disturbance of the sense of reality is indicative of the severity of the illness. These patients are not neurotics, they are "borderline" cases or ambulatory schizophrenics.' He comments that 'though the analytic situation is especially liable to such distortion, these patients try to convert every significant person into a parent'.

Rappaport, in expressing his agreement with Blitzsten that for such patients the analyst is the parent, nevertheless does not maintain that these patients are deluded or hallucinating to the degree that the analyst is *believed to be* the actual parent; there is definitely a special quality to their transferences. The transference is not hidden, and 'the patient screams out that he wants his fantasy to be reality'. The patient believes that in his analyst he can acquire a parent (presumably someone who will act and be like a real or wished-for parent in the patient's life). The view of the analyst *qua* analyst is lost.

It could be argued that such feelings and wishes are not transference at all. In 1951 Nunberg had put forward the view that the patient's attempts to transform the analyst into the parent do not constitute transference. He spoke of a patient whose 'particular fixation to her father created the wish to find his reincarnation in the person of the analyst, and, since her desire to transform the latter into a person *identical* with her father could not be fulfilled, the attempts to establish a working transference were futile'. If this patient had projected unconscious images of her past objects onto the person of the analyst, then, in Nunberg's view, we would be dealing with transference. However, 'She did not project the image of her father on to the analyst; she tried to change her analyst according to the image of her father'. Clearly Nunberg is referring to phenomena similar to those later described by Rappaport. Moreover, in chapter four we spoke of the 'concealed' repetition of earlier experiences and relationships in the transference, implying that the patient is not aware of the repetition of the past in the present. While this might argue against the use of the term 'transference' in regard to the phenomena described by Rappaport, it is equally possible for a patient to have an erotized transference of this sort without being aware that a repetition of the past is involved. Rappaport's main theme in his 1956 paper relates to the management of the patient who wishes to give sexual love to, and to receive it from, a therapist. The question of management is also considered by Menninger (1958) who regards erotized transference as a manifestation of resistance, characterized by demands for love and sexual gratification from the analyst, demands that are not felt by the patient to be alien or inappropriate (i.e. they are felt to be 'ego syntonic').

Technical considerations are also the central concern of a paper by Saul (1962). He connects the erotized transference, more specifically than Rappaport does, with real frustration in relationships in early life, suggesting that the hostility and anger engendered by such frustration may also be repeated in relation to the therapist. In addition, the extreme love is seen as, in part, a means of protecting the doctor from hostile feelings. The hostility and destructiveness in such patients has also been noted by others (e.g. Greenson, 1967; Nunberg, 1951). Greenson relates the erotized transference to other areas of disturbance, and comments, 'Patients who suffer from what is called an "eroticized" transference are prone to very destructive acting out. . . . All these patients have transference resistances that stem from underlying impulses of hatred. They seek only to discharge these feelings and oppose the analytic work.' In speaking of his own experience of such cases he says that 'they came to the hours eagerly, but not for insight, only to enjoy the physical proximity. My interventions seemed irrelevant to them.' An essentially similar point is made by Swartz (1967) when he speaks of the patient's expectation that the analyst will in fact reciprocate the patient's feelings. Patients with an erotized transference are on the whole not suitable for classical psychoanalytic treatment as they cannot tolerate the demands of classical psychoanalysis (Greenson, 1967; see also Wexler, 1960) and cannot maintain an adequate treatment alliance.

In 1973 Blum provided a comprehensive review of the status of the concept of erotized transference. He emphasized the need to distinguish it from erotic transference, a distinction which we fully endorse. Erotized transference is described by Blum as

> an intense, vivid, irrational, erotic preoccupation with the analyst, characterized by overt, seemingly ego syntonic demands for love and sexual fulfilment from the analyst. The erotic demands may not seem unreasonable or unjustified to the patient. The frequent flooding with erotic fantasy may continue into daily life or be displaced onto situations outside analysis, or onto fantasies [about what will happen] after analysis. . . . The intensity and tenacity of erotized transference, the resistance to interpretation, and the continuing attempts to seduce

the analyst into a joint acting out, as well as the frequent acting out of such a transference with a substitute for the analyst, confirm the complicated infantile reactions of these patients. These are not ordinary reactions of transference love, and these patients can resemble intractable love addicts. Their erotized transference is passionate, insistent, and urgent. . . . The conscious fear is not of regression or retribution, but of disappointment and the bitter anguish of unreciprocated love. Through projection and denial they can assume their analyst indeed loves them.

In agreement with a number of other authors (e.g. Lester, 1985; Swartz, 1967; Wrye & Welles, 1989), Blum stresses the role of pregenital factors and very early experiences in the genesis of erotized transference. He refers to

sexual seduction in childhood, especially during the oedipal phase; instinctual overstimulation with deprivation of parental, phase-appropriate protection and support; intense masturbatory conflict; family toleration of incestuous or homosexual behaviour in the bedroom, bathroom etc.; revival and repetition of precocious and incestuous sexual activity in adolescence,

and goes on to say that

these patients have often participated in seductive childhood games, e.g. 'playing doctor', group teasing and play in the parents' or grandparents' bed, etc. Analysis may be treated as a pleasurable and perilous 'game' of seduction. Narcissistic injury and fragility [are] associated with parental insensitivity and lack of empathy. The erotization frequently masked the trauma of repeated seduction and overstimulation with consequent distrust and sadomasochism.

A return to the seduction theory of neurosogenesis is not advocated by Blum, who nevertheless emphasizes the pathogenic role of seduction and trauma in the production of erotized transference. He also stresses the fact that narcissistic needs are prominent in these patients. These are demonstrated in fantasies of being the 'favourite' and very special. Such narcissistic needs 'may be disguised through erotized ingratiation in the service of maintenance of a fragile self-esteem'. Blum concludes that:

erotized transference has multiple determinants and a variable course. It resembles a vehemently exaggerated, distorted form of expectable erotic transference. Erotic transference is a relatively universal, though variably intense and recurrent phase of analysis. There is a continuum from feelings of affection to strong sexual attraction, from ubiquitous unconscious sexual transference wishes to conscious, ego syntonic, erotic transference preoccupation. It is this insistent, conscious, erotic, transference demand that is erotized transference 'proper'.

Erotized transferences of the sort discussed above have for the most part been reported in regard to female patients with male analysts. Lester (1985) remarks that, with the possible exception of Bibring-Lehner (1936), there is no literature on male patients developing an erotized transference towards a female analyst. She suggests that 'the expression of strong erotic urges to the female analyst by the male patient is somewhat inhibited by the fantasy of the overwhelming pre-oedipal mother. In contrast, such erotic feelings are fully expressed by the female patient' (see also Person, 1985; Wrye & Welles, 1989). While this is true in many cases, it is certainly not true in all.

Although many authors stress those elements that reflect the repetition of the past in the erotized transference, in our view the defensive aspects, especially the function of defending against the emergence of depressive affect, are extremely important.

Psychotic and borderline transference

The work of Rappaport (1956) and Greenson (1967) on the erotized transference appears to refer to forms of transference intermediate between the cases discussed by Freud and the cases of psychotic transference or transference psychosis described by such authors as Rosenfeld (1952, 1954, 1969) and Searles (1961, 1963), in which frankly psychotic features appear in the patient's relationship to his therapist.

We pointed out earlier (chapter four) that Freud (1911c, 1914c) took the view that transference did not occur in what he called the 'narcissistic neuroses' (the functional psychoses). He believed that psychotic psychopathology represented a return, in part, to a very early level of psychological functioning, a level at which the capacity to relate to and to love others as distinct from oneself had not developed. The psychotic's withdrawal of interest in the outside world was thought to be the result of a regression to the early 'narcissistic' level. Abraham (1908), too, believed that transference phenomena were absent in schizophrenia.

As Rosenfeld (1952, 1969) has shown, beginning with Nunberg's (1920) observations of transference phenomena in a patient with catatonic schizophrenia, an increasing number of psychoanalysts have disputed Freud's original contention and have made the point that transference does occur in psychotics. Notable among them have been Sullivan (1931), Federn, (1943) and Rosen (1946). A number of authors (Balint, 1968; Rosenfeld, 1952, 1965a, 1969; and Searles, 1961, 1963) have, from their different theoretical viewpoints, rejected the idea that the earliest stages of psychological development (which they believe to be recapitulated in aspects of the symptoms of schizophrenic patients) are free from the investment of emotional interest in others. Thus Rosenfeld (1952) comments, 'We are dealing here not with an absence of transference, but with the difficult problem of recognizing and interpreting schizophrenic transference phenomena'. He ascribes this difficulty to the fact that 'as soon as the schizophrenic approaches *any* object in love or hate he seems to become confused with this object . . . [which] throws some light on the infant's difficulty in distinguishing between the "me" and the "not me"'. The view that misidentifications and delusional ideas develop within the psychotic's relation to his doctor is extended and elaborated by Little (1960a), Searles (1963), and Balint (1968). Balint appears to be the only one of these authors who is alert to the dangers of reconstructing early psychological functioning on the basis of its being exactly like the behaviour of disturbed adults in psychoanalytic therapy.

The transference concept can legitimately be applied to aspects of the psychotic patient's interaction with his therapist. Even the most withdrawn catatonic schizophrenic may, after recovery of rationality, show evidence of considerable perceptiveness of events involving others at the time of his illness. Moreover, there is little doubt that some disturbed behaviour arises in response to the patient's perceptions of the conscious or unconscious attitudes of others. (In this context, the social psychiatric surveys of, for example, Brown, Bone, Dalison, and Wing, 1966, which show that the symptoms of schizophrenia have cultural determinants, are relevant.) Doctors and ward personnel alike are taken into the content of disordered thought processes. What Searles, Rosenfeld, and others (e.g. Fromm-Reichmann, 1950) seek to show by their detailed case presentations is that such thought processes represent repetitions of earlier interpersonal relationships. So Searles (1963) writes of the chronic schizophrenic patient: 'He is so incompletely differentiated in his ego functioning that he tends to feel not that the therapist reminds him of, or is like, his mother or father (or whomever, from his early life) but rather his functioning towards the therapist is couched in the unscrutinized assumption that the therapist is the mother or father.' But he adds, in line with Rosenfeld, that one of the major reasons for underestimating the role of transference in psychotics 'is that it may require a very long time for the transference to become not only sufficiently differentiated but also sufficiently integrated, sufficiently coherent, to be identifiable'.

Just as Freud thought that in the treatment of neurotic patients the internal problems that give rise to the neurosis become concentrated within the analytic treatment situation as a 'transference neurosis' (1914c, 1920g), so Rosenfeld and Searles believe that a parallel transference psychosis can be discerned. Searles (1963) designates four varieties of transference psychosis:

1. transference situations in which the therapist feels unrelated to the patient;

2. situations in which a clear-cut relatedness has been established between patient and therapist, and the therapist no longer feels unrelated to the patient, but the relatedness is a deeply ambivalent one;

3. instances in which the patient's psychosis represents, in the transference, an effort to complement the therapist's personality, or to help the 'therapist–parent' to become established as a separate and whole person;

4. situations where a chronically and deeply disturbed patient

tries to get the therapist to do his thinking for him, but at the same time tries to get away from such a close relationship.

Searles emphasizes countertransference perceptions by the doctor as a basis for assessing the type of psychotic disturbance (see chapter six). He relates each of the types of transference psychosis to actually damaging, although perhaps misperceived and misinterpreted, family patterns. Here he allies himself with the 'family theorists' of schizophrenia (Bateson, Jackson, Haley, & Wearland, 1956; Lidz, Fleck, & Cornelison, 1965; Mishler & Waxler, 1966; Wynne & Singer, 1963). Rosenfeld suggests that what is reproduced during the treatment is not an actual parent–child situation but a *version* of it which had been distorted by the infant's fantasy, not unlike the situation in the neuroses.

There does not, in our view, appear to be sufficient evidence that the *content* of the psychotic's transference is characteristic of or specific to psychosis. The evidence that the psychotic can relate to people (albeit in a psychotic way) is strong, as is the evidence that aspects of childhood relationships, whether these be real or fantasied, enter into the content of the transference. Nor is there reason to doubt the observation that the psychotic's relation to his therapist may become extremely intense. What seems to be the distinguishing feature in the transference of psychotic patients is the *form* that it takes—a form that is closely related to the psychotic mental state of the patient. A transference wish which might be resisted in the neurotic, or (being subject to reality testing) produced in a disguised form, might find expression as a delusional conviction in the psychotic. From a psychoanalytic point of view the differences could be attributed to defective functioning of the controlling and organizing part of the personality (the ego), in particular those functions connected with distinguishing 'real' from 'imaginary'. To put it very simply, everything that has been described in regard to the form of the transference in psychotics can be attributed to the general features of the psychosis. If parts of the schizophrenic patient's personality are relatively intact, then we can expect that aspects of his behaviour and attitudes based on those parts may remain intact. This would appear to be the basis for the capacity of certain psychotic patients to establish a treatment alliance of some sort. This capacity may only exist in regard to particular forms of treatment, and its assessment must inevitably determine the choice of therapeutic method. The fact that transferences occur in psychotic patients, that these transferences can be interpreted, and that the patient may react to transference interpretations, has led certain analysts (e.g. Rosenfeld and Searles) to conclude that psychotic patients can be more effectively treated by psychoanalytic methods than through other techniques. In our view, the evidence that analysis can bring about sustained improvement on its own is unconvincing, although it appears to be true that close daily contact with a therapist can bring about improvement in the chronic psychotic's condition.

We have been concerned, in this section of the chapter, with the concepts of psychotic transference and transference psychosis as forms of transference found in psychotic patients, but there is also another, completely different usage of the term 'transference psychosis' in the literature. In 1912 Ferenczi described transitory psychotic or near-psychotic symptoms occurring during the analytic session in patients who were not otherwise psychotic. These included, in rare cases, true hallucinations evoked in the analytic hour. In 1957 Reider published a paper on 'Transference Psychosis' in which he described the appearance of psychotic and delusional features in the transference of a non-psychotic patient. The literature on this topic has been ably summarized by Wallerstein (1967) who, like Reider, confined the usage of the term to 'patients deemed wholly within the neurotic range in terms of character structure and adjudged appropriate for classical analysis, in whom nevertheless a disorganizing reaction of psychotic intensity occurred within the transference'. Such symptoms as delusional hypochondriasis (Atkins, 1967), 'delusional' fantasies (Wallerstein, 1967), and paranoid delusional states (Romm, 1957) are most commonly described. While it may be possible to attribute the appearance of these psychotic features to the regression-inducing qualities of the analytic situation, they nevertheless only appear in certain patients. The concept of a transitory psychotic mental 'posture' might be useful here (Hill, 1968; Sandler & Joffe, 1970). By 'posture' in this connection is meant the particular organization or constellation of ego functions and defence mechanisms which the patient might adopt in order to deal with a situation that is extremely dangerous or painful. Usually this will be regressive, i.e. there will be a return to an earlier mode of ego functioning. With the disappearance of the painful state, or the threat to the patient, he may be able to resume a more adult mental 'posture'.

Little (1958) as well as Hammett (1961) make use of the term 'delusional transference' to describe a situation in which gross anomalies of the patient–therapist relationship develop; they consider that what is observed is a distorted but nonetheless discernible recapitulation of aspects of very early mother–child relationships. The problems posed by the assumption (made by a number of authors) of phases of 'childhood psychosis' as explanations of psychotic-like beliefs arising during analysis have been mentioned earlier and have been discussed by Frosch (1967), who more recently (1983), in an excellent review of the topic, has taken the view that when 'the terms "transference psychosis", and "delusional transference" have been applied to the appearance of psychotic and psychotic-like phenomena during analysis . . . these phenomena must be clearly distinguished from a psychotic transference, namely transference manifestations in which the patient simply extends his psychotic system to include the analyst'. Frosch contrasts this view with that of Rosenfeld (1952) and Searles (1963) who take the position that the term 'transference psychosis' can be applied when psychotic patients extend their delusional system to include the analyst. Frosch adds: 'To a large extent the choice of terminology depends on how one defines transference.'

We agree with this last remark because the view of transference as including the externalization of aspects of self and object fits well with the observations that can be made of the way in which psychotics relate to others. However, we are still left with a conceptual problem. Such externalizations occur outside therapy as well as within it, and this makes one wonder whether the intense delusional attitudes, which may develop in the psychotic towards the therapist, can really be properly considered to be transference, in that they do not entail a *development* of the transference as primitive aspects of the self are externalized onto the analyst. It is the critical distinction between the so-called 'unfolding of the transference' and the extension of the existing delusional system, that is important in this context.

A number of analysts, including Winnicott (1954, 1955), Khan (1960), and Little (1960a, 1966), have advised that the analyst should, with some patients, permit the development of disturbed (and disturbing) infantile dependent behaviour and of associated intense and primitive feelings. They have suggested (with Balint, 1968) that only in such states is it possible to relive, and hence undo, earlier failures of maternal care. Active encouragement of such regression is thought by some to be a latter-day version of the so-called 'corrective emotional experience' (Alexander & French, 1946) and does not have wide acceptance as a valid technical approach.

The great interest in 'psychotic' or 'delusional' transference shown in the 1960s has, in large part, given way to considerations of transference manifestations in cases with borderline and narcissistic pathology. Following Knight's introduction of the concept of borderline states in 1953, interest in the conditions labelled 'borderline' has grown. This has been stimulated particularly by the work of Kernberg (1967, 1975, 1976a, 1976b, 1980b) and a number of other authors (e.g. Abend, Porder, & Willick, 1983; Gunderson, 1977, 1984; Masterson, 1978; Meissner, 1978; Stone, 1980). While one use of the term 'borderline' refers to a state occurring during a process of movement in the direction of psychotic organization, another refers to a type of personality organization and personality disorder. Such conditions do not indicate that the individual is on the way to becoming psychotic. The person with a borderline personality organization or borderline personality disorder is usually described in terms of specific vulnerabilities of ego functions and a tendency to use primitive defences. *Identity diffusion* (Erikson, 1956; Kernberg, 1967, 1975), said to be a characteristic of the borderline personality and implying a deficiency in integrated self and object concepts, is regarded by Kernberg as a central problem in the borderline personality. He, along with other authors, takes the view that analytically orientated psychotherapy is an appropriate treatment for these conditions. The development of a transference is essential for such therapy and, in Kernberg's technique of expressive psychotherapy, primitive transferences, based on multiple con-

tradictory self and object images, are seen to develop. Such transferences arise rapidly in the treatment setting and need quick
interpretation in the 'here-and-now' of the session. The transferences serve as resistances and are often accompanied by severe
acting out, but Kernberg sees it as possible that they can be
worked through and their place taken by more typical 'neurotic'
transferences. The work of Adler and Buie (Adler, 1981, 1985;
Adler & Buie, 1979; Buie & Adler, 1982–83) also emphasizes the
exploration, discussion, and interpretation of the transference,
leading to improvement through the internalization of the 'holding introject'. The approaches of Rinsley (1977, 1978) and
Masterson (1972, 1976, 1978) place less emphasis on transference
interpretation and more on the active fostering of a treatment
alliance (see chapter three).

Despite many attempts at clarification, the diagnosis of
'borderline' remains imprecise; at the same time it is clear that a
need exists for such a diagnostic category and for further exploration of the role of transference and transference interpretation in
the treatment of patients falling within this category.

Transference in narcissistic pathology

Reference was made earlier in this chapter to Freud's view that
the 'narcissistic neuroses' could be distinguished from the 'transference neuroses', such as hysteria, in which an analysable
transference towards the analyst develops. We have progressed
far from this view and no longer speak of the narcissistic neuroses
but, rather, of borderline states, borderline personality disorder,
and pathological narcissism. Moreover, since Freud's day the
view has been taken that analysis of the transference is possible
in patients with such diagnoses.

Since a number of early psychoanalytic writers (e.g. Abraham,
1919; Reich, 1933) first considered pathological narcissism and its
analysis, the topic of the analytic treatment of patients with narcissistic pathology has come to the fore with the work of Kohut
(1966, 1968, 1971, 1977, 1984). In 1971 Kohut examined what he
referred to as narcissistic transference, but later he discarded the

term and replaced it with the notion of 'selfobject' transferences. Kohut is concerned with the patient's 'damaged self', which searches for 'development enhancing responses of an appropriate selfobject', and this search is always at the centre of the patient's experiences during analysis. In regard to the self, Kohut, in his final formulation (1984), says that it consists of three major constituents (the pole of ambitions, the pole of ideals, and the intermediate area of talents and skills). He subdivides the selfobject transferences into three groups:

1. those in which the damaged pole of ambitions attempts to elicit the confirming-approving responses of the selfobject (mirror transference);

2. those in which the damaged pole of ideals searches for a selfobject that will accept its idealization (idealizing transference);

3. those in which the damaged intermediate area of talents and skills seeks a selfobject that will make itself available for the reassuring experience of essential alikeness (twinship or alter ego transference).

Kohut's view of the selfobject is a very specific one, as succinctly described in Moore and Fine's *Glossary* (1990):

Both normal and pathological structures of the self are related to the internalisation of interactions between the self and selfobjects. The selfobject is one's subjective experience of another person who provides a sustaining function to the self within a relationship, evoking and maintaining the self and the experience of selfhood by his or her presence or activity. Though the term is loosely applied to the participating persons (objects), it is primarily useful in describing the intrapsychic experience of various types of relationships between the self and other objects. It also refers to one's experience of imagos needed for the sustenance of the self. Selfobject relationships are described in terms of the self-sustaining function performed by the other or the period during which the function was meaningful.

An essential part of Kohut's self psychological analytic technique is played by the analyst's empathy. This is seen as an important way of understanding the patient's inner state (see chapter eleven). On the basis of empathic understanding, the patient's internal condition can be explained in terms of his narcissistic needs and developmental disappointments, particularly in relation to archaic states of the self. Through the patient's experiences in the analysis he becomes aware of the separateness of the analyst and himself, an awareness brought about by the analyst's appropriate 'non-traumatic frustrations'. This leads to what Kohut calls 'transmuting internalization' in the patient (i.e. structural change), a consequence of which is his enhanced ability to take over and carry out important selfobject functions for himself. This has been well expressed by Tylim (1978) who remarks that 'The progress of treatment seems to rely upon the systematic working through process of the narcissistic bond which eventually will bring the figure of the analyst from the status of a selfobject or partial object to the status of a separate one, with realities and shortcomings of his own'.

A number of authors have considered problems of the transference in narcissistic pathology from somewhat different viewpoints (e.g. Hanly, 1982; van der Leeuw, 1979). Kernberg, in opposition to Kohut, does not place emphasis on the centrality of the self. He sees narcissistic pathology as the result of the development of certain adaptive psychopathological *intrapsychic structures* rather than the outcome of early deficit, which Kohut sees as the result of a lack of development of normal narcissistic regulatory processes. For Kernberg, the group of narcissistic patients overlaps with the borderline group and consequently his approach to narcissistic disorders is the same as that taken by him in the treatment of borderline patients.

Kohut's work has been of undoubted importance in drawing attention to, and providing an approach towards, the analysis of patients with narcissistic pathology. Nevertheless, as with all schools in psychoanalysis, this approach has, in our view, become over-encompassing, with too great an emphasis being placed on developmental deficit, as opposed to conflict, in the production of pathology (see chapter ten).

The distinguishing features
of the further varieties of transference

In the 'ordinary' transferences of neurotic and 'normal' patients, the capacity to test the transference illusion against reality exists, and the patient is able to view himself to some extent as if he were another person. Interpretations that take the form of 'you are reacting to me *as if* I were your father' are normally understood by the patient who can bring his reasonable and self-observing capacities to bear on what is happening. In such cases the patient possesses and employs the elements that make for a successful treatment alliance (chapter three). In those varieties of trans-ference described in this chapter, the patient may not possess or use these self-critical and self-scrutinizing elements, and it is of interest that writers on these forms of transference refer to the disappearance of the 'as if' quality of the transference. In our view what distinguishes such types of transference from the more usual forms *is the patient's attitude towards his own behaviour.* The same transference content may emerge in the analysis of a neurotic patient, who may bring it in a roundabout way (e.g. via a dream), whereas patients who are psychotic (even if only appearing temporarily so during the analytic hour) bring it more directly, perhaps in the form of a delusional belief. The difference would appear to reside in the formal aspects of the current mental state of the patient.

Statements to the effect that the patient with one or other form of erotized or psychotic transference sees and treats the analyst like the real parent could only be correct if the patient held the delusional conviction that the analyst *was in fact* his parent. Cases of this sort must be extremely rare, but it would appear that what is meant by such statements is that the patient loses sight of the professional role and function of the therapist and is unable to maintain a normal 'distance' from, and the capacity for insight into, what has been going on. Further, it should be noted that the content of the transference, whatever its form, should not be re-garded as a simple repetition of the past. A patient who develops a homosexual transference towards his analyst may react, if he is a neurotic, with anxiety and resistance. If he is psychotic, he might respond with delusions of persecution. In both cases he would be defending against the same unacceptable impulses and wishes.

It is impressive that the varieties of transference content described by certain psychoanalysts in regard to schizophrenia are extremely similar to those that may be found in psychoses which are undoubtedly of organic origin. This lends support to the view that psychotic productions, including transference manifestations of the sort discussed in this chapter, are not a consequence of a need to repeat inadequately resolved infantile psychotic states. It seems to us to be perfectly plausible to say that the distinguishing features in different types of transference relate to the way in which unconscious thoughts, impulses, and wishes tend to come into consciousness, and the way in which they are accepted, rejected, acted upon, or modified. It is likely, therefore, that the specific defects that lead to psychosis and to psychotic transferences lie in such areas as the controlling, organizing, synthesizing, analysing, and perceptual functions of the personality. It is true, of course, that there may be particular family situations which predispose subjects at risk to schizophrenic breakdown. The 'double bind' phenomenon (Bateson et al., 1956) is certainly observable, and the patient may attempt to recreate it with the therapist in the transference relationship. However, similar modes of relating are seen in families that do not contain a schizophrenic member.

In the previous chapter we suggested that the concept of transference was capable of extension outside the classical psychoanalytic situation, and that the differentiation between transference and non-transference elements in any patient–doctor relationship would be clinically useful. Similarly, the various forms of transference discussed in this chapter may be observed outside psychoanalysis and can often be traced in a whole variety of relationships. There is ample clinical evidence to conclude that erotization of transference elements can occur outside the psychoanalytic situation, that psychotic patients can show psychotic and delusional features in their relations with others, and that special situations may produce or release transient psychotic reactions in certain individuals.

CHAPTER SIX

Countertransference

In chapters three, four, and five we have discussed the *treatment alliance* and *transference,* concepts that have been used in connection with aspects of the relationship between the patient and therapist. These two clinical concepts originated within the psychoanalytic treatment situation, and we have indicated some possibilities of extension outside it. Both concepts emphasize processes occurring within the patient and tend to stress one side of the relationship only. Even the concept of treatment alliance, although nominally appearing to include the roles of both patient and therapist, has tended to be regarded from the point of view of processes and attitudes *within* the patient. However, there has been some change in this regard, particularly since the 1970s, in that the therapist's attitudes, feelings, and professional stance have increasingly been taken into account.

Just as the term 'transference' is often used loosely as a synonym for the totality of the patient's relation to his therapist, so the term 'countertransference' is often employed in a general sense (both within psychoanalysis and outside it) to describe all the therapist's feelings and attitudes towards his patient, even to indicate facets of ordinary non-therapeutic relationships (Kemper, 1966). Such a usage is very different from what was originally intended, and, as a consequence, confusion has arisen about the precise meaning of the term which was first used by Freud (1910d) in discussing the future prospects of psycho-analysis. He said of the psychoanalyst: 'We have become aware of the "counter-transference", which arises in him as a result of the patient's influence on his unconscious feelings, and we are almost inclined to insist that he shall recognize this counter-transference in himself and overcome it . . . no psychoanalyst goes further than his own complexes and internal resistances permit.'

In a letter on 6 October 1910 to his colleague Ferenczi, whom he had analysed, Freud (Jones, 1955) apologized for his failure to overcome countertransference feelings which had interfered with Ferenczi's analysis. Freud went on to develop the theme that the analyst should aim to show the patient as little as possible of his own personal life, and he warned analysts against discussing their own experiences and shortcomings with their patients: 'The doctor should be opaque to his patients, and, like a mirror, should show them nothing but what is shown to him.' He also warned the analyst against the danger of falling into 'the temptation of pro-jecting outwards some of the peculiarities of his own personality' (1912e). In the same paper Freud commented that the analyst 'must adjust himself to the patient as a telephone receiver is adjusted to the transmitting microphone. Just as the receiver converts back into sound-waves, so the doctor's unconscious is able, from the derivatives of the unconscious which are communi-cated to him, to reconstruct that unconscious, which has deter-mined the patient's free associations.'

Just as transference was, early on, seen by Freud as an obstruction to the patient's flow of free associations, so counter-transference was consistently regarded as an obstruction to the freedom of the analyst's understanding of the patient. Freud (1913i) regarded the analyst's mind as an 'instrument', its effec-tive functioning in the analytic situation being impeded by countertransference. Freud did not take the step (which he took in regard to transference) of regarding countertransference as a useful tool in psychoanalytic work.

The strength of Freud's views on the undesirability of counter-transference is evident in comments he made a few years later (1915a), in speaking of the physician's awareness of the patient's love for him:

> For the doctor the phenomenon signifies a valuable piece of enlightenment and a useful warning against any tendency to a countertransference which may be present in his own mind. He must recognise that the patient's falling in love is induced by the analytic situation and is not to be attributed to the charms of his own person; so that he has no grounds whatever for being proud of such a 'conquest', as it would be called outside analysis. And it is always well to be reminded of this . . . the experiment of letting oneself go a little way in tender feelings for the patient is not altogether without danger. Our control over ourselves is not so complete that we may not suddenly one day go further than we had intended. In my opinion, therefore, we ought not to give up the neutrality towards the patient, which we have acquired through keeping the counter-transference in check.

It should be emphasized that, for Freud, the fact that the psychoanalyst has feelings towards his patients, or conflicts aroused by his patients, did not in itself constitute countertransference. The analyst was to aim to function like a mirror in the analytic situation, reflecting (through his interpretations) the meaning of the material brought by the patient, including the meaning of the patient's transference distortions. For a response in the analyst to have been regarded as countertransference it had to constitute a sort of 'resistance' in the psychoanalyst towards the analytic work with his patient. The analyst may, through self-scrutiny, become aware of the existence of countertransference reactions and con-flicts in himself, and this was an indication for him to make every effort to recognize their nature and to eliminate their adverse consequences. In Freud's view, the conflicts were not in them-selves countertransference, but could give rise to it.

Freud repeatedly stressed the limitations imposed on the analytic work by the analyst's psychological blind spots (1912e, 1915a, 1931b, 1937d). He initially advocated (1910d) a continuous self-analysis for the analyst, but he soon took the view that this was difficult because of the analyst's own resistances to self-understanding and recommended that the analyst undergo an analysis himself ('training analysis') in order to gain insight and to overcome the psychological deficiencies created by unresolved unconscious conflicts (1912b). Later, believing even this to be inadequate, he suggested that analysts be re-analysed about every five years (1937c). This recommendation has not been commonly implemented, probably because training analyses have become much longer and, consequently, more thorough. However, second analyses are not uncommon among psychoanalysts, especially if they perceive difficulties in their own work or have personal problems for which they need analytic help.

Undoubtedly Freud included in countertransference more than the analyst's transference (in the sense in which he used the term) to his patient. While it is true that a patient may come to represent a figure of the analyst's past, countertransference might arise simply because of the analyst's inability to deal appropriately with those aspects of the patient's communications and behaviour that impinge on inner problems of his own. Thus if a psychoanalyst has not resolved problems connected with his own aggression, for example, he might need to placate his patient whenever he detects in that patient aggressive feelings or thoughts. Similarly, if the analyst is threatened by his own unconscious homosexual feelings, he may be unable to detect any homosexual implications in the patient's material; or, indeed, he may become unduly irritated with the patient, may unconsciously sidetrack him onto another topic, and so forth. The 'counter' in the countertransference may thus indicate a reaction in the analyst which implies a parallel to the patient's transference (as in 'counterpart') as well as being a reaction to it (as in 'counteract'). The etymology of the term has been discussed by Greenson (1967).

There have been a number of different lines of development in the psychoanalytic literature on countertransference after Freud. Several authors have maintained that the term should be employed in the exact sense in which it was first used, i.e. that it should be limited to those unresolved conflicts and problems aroused in the psychoanalyst as a consequence of his work with the patient and which then hinder the analyst's effectiveness

(Fliess, 1953; Stern, 1924). Fliess says, 'Countertransference, always resistance, must always be analysed'. Winnicott (1960) describes the countertransference as the analyst's 'neurotic features *which spoil the professional attitude* and disturb the course of the analytic process as determined by the patient'. Others, while adhering more or less to the original concept, emphasized that the origin of countertransference hindrances lies predominantly in the therapist's transference towards the patient (Gitelson, 1952; Hoffer, 1956; A. Reich, 1951; Tower, 1956). For example, A. Reich (1951) remarked that the analyst

> may like or dislike the patient. As far as these attitudes are conscious, they have not yet anything to do with counter-transference. If these feelings increase in intensity, we can be fairly certain that the unconscious feelings of the analyst, his own transferences onto the patient, i.e. countertransferences, are mixed in. . . . Countertransference thus comprises the effects of the analyst's own unconscious needs and conflicts on his understanding or technique. In such cases the patient represents for the analyst an object of the past on to whom past feelings and wishes are projected . . . this is counter-transference in the proper sense.

Unfortunately the views of those authors who regarded countertransference as being the outcome of the analyst's own transference to the patient were often rendered obscure by their failure to indicate the exact sense in which they made use of the concept of transference (chapter four). Some appeared to relate countertransference to Freud's original transference concept, while others regarded transference as referring to all aspects of relationships (e.g. English & Pearson, 1937). In line with this latter usage, M. Balint, in one of the earliest papers on countertransference (1933), equated it with the analyst's own transference to his patient, and later (M. Balint & A. Balint, 1939) broadened the use of the term to include anything (even the positioning of the cushions on the couch) which reveals the personality of the analyst. In a later paper, M. Balint (1949) uses the term 'countertransference' unambiguously to describe the totality of the analyst's attitudes and behaviour towards his patient. For Balint, unlike Freud, countertransference came to include the professional attitude of the analyst towards his patient. Langs (1975) has indicated how the way the ground rules of the analysis are managed conveys something of the analyst's state of mind to the patient.

A major development in psychoanalytic writings on counter-transference occurred when it began to be seen as a phenomenon of importance in helping the analyst to understand the hidden meaning of the patient's material. The essential idea was that the analyst has elements of understanding and appreciation of the processes occurring in his patient, that these elements are not immediately conscious, and that they can be discovered by the analyst if he monitors his own feelings and associations while listening to the patient. This is an idea that is implicit in descriptions by Freud (1909b, 1912e) of the value of the analyst's neutral or 'evenly-suspended' attention, but the first explicit statement of the positive value of countertransference was made by Heimann (1950, 1960), and was extended by others (e.g. Little, 1951, 1960b). Heimann began by regarding countertransference as including all the feelings that the analyst experiences towards his patient. The analyst has to be able to '*sustain* the feelings which are stirred up in him, as opposed to discharging them (as does the patient), in order to *subordinate* them to the analytic task in which he functions as the patient's mirror reflection'. Her basic assumption (1950) is 'that the analyst's unconscious understands that of his patient. This rapport on the deep level comes to the surface in the form of feelings which the analyst notices in response to his patient, in his "countertransference"'. She maintains that the analyst must use his emotional response to the patient—his countertransference—as a key to the understanding of the patient. The analyst's awareness of his own responses can thus provide an additional avenue of insight into the patient's unconscious mental processes. This extension of the concept of countertransference is similar to the change in Freud's view of the function of transference, first regarded only as a hindrance but later seen as an asset to therapy (chapter four)

Heimann's work on countertransference is of substantial significance. Although her orientation at the time was strictly Kleinian, she did not link countertransference with Klein's concept of projective identification (1946). This connection was made by Racker in a series of papers (Racker, 1953, 1957, 1968), in which the analyst's countertransference was looked at as a *response* to the patient's projective identifications (chapter four). Racker further distinguished between *concordant* and *complementary* identifications on the part of the analyst, resulting from the patient's projections. To put it simply: 'countertransference based on a concordant identification occurs when the analyst identifies with the patient's own fantasy self representation of the moment. Countertransference based on a complementary identification occurs when the analyst identifies with the object representation in the patient's transference fantasy' (Sandler, 1987).

A. Reich (1951) pointed out that 'countertransference is a necessary prerequisite of analysis. If it does not exist, the necessary talent and interest is lacking. But it has to remain shadowy and in the background.' A similar view was put forward by Spitz (1956) and Little (1960b) who said that 'without unconscious countertransference there would be neither empathy nor analysis itself'. Money-Kyrle (1956) referred to empathy as the 'normal' countertransference.

A persistent theme in the psychoanalytic literature is that countertransference phenomena are essential concomitants of psychoanalytic treatment. One of the clearest statements in this connection was made by Sharpe (1947) who says, 'To say that . . . an analyst will still have complexes, blind spots, limitations is only to say he remains a human being. When he ceases to be an ordinary human being he ceases to be a good analyst'. She adds, 'Countertransference is often spoken of as if it implied a love attitude. The countertransference that is likely to cause trouble is the unconscious one on the analyst's side, whether it be an infantile negative or positive one or both in alternation. . . . We deceive ourselves if we think we have no countertransference. It is its nature that matters.'

As with other psychoanalytic concepts, the attribution of additional meaning to the term 'countertransference' has led to a loss of precision in its use. While there can be little doubt that all the therapist's feelings towards his patient must be a subject of interest to those investigating the doctor–patient relationship in a variety of situations, we have to question whether the extension of the countertransference concept to cover all the feelings experienced towards a patient is useful.

Most of the psychoanalytic literature on countertransference in the 1950s and 1960s appears to reflect adherence to one or other or both of the two main views described above, i.e. that countertransference is either an obstacle to the analytic work or that it is a valuable tool. The problems arising from these opposing views were recognized in the psychoanalytic literature relatively early (e.g. Orr, 1954). Hoffer (1956) was one of the first to attempt to deal with the confusion connected with the term by distinguishing between the analyst's *transference to his patient* and the analyst's *countertransference*, but idiosyncratically relates the analyst's transference to his humanity and appreciation of the patient's realistic needs. Countertransference, on the other hand, relates to the analyst's intrapsychic reactions, including his limitations in comprehending the patient's material.

Kernberg (1965), in a review of the writings on countertransference, pointed out that the broadening of the term to include all emotional responses in the analyst is confusing and causes it to lose all specific meaning. However, he also cited criticisms of the earlier view of countertransference as a 'resistance' or 'blind spot' in the analyst, pointing out that such a judgement may obscure the importance of countertransference by implying that it is something 'wrong'. This may encourage a 'phobic' attitude in the analyst towards his own emotional reactions and thus limit his understanding of the patient. He points out, in accord with views expressed by others (e.g. Winnicott, 1949), that the full use of the analyst's emotional response can be considered to be of particular diagnostic importance in the assessment of the suitability for treatment of patients with profound personality disorders and other very disturbed or psychotic patients.

The insights gained in the psychoanalytic treatment of borderline, delinquent, and psychotic patients, a consequence of the so-called 'widening scope of psychoanalysis', gradually came to be applied more generally. This is most strikingly seen in regard to the understanding and use of the countertransference within the context of the interpersonal relationship between patient and analyst. Thus Kernberg (1975), in writing on the treatment of borderline patients, points out that the patient's primitive internalized object relations mobilize, through projective identification, parallel primitive object relations in the analyst. The analyst subjectively experiences the projected aspects of the patient's self. From the side of the patient the projective identification is a way of managing the projected parts by controlling the analyst, so that the analyst is experienced by the patient as possessing the split-off and projected aspects of the patient's own self. The analyst's empathy with the patient is due to the fact that he also possesses primitive object relations which can be mobilized by the patient's projections.

Grinberg (1962) describes as 'projective counter-identification' the analyst's reactions to his own unconscious counter-transference responses. Grinberg's notion draws attention to the importance of seeing countertransference in its most general sense, as including the analyst's defensive reactions against feelings being aroused by the patient. So, for example, erotic feelings aroused in the analyst by the patient may be defended against by feelings of distaste for and hostility against the patient.

We have previously traced (chapter four) the development of the Kleinian theory of transference with its particular emphasis on projective identification, which is seen as a normal as well as a pathological phenomenon. Linked with this is the tendency in recent years for Kleinian analysts to place increasing emphasis on the constructive use of countertransference by the analyst. Reference was made to Joseph's view that the main path to the understanding and interpretation of transference was by way of the analyst's countertransference. Bion (1959, 1962) had described the functioning of projective identification in the analytic situation as parallelling the way in which the crying child projects its distress into the mother who 'contains' it and can then respond appropriately. The projected distress is then subject to what Bion calls 'reverie', i.e. the work of the mother in assessing the problem and then handling it appropriately. The analyst's function is the same; he 'contains' the patient's projections in a state of 'reverie' and responds with appropriate interpretations (see Hinshelwood, 1989).

Segal (1977) points out that the analyst's function of containing the patient's projections can be disrupted in a number of ways:

There is a whole area of the patient's pathology ... which specifically aims at disrupting this situation of containment, such as: invasion of the analyst's mind in a seductive or aggressive way, creating confusion and anxiety, and attacking links in the analyst's mind. We have to try to turn this situation to good account and learn about the interaction between the patient and ourselves from the very fact that our containment has been disturbed. It is from such disturbances in the analyst's capacity to function that one first gets an inkling of such psychotic processes.

It is worth noting that in the Kleinian view psychotic processes are thought to occur in everyone.

Although developments in Kleinian theory and technique represent a major trend in the development of views on countertransference, other psychoanalysts, from quite different theoretical positions, have also emphasized the interpersonal perspective of transference–countertransference interactions. Loewald (1986) put it nicely when he remarked that transference and countertransference cannot be treated as separate issues. He writes, 'They are the two faces of the same dynamic, rooted in the inextricable intertwinings with others in which individual life originates and remains throughout the life of the individual in numberless elaborations, derivatives, and transformations. One of these transformations shows itself in the encounter of the psychoanalytic situation.'

It has been pointed out by McLaughlin (1981) that it has become increasingly evident 'that both parties are caught up in a communicative field of incredible sensitivity and subtlety, with transferential–countertransferential shadings constantly at play in enormous affective intensities—a field in which the possibility of a neutral or catalytic comment, given or received, is remote indeed'. Similarly, Langs (1978) uses the concept of the 'bipersonal field' and sees countertransference as an interactional product. Langs refers to the bipersonal field as

the temporal–physical space within which the analytic interaction takes place. The patient is one term of the polarity; the analyst is the other. The field embodies both interactional and intrapsychic mechanisms, and every event within the field receives vectors from both participants. The field itself is defined by a framework—the ground rules of psychoanalysis—which not only delimits the field, but also, in a major way, contributes to the communicative properties of the field and to the analyst's hold of the patient and containment of his projective identifications.

Sandler (1976), in writing on countertransference and 'role-responsiveness', put forward the view that the patient will attempt to actualize, to bring about in reality, the self-object interaction represented in his dominant unconscious wishful fantasy. This interaction, involving a role for the subject and another for the object (the 'role relationship'), will tend to be actualized through manipulation of the analyst in the transference via rapid unconscious (including non-verbal) signals. This pressure from the side of the patient to provoke or evoke a particular response in the analyst may lead to countertransference experiences or even to a countertransference enactment on the part of the analyst (a reflection of his 'role responsiveness'). Such enactments should be considered as compromises between the role the patient is attempting to force upon the analyst and the analyst's own propensities. The analyst's awareness of such role-responses can be a vital clue to the dominant transference conflict and associated transference fantasies in the patient. In this connection Sandler introduces the concept of the 'free-floating responsiveness' of the analyst (normally kept within well-defined limits set by the ground rules of the analytic situation). Moeller (1977a, b) emphasizes that the analyst needs 'to grasp *both sides* of the role relationship, subject *and* object; grasp, that is, the whole relationship intrapsychically before he can be in any position to understand the situation of the patient'.

In an attempt to differentiate countertransference from other reactions of the analyst, Chediak (1979) points out that countertransference is only one of a number of what he calls *counter-reactions* of the analyst towards the patient. He proposes that such counter-reactions arise from different sources within the analyst–patient relationship and suggests that it is clinically useful to distinguish them. He divides the analyst's reactions (the first of which is not regarded as a counter-reaction) as follows:

1. *intellectual understanding* based on information given by the patient and intellectual knowledge possessed by the analyst;

2. *the general response to the patient as a person*, the counterpart of what Strupp (1960) stresses when talking about the patient's reaction to the analyst's personality;

3. *the analyst's transference* to the patient, i.e. reliving of early part object relationships as elicited by certain features in the patient;

4. *the analyst's countertransference*, i.e. the reaction in the analyst to the role he is assigned by the patient's transference;

5. *empathic identification* with the patient.

Whatever form it takes, countertransference is inevitable. Silverman (1985) remarks that this is so 'because of the very nature of the psychoanalytic process and because of the impossibility of any analyst's gaining so thorough an understanding of and control over his own unconscious inclinations from his training analyst that he will be completely impervious to the skilful efforts of his analysands to draw him into acting out their neurotic conflicts with them rather than analysing them'. Consequently analysts 'must be vigilant to the emergence of countertransference reactions so that they can analyse and overcome them'.

The analyst's countertransference is linked by Jacobs (1983) to his attitude towards the objects of the patient's present and past life. These responses 'are a product of complex interactions between the impulses, affects, fantasies, and defences evoked in the therapist by the mental representations he has formed of these objects'. A similar point is made by Bernstein and Glenn (1988) in regard to child analysis, in which the analyst may develop strong feelings about members of the child's family (see also Racker, 1968).

Events in the analyst's life may affect the countertransference profoundly (see van Dam, 1987). For example, illness in the analyst may lead to denial on his part, in which case the countertransference will have an unconscious defensive slant (Dewald, 1982). Abend (1982) put it well when he said,

It is my contention that the chief significance of the powerful countertransference elements mobilized by the analyst's experience of serious illness is their tendency to influence analytic technique. This means, among other things, that the very clinical judgement relied upon to assess the specific needs of patients ... is exactly what is under pressure from the countertransference; at no other time is the analyst's judgement about this technical problem *less* likely to be objective and reliable. Countertransference reactions are liable to affect the analyst's perception, understanding, capacity for instinctual control, and judgement in subtle, or sometimes not so subtle ways, and therefore may well colour his opinion of his patient's needs and capabilities.

Other special elements in the countertransference are described in the literature in relation to the analysis of special types of patient. Thus P. Tyson (1980) draws attention to the fact that the gender of the analyst plays a role in transference–countertransference reactions in child analysis at particular phases in the child's development. The tendency for analysts working with older patients to equate the patients with their own parents has been remarked upon (King, 1974). This is a countertransference manifestation which is not 'put into the analyst by the patient' (see also Wylie & Wylie, 1987). McDougall (1978) describes how the ideas, fantasies, and feelings of certain patients, traumatized at an early pre-verbal stage, can be discerned first in the countertransference. She says, 'In these cases it is permissible to deduce the existence of sequelae to early psychic trauma which will require specific handling in the analytic situation. This "screen-discourse", impregnated with messages that have never been elaborated verbally, can in the first instance only be captured by the arousal of countertransference affect.'

It is worth mentioning that empathy, so important a part of psychoanalytic technique, is not to be equated with countertransference (see Beres & Arlow, 1974; Arlow, 1985; Blum, 1986). Fliess (1942, 1953) had, relatively early on, pointed out that the analyst's capacity for empathy can be regarded as being based on 'trial' identification with the patient and that this reflects the analyst's capacity to place himself in another person's shoes. Knight (1940) also links empathy with those projective and introjective processes which contribute to 'trial identification'. The capacity for empathy is regarded as a prerequisite for the constructive use of countertransference (Rosenfeld, 1952), yet countertransference reactions can lead to a failure of empathy in the analysis (Wolf, 1979). It would seem that there is a two-way relationship between empathy and countertransference, reflecting the double aspect of countertransference, as a vehicle for gaining insight into the unconscious processes in the patient on the one hand, and as an impediment to empathic understanding on the other. Abend (1986) distinguishes in this context between 'beneficial empathy' and 'disadvantageous countertransference'. Clearly the unconscious and subtle aspects of the countertransference are important, particularly as these may be camouflaged and rationalised by the analyst. Jacobs (1986) remarks, 'Even today the idea of countertransference, for many colleagues, is synonymous with overt actions and with an identifiable piece of acting out on the part of the analyst'. He goes on to say that it 'is precisely those subtle, often scarcely visible countertransference reactions, so easily rationalized as parts of our standard operating procedures and so easily overlooked, that may in the end have the greatest impact on our analytic work'. However, the awareness by the analyst of his own bodily responses (movements, posture) can give him a clue to his countertransference (Jacobs, 1973).

Another line of thought about countertransference relates to developments in self psychology stemming from the work of Kohut. In the previous chapter the self psychological view of transference was described, with special reference to the role of the analyst as a 'selfobject'. The analyst, too, will treat the patient as a selfobject and will be dependent on him for validation. If the patient does not respond in this regard, the analyst can feel that he has failed as a soothing and understanding selfobject (Adler, 1984). Kohut had previously (1971, 1977) referred to the stimulation in the analyst of primitive grandiose countertransference feelings as a consequence of the patient's idealizing transference (see chapter five). Moreover, analysts whose development has been characterised by archaic grandiosity may find themselves angry and rejecting because their own grandiose wishes have been activated. Similarly, the patient may react with rage towards, or withdrawal from, an analyst who fails to function adequately in the mirror transference (see chapter five).

We can see that the concept of countertransference has been broadened over the years to include a number of different meanings, inevitably diminishing the precision with which it was originally used. In present usage the following main elements or meanings can be discerned (some of which have been listed by Little, 1951):

1. 'resistances' in the analyst due to the activation of inner conflicts within him—these disturb his understanding and conduct of the analysis, producing 'blind spots' (Freud 1910d, 1912e);

2. the 'transferences' of the analyst to his patient—here the patient becomes a present-day substitute for an important figure in the childhood of the analyst (e.g. A. Reich, 1951, 1960; Brenner, 1976, 1985); the projections of the analyst onto his patient should also be included;

3. the consequence of externalization or projective identification on the part of the patient, in which the analyst comes to experience a response to the patient in which the analyst is then the vehicle either for an aspect of the patient's own self or for an aspect of the object (e.g. Racker, 1953, 1957, 1968; Bion, 1959, 1962; Kernberg, 1975; Sandler, 1976, 1990a, 1990b; Segal, 1977);

4. the reaction of the analyst to the patient's transferences (Gitelson, 1952) and to his own countertransference responses (Grinberg, 1962);

5. countertransference as an interactional product of the 'communicative field' in which both the analyst and patient are involved (Langs, 1978; McLaughlin, 1981);

6. the analyst's dependency on the patient for 'validation' (Kohut, 1971, 1977; Adler, 1984);

7. the disturbance of communication between the analyst and patient due to anxiety aroused in the analyst by the patient–analyst relationship (Cohen, 1952);

8. personality characteristics of the analyst or events in the analyst's life (e.g. illness) which are reflected in his work and which may or may not lead to difficulties in the patient's therapy (e.g. M. Balint & A. Balint, 1939; Abend, 1982; Dewald, 1982; van Dam, 1987);

9. the whole of the analyst's conscious and unconscious attitudes to his patients (e.g. Balint, 1949; Kemper, 1966);

10. specific limitations in the psychoanalyst brought out by particular patients;

11. the 'appropriate' or 'normal' emotional response of the analyst to his patient—this can be an important therapeutic tool (Heimann, 1950, 1960; Little, 1951) and a basis for empathy and understanding (Heimann, 1950, 1960; Money-Kyrle, 1956).

Undoubtedly the restriction of the clinical concept of countertransference to the analyst's transference to his patient provides us with too narrow a definition, and one which is too closely tied to the particular meanings attributed to transference (chapters four and five). The broadening of the concept to include all the analyst's conscious or unconscious attitudes, and even all his personality traits, renders the term practically meaningless. On the other hand, it is appropriate to take into account the useful extension of the concept to include those aspects of the analyst's emotional responses to his patient which do not lead to 'resistances' or 'blind spots' in the analyst, but which may be employed by him, as far as he is able to become conscious of them, as a means of gaining insight, through an examination of his own mental reactions, into the meaning of the patient's communications and behaviour (see chapter eleven).

It would follow from this that a useful view of countertransference might be to take it as referring to the specific emotionally based responses aroused in the analyst by the specific qualities of his patient. This would exclude *general* features of the analyst's personality and internal psychological structure (which would colour or affect his work with all his patients) and would imply

1. that there are countertransference responses in the analyst, and that these exist throughout the analysis;

2. that countertransference can lead to difficulties in, or inappropriate handling of, the analysis—this will occur if and when the analyst fails to become aware of aspects of his countertransference reactions to the patient, or fails to cope with them even if he is aware of them;

3. that constant scrutiny by the analyst of variations in his feelings and attitudes towards the patient can lead to increased insight into processes occurring in the patient.

Although it has not been stressed as such in the literature, we would suggest that the *professional attitude* of the therapist, which allows him to take a certain 'distance' from the patient and yet remain in touch with his own and the patient's feelings, is of the greatest service in the conducting of the analytic work. Arlow (1985) speaks of the 'analytic stance'. Relevant to this is the concept of the analyst's 'work ego' (Fliess, 1942; McLaughlin, 1981; Olinick, Poland, Grigg, & Granatir, 1973). Closely associated with the analyst's 'work ego' and professional attitude is the effective exercise by the analyst of his capacity for self-scrutiny and self-analysis. In this connection, Kramer (1959) has spoken of the use of an 'auto-analytic function' (see R. L. Tyson, 1986). The professional stance of the analyst (which is not at all the same as aloofness) is one of the factors that allows analysts to understand material in their patients which had not been adequately analysed in their own training analysis, nor adequately internalized in their training. It is also one of the factors, apart from intellectual insight, which enables certain therapists who have not been analysed to do adequate psychotherapy, especially under the supervision of an analyst. In putting forward this idea, we would emphasize that we do not underestimate the importance of the personal analysis in the training of the psychoanalyst, nor the significance of countertransference resistances in the analyst due to unanalysed inner conflicts.

The concept of countertransference can readily be extended outside psychoanalytic treatment, and awareness of it can be regarded as a useful element in any doctor–patient or therapist–patient relationship. It follows that it can be of potential value for the clinician to monitor his reactions to his patients, and this can be extended to include the monitoring by the clinician of the reaction of other members of the staff of a therapeutic institution. For example, Main (1957, 1989) has described a group of patients who evoke a particular type of response in the medical and nursing staff of a psychiatric hospital. He suggests that this reaction, although it may be related to the internal problems and conflicts stimulated in the staff by such patients, is also the manifestation of an area of psychopathology in the patients themselves. Thus the observation of countertransference reactions may also be of diagnostic importance.

CHAPTER SEVEN

Resistance

W hile the *treatment alliance* (chapter three) and some aspects of *transference* (chapters four and five) relate to tendencies within the patient which act to maintain the treatment relationship, the concept of *resistance* is concerned with elements and forces in the patient that oppose the treatment process. Although resistance is a clinical, rather than a psychological, concept originally described in connection with psychoanalytic treatment, it is one that can readily be extended, without substantial revision, to other clinical situations.

Resistance as a clinical concept emerged in Freud's discussion of his early attempts to elicit 'forgotten' memories from his hysterical patients. Before the development of the psychoanalytic technique of free association, when Freud was still employing hypnosis and the 'pressure' technique (chapter two), resistance was regarded as anything in the patient which opposed the physician's attempts to influence him. Freud saw these opposing tendencies as being the reflection, in the treatment situation, of the same forces which brought about and maintained the dissociation (repression) of painful memories from consciousness. He commented (1895), 'Thus a psychical force . . . had originally driven the pathogenic idea out of association and was now opposing its return to memory. The hysterical patient's "not knowing" was in fact a "not wanting to know"—a not wanting which might be to a greater or less extent conscious. The task of the therapist, therefore, lies in overcoming . . . this resistance to association.'

Resistance was regarded by Freud as being present in pathological states other than hysteria or obsessional neurosis (the 'defence neuroses'), e.g. in psychotic conditions. In describing a case of chronic paranoia (1896b) he remarked that

> in this case of paranoia, just as in the two other defence neuroses with which I was familiar, there must be unconscious thoughts and repressed memories which could be brought into consciousness in the same way as they were in those neuroses, by overcoming a certain resistance. . . . The only peculiarity was that the thoughts which arose . . . were for the most part heard inwardly or hallucinated by the patient, in the same way as her voices.

In Freud's discussion of this case it becomes clear that he viewed the difference between the productions of the psychotic and those of the neurotic as being differences in form rather than content. What might emerge in the neurotic as a fantasy or in a dream, emerges in the psychotic patient as a belief (see the discussion of the psychotic transference in chapter five). Freud could assert in 1900 that 'Whatever interrupts the progress of analytic work is a resistance'.

The motives for resistance were seen to be the threat of arousal of unpleasant ideas and affects. The ideas that had been repressed (and resisted recollection) were characterized as being 'all of a distressing nature, calculated to arouse the affects of shame, of self-reproach and of physical pain, and the feeling of being harmed' (1895d). The entry of psychoanalysis into what has been described as its second phase (chapter one) and the recognition of the importance of inner impulses and wishes (in contrast to painful real experiences) in causing conflict and in motivating defence brought no fundamental change in the concept of resistance. Nevertheless resistance was now seen as being directed not only against the recall of distressing memories but also against the awareness of unacceptable impulses. In a paper on 'Freud's Psycho-Analytic Procedure' (1904a), written by Freud himself, he states, 'The factor of resistance has become one of the cornerstones of his theory. The ideas which are normally pushed aside on every sort of excuse . . . are regarded by him as derivatives of the repressed psychical phenomena (thoughts and impulses), distorted owing to the resistance against their reproduction. . . . The greater the resistance, the greater is the distortion.'

In this formulation a new element can be seen. Resistance was no longer regarded as a complete suppression of unacceptable mental content, but as being responsible for the *distortion* of unconscious impulses and memories so that they appear *in disguise* in the free associations of the patient. In this context, resistance was seen to operate in exactly the same way as the 'censor' in dreaming (Freud, 1900a), i.e. it was thought to function to prevent unacceptable thoughts, feelings, or wishes from becoming conscious.

The link between the clinical phenomenon of resistance and such 'distorting' or 'censoring' processes led naturally to the formulation that resistance is not something that appears from time to time during analysis—it is constantly present during that treatment. The patient 'must never lose sight of the fact that a treatment like ours proceeded to the accompaniment of a *constant resistance*' (Freud, 1909c). Freud also commented in that paper on the satisfaction that patients receive from their sufferings, a point which he amplified elsewhere, and to which we will return later in this chapter when we come to speak of the gratification obtained through suffering and through the satisfaction of a need for punishment.

In chapter four we commented on the importance Freud attached to the relation between transference and resistance. The so-called 'transference resistances' were regarded as the most powerful obstacles in the path of psychoanalytic treatment (1912b, 1940a [1938]). Thoughts and feelings involving the therapist may arise as a consequence of the patient's tendency to re-experience repressed earlier important attitudes, feelings, and experiences instead of recalling them. These will tend to arise anew in the here-and-now of the analytic situation. The development of such transferences from past figures to the analyst may unconsciously be felt to be extremely threatening. Freud commented (1912b):

> The patient who becomes dominated by a strong transference resistance is flung out of his real relation to the doctor . . . feels at liberty then to disregard the fundamental rule of psychoanalysis which lays it down that whatever comes into one's head must be reported without criticizing it . . . forgets the intentions with which he started the treatment, and . . . regards with indifference logical arguments and conclusions which only a short time before had made a great impression on him.

Sources and forms of resistance

By 1912, the major distinction made by Freud in regard to the sources of resistance in patients undergoing psychoanalysis was between *transference resistance* and *repression resistance,* the latter being the resistance, inherent in the psychological structure of the patient, to the awareness of painful or dangerous impulses and memories. While transference resistances may disappear, and even be replaced by transference attachments which reinforce the treatment alliance, repression resistances can be conceived of as an ever-present (though fluctuating) internal force that acts in opposition to the aims of treatment.

The third phase of psychoanalysis, beginning with the 'structural' theory described in *The Ego and the Id* (Freud, 1923b) brought about a significant change in the notion of resistance. In Freud's important work, *Inhibitions, Symptoms and Anxiety* (1926d), he pointed out that danger to the ego arises not only from instinctual sources but from the superego and the external world as well. At this time he introduced his second theory of anxiety in which anxiety was seen as a *signal* of danger to the ego rather than being, as he had originally said, a transformation of libido into anxiety following repression of a sexual impulse. In the new theory the danger signal could prompt the ego's defensive activity, which in turn could lead to resistance in the analysis. Freud was now in a position to distinguish between five major types and sources of resistance (1926d):

(1) *Repression resistance,* which can be regarded as the clinical manifestation of the individual's need to defend himself against impulses, memories, and feelings which, were they to emerge from the depths into consciousness, would bring about a painful state, or would threaten to cause such a state. The repression resistance can also be seen as a reflection of the so-called 'primary gain' from the neurotic illness. 'Primary gain' refers here to the gain resulting from the resolution of painful intrapsychic conflict through the formation of a neurotic symptom. If the mechanisms of defence cannot cope with the conflict, neurotic symptoms are formed as 'last resort' formations aimed at dealing with conflict and at protecting the individual from conscious awareness of distressing and painful mental content. The process of free association during psychoanalysis creates a constant potential danger situation for the patient because of the invitation offered to the repressed by the process of free association. This in turn promotes the repression resistance. The closer the repressed material comes to consciousness, the greater the resistance, and it is the analyst's task to facilitate, through his interpretations, the emergence of such content into consciousness in a form that can be tolerated by the patient (chapter twelve).

(2) *Transference resistance,* which, although essentially similar to the repression resistance, has the special quality that it reflects the struggle against infantile impulses that have emerged in direct or modified form in relation to the analyst (chapter four). The analytic situation reanimates, in the form of a current distortion of reality, material that had been repressed or had been dealt with in some other way (e.g. by being channelled into the neurotic symptom itself). This revival of the past in the psychoanalytic relationship can lead to the transference resistance. Here, too, it is the analyst's task to assist the emergence of transference content into consciousness in a tolerable form by means of his interventions. Transference resistances include the conscious withholding by the patient of thoughts about the analyst, as well as reflecting unconscious transference thoughts which are defended against.

(3) Resistance can derive from *the gain from illness* (secondary gain). Although in the first instance the symptom may be felt as a 'foreign body' and undesirable, a process of 'assimilation' of the symptom into the individual's psychological organization may, and often does, occur. Freud put it thus: 'The ego now proceeds to behave as though it recognized that the symptom had come to stay and that the only thing to do was to accept the situation in good part and draw as much advantage from it as possible' (1926a). Such secondary gains from symptoms are familiar in the form of the advantages and gratifications obtained from being ill and cared for or pitied by others, or in the gratification of aggressive and revengeful impulses towards those who are then forced to share in the patient's suffering. Secondary gain may also accrue through the satisfaction of a patient's need for punishment, or of concealed masochistic trends. Gross examples of gain from illness may be seen in patients with 'compensation neuroses', or those who remain ill because of the secondary gain from society, e.g. where 'welfare' payments exceed the wage that could be earned. The patient's unconscious reluctance to abandon these secondary advantages from illness, during the course of treatment, constitutes this particular form of resistance.

(4) *Id resistance* is due to the resistance of instinctual impulses to any change in their mode and form of expression. As Freud said (1926e): 'As you can imagine, there are likely to be difficulties if an instinctual process which has been going along a particular path for whole decades is suddenly expected to take a new path that has just been made open for it.' This form of resistance necessitates what Freud called 'working through' for its elimination (chapter ten). In our view this resistance in treatment can be regarded as part of the more general psychological resistance to giving up acquired habits and modes of functioning—the resistance to 'unlearning'. An aspect of the concept of 'working through' would be the process of acquiring new patterns of functioning, and learning to inhibit the older, more firmly established patterns. This process is regarded as constituting an important part of the analytic work. The 'id resistance' has also been considered in some psychoanalytic writings as being due to 'sluggishness', 'adhesiveness' or 'stickiness' of the libido.

(5) *Superego resistance* is the resistance stemming from the patient's sense of guilt or his need for punishment. Freud regarded the 'superego resistance' as being the most difficult for the analyst to discern and to deal with. It reflects the operation of an unconscious sense of guilt (1923b), and accounts for the apparently paradoxical reaction of the patient to any step in the analytic work which represents the fulfilment of one or other impulse that he has defended against because of the promptings of his own conscience. Thus a patient who has strong guilt feelings related, for example, to the wish to be the most-loved son and to triumph over his siblings may react with resistance to any change that threatens to bring about a situation in which he can become more successful than his rivals. Or a patient who has intense unconscious feelings of guilt about his particular sexual wishes may react with strong resistance following the freeing of such wishes through the analytic process. Superego resistance can be exemplified by the patient who allows himself to have a thought that arouses guilt, represses this thought, and comes to the session with an uneasy feeling which is eventually identified as a feeling of guilt that makes him resistant to the work of analysis. The most intense form of such superego resistance can be seen in the negative therapeutic reaction, to be discussed in chapter eight.

Freud saw the clinical phenomena of resistance as being intimately, though not exclusively, related to the whole range of the patient's mechanisms of defence. It was not specifically linked with repression, although he often used the term 'repression' as a synonym for defence in general. The defence mechanisms are developed and utilized to deal with situations of danger (in particular, the dangers that would arise if unconscious sexual or aggressive wishes were to be allowed free and direct expression in consciousness or in behaviour) and include such mechanisms as projection, undoing, intellectualization, rationalization, identification with the aggressor, reaction formation, and so forth. Freud commented (1937c) that 'the defensive mechanisms directed against former danger recur in the treatment as *resistances* against recovery. It follows from this that the ego treats recovery itself as a new danger'.

Freud had made a number of references to the relation between the form of the resistance shown by the patient and the nature of the underlying defensive organization. For example, he had described particular distortions of free association which were thought to be characteristic of obsessional neurotics (1909d). But while the types of resistance were felt to be indicative of aspects of the patient's psychopathology (1926d), they were, in the main, regarded by Freud as obstacles to the work of analysis.

In 1936 Anna Freud, in her book, *The Ego and the Mechanisms of Defence,* emphasized the extent to which the resistances can provide information about the patient's mental functioning. Thus resistances, insofar as they reflect the type of conflict and the defences used, became an object of analytic study in themselves. Analysis of resistances could be seen as essentially the analysis of those aspects of the patient's defences which entered into and contributed to the pathological outcome of his conflicts. 'Defence analysis', through the analysis of resistances, has come to play an increasingly important part in psychoanalytic technique (A. Freud, 1965; Glover, 1955; Hartmann, 1951; Sandler & A. Freud, 1985). Gillman (1987), writing about the analysis of dreams, has remarked that from one point of view all dreams are 'resistance dreams', in that their content obscures unconscious material which is defended against. At the same time the dream is seen as 'a window to material that otherwise might be unavailable'. Gillman goes on to say that dreams reflect the characteristic defences that patients use to ward off awareness of unpleasant mental content.

In a number of important publications, Reich (1928, 1929, 1933) demonstrated that certain patients had developed fixed character traits that were the outcome of past defensive processes, and which showed themselves both in the personality and in the psychoanalytic process as characteristic 'fixed' attitudes. Reich referred to these as the 'armour-plating of character' [*Charakterpanzerung*]. While he maintained that resistances resulting from such 'fixed' personality characteristics should initially be the main focus of the psychoanalytic work, Anna Freud (1936) took the view that these particular resistances should be placed in the foreground of the analysis only when no trace of a current conflict, involving ego, drive, and affect, could be detected—a view that was expanded on by Sterba (1953).

In 1937 Freud published 'Analysis terminable and interminable' (1937a), in which he discussed a number of different factors that could limit the success of the analytic work. Among these was the innate constitutional strength of the drives, which contributed to an unchangeable 'bedrock' of the patient's personality. A further factor was the inaccessibility of dormant conflicts which did not appear in revived form in the transference and could therefore not be successfully analysed. Freud also suggested that the specific qualities of mobility and adhesiveness of the libido, and biologically determined sources of conflict—e.g., penis envy in the female and the male's constitutional passivity—contributed to the resistance to change.

Shortly afterwards, Deutsch (1939) proposed a three-fold classification of forms of resistance into (1) the intellectual or 'intellectualizing' resistances, (2) the transference resistances, and (3) those resistances that emerge as a consequence of the patient's need to defend himself against the recollection of childhood material. She discussed the first group *in extenso,* commenting that patients who show the intellectual resistances attempt to replace analytic *experiencing* with intellectual *understanding.* Such resistances may be found in highly intellectual individuals, in obsessional neurotics, and in patients 'with blocked or disturbed affects, who, having repressed the affective side of their life, have retained the intellectual side as the sole means of expressing their . . . personality'.

In spite of the close link between resistance and defence, it has been repeatedly emphasized that resistance is not synonymous with defence (Brenner, 1981; Gero, 1951; Laplanche & Pontalis, 1973; Loewenstein, 1954; Lorand, 1958; Stone, 1973). Blum (1985) aptly says,

> The concept of defence is broader than that of resistance since resistance is a treatment function that takes its meaning from the analytic process. Resistance may usually be seen in its influence on free association and the patient's cooperation with the analytic effort in the therapeutic alliance, but resistance may also be defined and described from many other points of

view, e.g., transference resistance, superego resistance, id resistance, negative therapeutic reaction, repetition and regression tendencies, etc. In a broad sense, defence impedes insight, and insight permits the awareness and lifting of defensive operations serving as resistance within the analytic process.

Whereas the patient's defences are an integral part of his psychological structure, resistance represents the patient's attempts to protect himself against the threats to his psychological equilibrium posed by the analytic procedure. As Greenson (1967) puts it: 'The resistances defend the *status quo* of the patient's neurosis. The resistances oppose the analyst, the analytic work, and the patient's reasonable ego'. In Rangell's view (1985) resistance can be regarded as a second layer of defence activated by the ego when existing defences are too weak to cope.

A different aspect is emphasized by Stone (1973), who draws attention to the fact that

the phenomena of resistance are largely, if not exclusively, of self-protective, conservative orientation. That their purposes are usually irrational in derivation, and largely ego dystonic, renders them amenable to analytic work. It must be recalled that they exist, in a subjectively purposive sense, to protect the encapsulated unconscious aspects of the personality, and, reciprocally, to protect the adult functioning personality . . . from the potentially disruptive intrusions and demands of hitherto unconscious content.

He adds: 'The analyst is from the beginning experienced as a threat by the infantile aspect of the ego.' This reflects the point that the analytic setting offers an invitation to regress, resulting in an intensification of a previously repressed wish or impulse, followed by increased conflict and heightened resistance.

An examination of the psychoanalytic literature since Freud indicates that the *concept* of resistance in psychoanalysis has in its central aspects remained essentially unchanged. However, the many *forms* which resistance can take have been described in detail, and there is little doubt that the sensitivity to subtle signs of resistance has come to be regarded as an increasingly important part of the psychoanalyst's repertoire of technical skills. It is important to differentiate between (1) the concept of an internal psychic state of resistance, which is not directly observable, and (2) the observable *signs* of this resistance, also usually referred to as 'resistances'. The failure to make this differentiation between the two meanings of 'resistance' has been a source of considerable confusion, because the second category of 'resistances' are products of a heightened internal state of resistance, and the analyst needs to be orientated towards the cause of the inner state rather than the specific manifestation of that state (although this should not be neglected). It is worth noting that some behaviours, usually considered to be signs of resistance—e.g. falling asleep and silence—may, at certain points in the analysis, be seen not only as resistance but as non-verbal forms of expression of repressed wishes, fantasies, or memories (see Ferenczi, 1914; Khan, 1963).

It might be of some use to follow the descriptive differentiation made by Glover (1955) between the 'obvious' or 'crass' resistances on the one hand, and the 'unobtrusive' resistances on the other. The 'crass' resistances include breaking-off treatment, lateness, missing appointments, silences, circumlocution, automatic rejection or misinterpretation of everything the analyst says, assumed stupidity, a persistent mood of abstraction, and falling asleep. The less obtrusive resistances are hidden beneath an apparent compliance with the requirements of the analytic situation. They may show themselves in the form of agreement with everything the analyst says, in the bringing of material (e.g. dreams) in which the patient believes the analyst to have a special interest, and in many other forms. As Glover remarks, 'On the whole, the characteristic of these unobtrusive resistances is just that they are not explosive, do not break through or disrupt the superficies of the analytic situation, but rather infiltrate the situation, exude through it, or, to vary the expression, move with the stream rather than against it, snagwise'. Fenichel (1945a) has distinguished between 'acute' resistances as opposed to the more hidden forms, the latter showing themselves mainly in the lack of change in the patient, even though the psychoanalytic work appears to be proceeding without hindrance. A significant clinical distinction, particularly in the context of the so-called 'character' analysis, has been made between ego syntonic and ego dystonic (or ego alien) resistances (Dewald, 1980; Gill, 1988; Reich, 1933;

Stone, 1973). Ego dystonic resistances are felt by the patient to intrude into the analytic work. Ego syntonic resistances, on the other hand, are not seen by the patient as resistances, but are felt to be appropriate reactions to the analytic situation. The terms 'ego syntonic' and 'ego dystonic' antedate the structural theory (Freud, 1923b) and should be read as 'consciousness syntonic' and 'consciousness dystonic'.

More recently, Stone (1973) and Dewald (1980) have made similar points by distinguishing between *tactical* and *strategic* resistances. Dewald says,

> Strategic resistances would be those basic unconscious core psychic operations through which the patient continues to seek satisfaction of infantile and early childhood drives and drive derivatives, object choices, or adaptive and defensive psychic operations. . . . The tactical resistances represent superimposed individual intrapsychic and interpersonal behaviour patterns in various hierarchies of organization by which patients defend themselves against conscious awareness of the strategic core resistances and the conflicts with which they are interlocked. . . . Their understanding and elaboration during the analytic process represent an important mode of access to the analysis of the ego, its synthetic operations, and the overall maintenance of characteristic psychic organization.

Any attempt to classify the forms of resistance must be in the nature of an academic exercise, although clinical illustrations can be extremely useful (Boesky, 1985; Boschán, 1987; Frank, 1985; Gill, 1988; Gillman, 1987; Lipton, 1977; Vianna, 1974, 1975). The range of forms that resistances can take is probably infinite, and it would appear to be more fruitful to investigate the different *sources* of resistances, as these are more limited in number, and indicate something of the motivation for the particular resistance and its function at a particular time. As Dewald remarks (1980), 'the manifestations of resistance are protean, and highly variable among different patients and also within the same patient during different periods of the analysis'.

As far as the *sources* of resistance are concerned, those outlined by Freud (1926d) remain central in the theory of psychoanalytic technique. However, the list needs to be extended and modified in the light of later contributions. An attempt at this follows, but the categories listed below overlap greatly.

(1) Resistances resulting from the threat posed, by the analytic procedure and its aims, to the particular adaptations made by the patient. In this context the concept of adaptation is used as referring to the individual's adaptation to forces arising both from the external world and from within himself (Hartmann, 1939; Sandler & Joffe, 1969). The repression resistance, being a specific case of what might be termed 'defence resistance', can be included here, for defences other than repression can give rise to resistance. The mechanisms of defence can, in turn, be regarded as mechanisms of adaptation and are essential for normal functioning as well as being involved in pathogenic processes (A. Freud, 1936).

(2) Transference resistances, essentially as described by Freud. Stone (1973) has summarized the relationship between resistance and transference as follows:

> First, the resistance to awareness of the transference, and its subjective elaboration in the transference neurosis. Second, the resistance to the dynamic and genetic [Stone refers here to the dissection of transference conflict and the understanding of its development] reductions of the transference neurosis, and ultimately the transference attachment itself, once established in awareness. Third, the transference presentation of the analyst to the 'experiencing' portion of the patient's ego, as id object and as externalized superego simultaneously, in juxtaposition to the therapeutic alliance between the analyst in his real function and the rational 'observing' portion of the patient's ego.

Stone (1973) observes that, 'what is of the first importance, however, is the establishment of a viable scientific and working concept of resistance to the therapeutic process as a manifestation of a reactivated intrapsychic conflict in a new interpersonal context'. It is of interest to recall that James Strachey wrote in 1934 that 'it is, of course, one of the characteristics of a resistance that it arises in relation to the analyst; and thus the interpretation of a resistance will almost inevitably be a transference interpretation'. Since then, there have been substantial developments in our knowledge of the relation between transference and resistance. Both Stone (1973) and Gill (1982) distinguish between 'resistance to the awareness of transference'—the patient's reluctance to become aware of his transference feelings and attitudes—and 'resistance to the resolution of transference'.

The emphasis in recent years on the interpersonal perspective of the analytic situation has led naturally to the consideration of the role of those factors in the analyst which may contribute to the patient's resistance. Stone (1973) points out that a 'rejecting or hostile or unruly attitude of the patient, sometimes [evokes] spontaneous antagonistic reactions in the physician'. He goes on to refer to this as the 'counter resistance' of the analyst. Such counter resistance can be quite unconscious and projected onto the patient (Vianna, 1975), producing resistance in him as a direct consequence. Anna Freud (1954) has suggested that 'with due respect for the necessary strictest handling and interpretation of the transference, I feel still that we should leave room somewhere for the realization that analyst and patient are also two real people, of equal adult status, in a real personal relationship to each other. I wonder whether our—at times complete—neglect of this side of the matter is not responsible for some of the hostile reactions which we get from our patients and which we are apt to ascribe to "true transference" only.' Anna Freud cautions that 'these are technically subversive thoughts and ought to be "handled with care"'.

Thomä and Kächele (1987) remark that 'the influence of the analyst and his treatment technique on the development of negative and erotized transferences is often mentioned only in passing. . . . This occurs despite the general recognition of how strongly negative transferences—and the same is true for erotized transferences—are dependent on countertransference, treatment technique, and the analyst's theoretical position.'

(3) Resistance deriving from secondary gains, as discussed by Freud.

(4) Superego resistance, as described by Freud. Later developments, particularly stimulated by Fairbairn's work on the rela-

tion between object relations and resistance, have led object relations theorists to think less and less in terms of Freud's structural
theory and to conceive of intra-psychic life essentially in terms of
internal object relationships. Superego resistance is seen by object relations theorists in terms of the relation to and interaction
with an internalized critical, or even persecutory, figure. The
connection between internal object relationships and psychoanalytic treatment is beautifully described by Fairbairn (1958), who
points out that 'in a sense, psychoanalytical treatment resolves
itself into a struggle on the part of the patient to press-gang his
relationship with the inner world through the agency of transference, and a determination on the part of the analyst to effect a
breach in this closed system and to provide conditions under
which in the setting of a therapeutic relationship, the patient may
be induced to accept the open system of outer reality'. Kernberg
(1985) makes a similar point when he says, in regard to understanding the patient's character, that the related conflicting
internalized object relations may become reactivated in the transference, in which case character defences become transference
resistances.

There can be little doubt that a sense of security is gained in the
internal reciprocal arrangement between the self and its objects,
even though this relationship may be a source of pain. Consequently the very existence of organized internal relationships
must provide resistance to change through analysis (Sandler,
1990a, 1990b).

(5) Resistance arising from faulty procedures and inappropriate technical measures adopted by the psychoanalyst. Such
resistances may be dealt with during the normal course of the
analysis if their source is realized and acknowledged by both
analyst and patient. If this does not occur, these resistances may
lead to a breakdown of treatment or its continuation on a spurious
basis (Glover, 1955; Greenson, 1967).

(6) Resistances due to the fact that changes in the patient
brought about by the analysis may lead to real difficulties in the
patient's relationships with important persons in his environment (Freud, 1916–1917; Gill, 1988; Stone, 1973). Thus a maso-

chistic and subservient spouse may offer a resistance to insight and change because such a change would threaten the marriage.

(7) Resistances prompted by the danger of cure and the loss of the analyst which this might entail. Many patients remain in analysis because of concealed gratifications obtained from the procedure and the analytic relationship. This is most likely to happen when the patient has come to depend on the analyst as an important figure in his life. A patient may unconsciously re-experience the analyst as a protecting or nurturing parent, and the resistance to cure may reflect a fear of giving up the relationship. Such patients may get worse when termination of treatment is considered, but this is not the same as the negative therapeutic reaction (chapter eight).

(8) Resistances that occur because the analytic work is a threat to the patient's self-esteem (Abraham, 1919). This is particularly important in those patients in whom the arousal of *shame* is a major motive for defensive activity. Such patients may have difficulties in tolerating the infantile aspects of themselves that emerge during the course of treatment because they regard these aspects as shameful.

As long ago as 1919, Abraham wrote of the problem of some patients who show continual resistance to the analysis through controlling their associations. Their essentially narcissistic personalities allow them to hide their defiance towards the analysis behind an external eagerness to be analysed. The work is impeded, according to Abraham, by the fact that their narcissistic love for themselves cannot be satisfied and so a satisfactorily functioning positive transference cannot be established. Following Abraham, increasing attention has been paid to the analysis of resistance in narcissistic patients and in those with severe personality disorders with borderline pathology (see Vianna, 1974; Boschán, 1987; Kernberg, 1988). Particularly significant in this connection is the work of Melanie Klein (1946, 1957), Rosenfeld (1965b, 1971) and Kohut (1971, 1977, 1984).

Rosenfeld suggests that resistances in the narcissistic patient can be approached 'only by a detailed and meticulous analysis of aggression and envy in the analytic transference relationship, as with the interpretation of the related persecutory anxieties projected onto the analyst' (in Vianna, 1974). Kernberg (1988) has traced the ramifications of narcissistic impulses from the point of view of object relations theory, and in speaking of the analysis of the resistances of patients with narcissistic personality structures, says, 'the emergence in the transference of the various features of the pathological grandiose self and the correspondingly admiring, devalued, or suspiciously feared object representations may permit the gradual clarification of the component internalized object relations that have led to the condensation of the grandiose self on the basis of its constituent real self, ideal self, and ideal object representations'. Many analysts now hold the view that narcissism should not be contrasted with object relationships, but should, rather, be conceived of in terms of very specific types of internal object relationship, including the relation of the individual to his own self.

(9) Resistance to the giving up of past adaptive solutions (including neurotic symptoms) because of the fact that such solutions need to be 'unlearned' or extinguished. This process of extinction takes time and is an integral part of the process of working through (chapter twelve). While this includes the so-called 'id-resistance', it also encompasses sources of resistance to change in modes of functioning of the more organized and controlling aspects of the personality (i.e. of the ego and superego). There has been increasing emphasis in recent years (e.g. Stone, 1973; Thomä & Kächele, 1987) on resistance being directed against 'the integration of experience, rather than against the explicitly and exclusively infantile or against the past' (Stone, 1973). This can be linked with a view expressed by Erikson (1968) that there is an 'identity resistance' based on a reluctance to lose feelings of identity bound up with the representation of the self. The less well organized the patient's self, the greater the threat, and therefore the greater the resistance. Similarly, Ogden (1983) discusses how the patient resists altering internal object relationships in the face of current experience. In addition, resistance can be used by the patient as a way of controlling the 'distance' between himself and the analyst in order to prevent a loss of control and therefore a loss of feelings of safety (see Sandler, 1968; Thomä & Kächele,

1987). While most analysts (e.g. Fenichel, 1941) would not accept the id resistance as a viable concept, others (e.g. Frank, 1985; Stone, 1973; Thomä & Kächele, 1987) take the view that id resistance can be a reflection of quantitative variations in the intensity of the instinctual drives.

(10) Character resistances, of the sort described by Reich (1928, 1929, 1933), resulting from the 'fixed' nature of character traits which may persist after the original conflicts that brought them into being have diminished or disappeared. These traits are acceptable to the patient because they do not give rise to distress. Boesky (1985) has expressed the view that the whole notion of character resistance should be abandoned and that, 'It is misleading to suggest that so-called character resistances should be dealt with differently than any other resistance'. On the other hand, Kernberg (1980a) is very much for the retention of the concept and stresses the importance of evaluating such resistances in relation to analysability.

Resistances that result from unchangeable aspects of the patient's character structure are, without doubt, of great significance in analysis. Sandler (1988) puts forward the view that the unalterable 'bedrock' in patients (Freud, 1937c) can be seen as 'a *specific* psychobiological bedrock which involves, to a very large degree, the structures created by the *specific* individual's development within the *specific* reciprocal relation between the person and his environment—in particular as a result of the infant–caregiver interaction. This certainly puts a limit on what analysis can achieve. . . . [It is] poor technique to disregard such factors and to view everything as "analysable".' Anna Freud's concept of ego restriction is relevant here. She (Sandler with A. Freud, 1985) says:

> Restriction of the ego deals with unpleasurable affect that is aroused by an external experience. The idea is that after the child has once had the experience that such an affect can be aroused, the easiest thing for him is not to enter the same situation again. This is by no means a neurotic mechanism, but really one of the mechanisms which help us to build up our different personalities. From the earliest time there is a more

or less automatic avoidance of the disagreeable, and after all, why *should* we have disagreeable experiences? The ego feels that there are other things one can do instead.

The role of resistance in childhood analysis is discussed in detail by Sandler, Kennedy, and Tyson (1980). They remark that in child analysis 'it is necessary to look for resistances to communication or to cooperation in general rather than resistances to verbal free association'.

While the last two forms of resistance are obviously related and may even be considered to be forms of 'secondary gain', their basis is different from that usually conceived of for 'secondary gain'. It has been suggested that an adaptive solution, be it a neurotic symptom, a character trait, or some other method of functioning, can be reinforced by the fact that its predictability and availability as a pattern of functioning creates an increment in the individual's feelings of safety and thus offers a resistance to change once the original 'primary gain' has disappeared (Sandler, 1960a). As described by Sandler and Joffe (1968) in relation to the persistence of the psychological 'structures' which are regarded as giving a pattern to aspects of behaviour:

> some structures may evolve in order to solve ongoing conflict. But they may persist and be utilized in order to maintain a feeling of safety even though the original impulses which entered into their formation are no longer operative in the same way. It is likely that the latter structures are [those] most amenable to change through behaviour therapy. Thus a neurotic symptom (and the structures which subserve it) may be directed towards solving, for example, an ongoing conflict between an instinctual wish and internal (superego) standards of the individual. But it may equally function at a later date as a method of producing a feeling of safety, and if other methods of providing safety feeling are available then a different and more comfortable solution may be created and utilized, and the employment of the older symptom structure inhibited. . . . All systems and techniques of psychotherapy (including behaviour therapy) abound with potential alternative safety-giving solutions which can be adopted by the patient.

There is general agreement among psychoanalysts that it is an important part of the analytic process for the analyst to make the patient aware of his resistances, to attempt to get him to view them as obstacles that have to be understood and overcome. This can be a far from easy task, for the patient will often make every attempt to justify or rationalize his resistance and to view it as appropriate in the circumstances. The prospect of successful analytic work may be unconsciously viewed by the patient as a threat to the safe neurotic equilibrium he has established. This threat may be so great that he may even manifest his resistance through a 'flight into health' and justify the cessation of treatment by the fact that his symptoms have, for the time being at least, disappeared. The fear of what might occur as a consequence of the analysis would appear to be so great as to outweigh the primary and secondary gains from the symptoms. The mechanisms whereby the 'flight into health' can be accomplished are, in our view, insufficiently understood, but it seems more likely that this process can take place when the secondary gains from illness have played an important part in maintaining the patient's symptoms after the primary gain from the symptoms has receded or disappeared. The 'flight into health' should be distinguished from the denial of symptoms, which may be part of the patient's justification for stopping treatment when the resistances aroused outweigh the treatment alliance.

While resistance was originally conceived of in terms of the patient's resistances to recollection and to free association, it is clear that the concept was soon extended to include all the obstacles to the aims and procedures of treatment that arise from within the patient. In psychoanalysis and psychoanalytic psychotherapy resistances are overcome by means of the analyst's interpretations and other interventions (chapter ten). In addition, the form and context of the resistance have come to be seen as a useful source of information to the therapist. Such a view of resistance enables the concept to be extended from psychoanalysis to all forms of treatment, and we can see the manifestations of resistance even in ordinary medical practice, in the form of forgotten appointments, misunderstandings of the doctor's instructions, rationalizations for breaking off treatment, and the like. Different methods of treatment may stimulate different sources of resistance, and this may account for the fact that one method may succeed with a patient when another would not. Indeed, some methods of treatment may owe their success to the fact that they by-pass certain sources of resistance, but it must be equally true that others may fail because no provision has been made for the adequate handling of the resistances that arise. Even in all these different situations, the resistance can itself be a source of useful information.

CHAPTER EIGHT

The negative therapeutic reaction

The clinical concept of the *negative therapeutic reaction* has been included in this book for a number of reasons. It is a concept of particular importance in the history of psychoanalysis, for it represents the clinical phenomenon chosen by Freud (1923b) to illustrate the workings of an 'unconscious sense of guilt' and to indicate the existence of what he conceived of as a special mental agency—the *superego*. Moreover, it is a concept widely used in clinical psychoanalysis, and significant papers have been written on the subject since Freud's original formulation. Unlike such concepts as *transference* (chapters four and five) and *acting out* (chapter nine), it has not been extensively applied outside clinical psychoanalysis. This may be regarded as surprising in view of the fact that it would seem to be readily applicable without alteration to a wide variety of clinical situations.

The phenomenon of the negative therapeutic reaction in psychoanalytic treatment was first described and explained by Freud (1923b):

There are certain people who behave in a quite peculiar fashion during the work of analysis. When one speaks hopefully to them or expresses satisfaction with the progress of the treatment they show signs of discontent and their condition invariably becomes worse. One begins by regarding this as defiance and as an attempt to prove their superiority to the physician, but later one comes to take a deeper and juster view. One becomes convinced, not only that such people cannot endure any praise or appreciation, but that they react inversely to the progress of the treatment. Every partial solution that ought to result, and in other people does result, in an improvement or a temporary suspension of symptoms produces in them for the time being an exacerbation of their illness; they get worse during the treatment instead of getting better.

Freud linked this with the operation of what he conceived of as an unconscious sense of guilt, due to the operation of the patient's conscience (an aspect of the superego). In these cases the illness can be regarded, in part at least, as serving the function of allaying or reducing the patient's sense of guilt. His symptoms may represent a need for punishment or suffering, an attempt to appease an unduly harsh and critical conscience. It follows that recovery, or the promise of recovery, represents a particular type of threat to these patients, viz. the danger of experiencing acute and perhaps unbearable feelings of guilt. It is suggested that in some way the state of being free from symptoms must in such patients represent the fulfilment of unconscious childhood wishes, the gratification of which is felt to be internally forbidden.

Freud unambiguously linked the negative therapeutic reaction with an unconscious sense of guilt, and while he maintained that feelings cannot appropriately be described as 'unconscious' (1923b, 1924c) he believed that the same factors that produce conscious feelings of guilt can operate outside conscious awareness, and that the concept of an 'unconscious sense of guilt' is useful in spite of philosophical and semantic objections to it. In 'The Economic Problem of Masochism' (1924), Freud added that the unconscious sense of guilt leading to the negative therapeutic reaction, might in some cases be reinforced by a concealed masochistic tendency (Loewald, 1972, discusses the role of the so-called death instinct in the context of masochism and the negative therapeutic reaction.) This would result in a further gain from the suffering brought about by the illness and present an increased resistance to recovery. He suggests that 'the suffering entailed by neuroses is precisely the factor that makes them valuable to the masochistic trend', and added that 'contrary to all theory and expectation . . . a neurosis which has defied every therapeutic effort may vanish if the subject becomes involved in the misery of an unhappy marriage, or loses all his money, or develops a dangerous organic disease. In such instances, one form of suffering has been replaced by another.' Freud also suggested in this paper that the idea of an unconscious sense of guilt is one that is difficult to explain to patients and is, in fact, psychologically incorrect. He remarked that the idea of a 'need for punishment' aptly covers the observed state of affairs. In 1923 Freud commented that when the negative therapeutic reaction is based on a 'borrowed' sense of guilt, one may achieve a brilliant therapeutic result. By 'borrowed sense of guilt' Freud meant guilt taken over from a love object by identification with that object's guilt. This phenomenon has been further discussed and its dynamic explored by Levy (1982).

Freud thus used 'negative therapeutic reaction' both descriptively and as an explanation. He used the notion as a *description* of a particular clinical phenomenon, i.e. the worsening of the patient's condition following some encouraging experience (e.g. the analyst's expression of satisfaction with the progress of the analytic work or the patient's own realization that progress had been made through the elucidation of some problem). This occurs when we might normally expect him to experience relief. On the other hand, he regarded the negative therapeutic reaction as an *explanation* of a clinical phenomenon in terms of a psychological mechanism, i.e. a reaction taking the form of getting or feeling worse instead of better, aimed at reducing the guilt feelings evoked by improvement.

The reaction was thought by Freud to be a characteristic of a certain type of patient in analysis, and it is of interest that he had, some years earlier, described essentially the same mechanism in an entirely different context. In 1916 he had included, in the description of a number of different character types, 'those wrecked by success'. Beginning from the comment that neurosis originates in the frustration of an instinctual wish, he goes on to comment: 'So much the more surprising, and indeed bewildering, must it appear when as a doctor one makes the discovery that people occasionally fall ill precisely when a deeply rooted and long cherished wish has come to fulfilment. It seems then as though they were not able to tolerate their happiness; for there can be no question that there is a causal connection between their success and their falling ill.' Freud illustrated his thesis by reference to the case of a woman who had lived happily with her lover for many years, seeming only to need legalization of their union to achieve complete happiness. When, finally, they were married, she broke down completely, developing an incurable paranoid illness. Freud also cites the case of a teacher who had for many years cherished the wish to succeed the master who had initiated him into his studies. When he was in fact chosen as the successor, he developed feelings of doubt and unworthiness and succumbed to a depressive illness which lasted for some years. (Freud cited Lady Macbeth as well as Rebecca West in Ibsen's *Rosmersholm* as examples.) 'Analytic work', said Freud, 'has no difficulty in showing us that it is forces of conscience which forbid the subject to gain the long hoped-for advantage from the fortunate change in reality' (1916d).

The early psychoanalytic literature on the negative therapeutic reaction was relatively sparse. Wilhelm Reich (1934) suggested that its occurrence was due to faulty analytic technique, particularly the failure to analyse the negative transference, and a paper by Feigenbaum (1934) describes a relevant clinical fragment. However, two important papers published shortly afterwards extended Freud's original concept to include a number of different mechanisms (Horney, 1936; Riviere, 1936).

In 1936 Riviere pointed out that the negative therapeutic reaction as described by Freud did not mean that the patient was necessarily unanalysable. The person who reacts in this way does not always break off treatment, and changes may be brought about in him through appropriate analytic work. Riviere went on to suggest that 'Freud's title for this reaction, however, is not actually very specific; a negative therapeutic reaction would just as well describe the case of any patient who does not benefit from a treatment'. She appears to have treated the concept more broadly than Freud did; she included in it a number of types of severe resistance to analysis and, in common with a number of later authors (e.g. Rosenfeld, 1968), certain forms of resistance in which the patient either explicitly or implicitly rejects the analyst's interpretations. Much of Riviere's discussion relates to what we have described as resistance caused by the threat of the analytic work to the patient's self-esteem and those due to 'fixed' character traits (chapter seven). Other aspects relate to the absence of an adequate treatment alliance in certain types of patient (chapter three).

In contrast to Riviere, Horney (1936) begins with the formulation that the negative therapeutic reaction is not, indiscriminately, every deterioration of the patient's condition. She suggests that only those instances ought to be included in which one might reasonably have expected the patient to feel relief. She goes on to say that in many cases of negative therapeutic reaction

> the patient very often actually feels this relief distinctly, and then after a short while reacts as described, e.g. with an increase in symptoms, discouragement, a wish to break off treatment, etc. A definite sequence of reactions appears, in principle, to be present. First, the patient experiences a definite relief, followed by a shrinking back from the prospect of improvement, discouragement, doubts (about himself or the analyst), hopelessness, wishes to break off, and makes remarks like 'I am too old to change'.

Horney suggested that the negative therapeutic reaction is embedded in persons with a particular type of masochistic personality structure. In such persons the effect of a 'good' interpretation by the analyst (in the sense that the interpretation is felt by the patient to be correct) may be considered to be of five kinds, which are not always present nor equally strong, but may exist in different combinations:

(1) Such patients receive a 'good' interpretation as a stimulus to compete with the analyst. The patient is resentful of what he feels to be the analyst's superiority. Horney considers competitiveness and rivalry to be above average in such patients, who are extremely ambitious. Fused with their ambition is an inordinate amount of hostility. They often express their hostility and their

sense of defeat by belittling the analyst and attempting to defeat him. The patient's reaction in this case is not to the content of the interpretation but to the skill shown by the analyst.

(2) The interpretation may also be regarded as a blow to the patient's self-esteem when it reveals to him that he is not perfect and has 'ordinary' anxieties. He feels reproached and may show a negative reaction in an attempt to turn the tables by reproaching the analyst.

(3) The interpretation is followed by a feeling of relief, however fleeting, and the patient reacts as if the solution means a move towards recovery and success. This reaction would appear to embody both a fear of success and a fear of failure. On the one hand, the patient feels that if he attains success he will incur the same sort of envy and rage that he feels towards the success of others, whereas on the other, he fears that if he makes a move towards ambitious aims and fails, others will crush him as he would like to crush them. Such patients recoil from all aims involving competition and impose a constant inhibiting or checking process on themselves.

(4) The interpretation is felt as an unjust accusation, and the patient constantly feels as if the analysis is a trial. The interpretation reinforces existing feelings of self-condemnation, and the patient reacts by accusations directed against the analyst.

(5) The patient feels the interpretation to be a rebuff and takes the uncovering of his own difficulties as an expression of dislike or disdain on the part of the analyst. This type of reaction is related to a strong need for affection and an equally strong sensitivity to rejection.

These reactions to interpretation are elaborated on by Horney, and we have mentioned them here at some length because of their obvious clinical importance. However, in spite of her initial precise description of the negative therapeutic reaction, Horney (like Riviere) includes other 'negative' responses based upon different underlying psychological processes. While these are important from the point of view of the treatment of patients with narcissistic and masochistic personality structures, they differ in quality from the reaction as described by Freud. The patient who shows the negative therapeutic reaction *deteriorates* when he might be expected to improve, and this is quite different from the patient who *resents* a 'correct' interpretation, or who shows some form of aggressive 'contrariness'. Clinical evidence of the existence of a negative therapeutic reaction in patients who have strong guilt feelings and a 'need for punishment' may sometimes be gained from the paradoxical reaction of such patients to interpretations that are felt by them to be an attack, criticism, or punishment. Sandler (1959), describing a case of a very masochistic patient who exhibited what he called a 'positive' therapeutic reaction, remarked:

> Much of her silence and difficulty in association was meant to provoke me to anger and being relatively inexperienced at the time, I occasionally . . . betrayed my irritation with her either by my comments or in the tone of my voice. Whenever this happened, she would relax and the following session would be a 'good' one; she would associate well and new material would emerge. This I understood at the time as being a result of having involuntarily satisfied her 'need for punishment'.

Until the 1960s, the psychoanalytic writings on or relevant to this topic (e.g. Arkin, 1960; Brenner, 1959; Cesio, 1956, 1958, 1960a, 1960b; Eidelberg, 1948; Feigenbaum, 1934; Greenbaum, 1956; Horney, 1936; Ivimey, 1948; Lewin, 1950; Riviere, 1936; Salzman, 1960) have, it appears to us, added little to our knowledge and understanding of this mechanism in the form in which it was described by Freud; rather, the meaning of the concept was extended. As a result it was applied in a variety of ways. A notably useful paper by Olinick (1964) reviews the many misconceptions that exist among analysts as to the nature of the negative therapeutic reaction. He expresses his concern about the tendency to blur the term and comments, 'One occasionally still hears the term employed as a designation for any and all worsenings of the patient's condition during treatment'. Olinick speaks of 'counterfeit' negative therapeutic reactions to describe the effect of faulty technique when an interpretation of an unconscious wish is given before the patient has been adequately prepared for it. Instead of experiencing relief, the patient feel worse because of the premature interpretation, but this is not a negative therapeutic reaction in the sense described by Freud. Olinick goes on to consider the negative therapeutic reaction as a special case of negativism. He traces the origins of a negativistic attitude to the early years of life and links it with situations that foster feelings of resentful aggressiveness and contrariness in the child.

There has been an increasing tendency to conceptualize the negative therapeutic reaction in terms of the vicissitudes of the child's relationships in the first years of life. A number of authors (e.g. Asch, 1976; Lampl-de-Groot, 1967; Limentani, 1981; Olinick, 1964, 1970, 1978;) have drawn attention to a predisposition to the reaction based on a regressive pull within the patient towards fusion with the internal image of a depressed, ambivalently loved and hated mother. In particular, Limentani (1981) refers to the fear of re-experiencing the psychic pain associated with traumatic early experiences. It is likely that the experiencing of guilt at the idea of abandoning the tie to the figure of early childhood plays a significant role in bringing about a negative therapeutic reaction. These close internal ties may be self-punitive and masochistic in nature, and the later occurrence of a negative therapeutic reaction may reflect the need of the patient to reaffirm the masochistic self-damaging bond to the object (Loewald, 1972). The patient's failure to individuate and separate from the early figures (Mahler, 1968; Mahler, Pine, & Bergman, 1975) has been emphasized in recent years, and a number of authors have made use of the separation–individuation frame of reference in their consideration of the negative therapeutic reaction (e.g. Valenstein, 1973; Asch, 1976; Grunert, 1979; Roussillon, 1985).

Asch (1976), in a discussion of the negative therapeutic reaction, draws attention to the link between the early masochistic relationship and the gaining of narcissistic rewards:

> A person who has developed under the aegis of a parent who had seemed to idealize a life of suffering with avoidance of gratification, and who has then introjected these aspects of the (loved) parental image, will resist improvements through analysis and will especially resist interpretations that tend toward removing obstacles to pleasure. Once a moral system has been integrated, obedience to it not only removes guilt

feelings, it also produces a narcissistic gratification that can become an end in itself.

We would add that the patient may fear a loss of so-called 'narcissistic omnipotence', a loss of the feeling of being master in his own house, if he accepts improvement following interpretation, because improvement represents a giving up of independence and self-control, resulting in a loss of self-esteem (Kernberg, 1975; de Saussure, 1979; Brandchaft, 1983).

Kohut, in the course of developing his theories of self psychology, postulated that the patient with a narcissistic disturbance has had 'deficits' in his early object relationships, and Brandchaft (1983), following Kohut, traces the negative therapeutic reaction to a failure in the patient to develop and sustain a 'cohesive and vigorous' self. He speaks of the need of the patient with a vulnerable self to maintain a tie with an analyst who is experienced as a relentlessly failing figure, and he considers this to be at the root of the negative therapeutic reaction.

The occurrence of the negative therapeutic reaction in patients who are prone to depression is a theme that has been referred to in the literature from 1936 onwards (e.g. Gero, 1936; Horney, 1936; Lewin, 1950, 1961; Olinick, 1970; Riviere, 1936). It has been noted that for some patients success represents, paradoxically, a move away from, or a loss of, an 'ideal' state of the self connected with certain harsh demands of the patient's conscience. It is probably the pain associated with the loss of this 'ideal' state that may lead to the development of a depressive reaction (Joffe & Sandler, 1965) in those who are prone to such reactions. A further, though less direct, link between the negative therapeutic reaction and depression can be traced, in our own clinical experience, to the attempts made by certain patients, who show a tendency to the negative therapeutic reaction, to develop psychological and physical symptoms which are aimed at warding off or preventing the development of a depressive state. The production of such symptoms has been described in relation to psychogenic pain (Joffe & Sandler, 1967).

Since Melanie Klein's book *Envy and Gratitude* (1957), increasing importance has been attached to the role of envy and associated destructiveness in development and pathology. In narcissistic and borderline patients the role of envy in bringing about the negative therapeutic reaction has been stressed (Bégoin & Bégoin, 1979; Kernberg, 1975; Rosenfeld, 1975; Segal, 1983; Spillius, 1979). The patient may envy and resent the analyst's capacity to make correct interpretations and as a consequence may need to destroy the analyst's power by developing a negative therapeutic reaction. Interestingly, this is reminiscent of the view put forward by Horney in 1936. Kernberg (1975) speaks of patients who have a narcissistic need to defeat the therapist, to 'destroy other people's efforts to help them, even though they themselves succumb in the process'.

Baranger (1974) has given a good description of Melanie Klein's views on the negative therapeutic reaction:

> Melanie Klein . . . provides us in *Envy and Gratitude* with invaluable indications that envy is always at the origin of a negative therapeutic reaction: for it is precisely at this point, when the analyst feels sure that he understands the analysand and when the latter shares this assurance, that the problem of the negative therapeutic reaction actually emerges; through it the analysand frustrates the analyst's success and triumphs over him. It is a last resource on the part of the analysand: after all, he is still capable of making the analyst fail, even at the cost of his own failure.

In earlier chapters the increasing emphasis on the interpersonal aspects of the analytic situation has been commented on. Olinick (1970), in regard to the negative therapeutic reaction, says that 'although it may be construed in one-person, intrapsychic terms, the negative therapeutic reaction requires for its actual appearance the presence of another person . . . the negative therapeutic reaction entails a seeking of one who will punish'. This has obvious implications for the analytic situation where it can arouse countertransference reactions in the analyst (chapter six). Olinick comments that 'countertransferences occur in all analysts, and may be particularly liable to occur in response to the prevalent characterology of the negative therapeutic reactor'. The transference and countertransference aspects of the reaction have been commented on by a number of authors (Asch, 1976; Brenner, 1959; Kernberg, 1975; Langs, 1976; Limentani, 1981;

Loewald, 1972; Olinick, 1964, 1970; Spillius, 1979). Negative therapeutic reactions may cause the analyst to be disappointed and place strain on his analytic neutrality, and could thus be seen as a way of evoking or provoking a response in the analyst. Langs (1976) points out that normally in analysis the patient responds to an interpretation in a way that validates that interpretation for the analyst. In the case of a negative therapeutic reaction, however, the patient may go on to undo this and thus deny the analyst any validation of this sort.

We have no doubt that the propensity for negative therapeutic reactions resides in the character of the individual, rather than being a specific function of the psychoanalytic treatment situation; these apparently paradoxical reactions to the threat of recovery or success can be regarded as occurring in other clinical situations. Thus it is to be expected that they can be detected as responses in certain individuals to progress (or to expressions of satisfaction by the therapist) in treatment of any sort. It would also follow that the previous histories of these individuals would indicate similar 'negative' reactions to experiences of success and achievement.

There are a number of other reasons for a patient's relapsing in situations in which improvement has occurred, and these may be quite distinct from the negative therapeutic reaction as described by Freud. For example, at the time of the termination of treatment, a temporary return of symptoms may occur. This is observed in other treatment situations, as when discharge from hospital or the cessation of outpatient attendance is discussed with the patient. Some relapses may be thought of in such terms as unresolved dependency of the patient upon the person of the doctor. Similarly, relapses may also represent attempts to deal with fears of breakdown after cessation of treatment, which are coped with by falling ill again before the end of treatment.

The negative therapeutic reaction is a clinical phenomenon that does not necessarily indicate faulty technique or inappropriate intervention on the part of the therapist. However, we would emphasize again that there are many reasons for the failure of treatment, and not all failures should be ascribed to the negative therapeutic reaction. Knowledge of the mechanism, and of the prognostic significance of the particular type of character structure in which the reaction may occur, has a wide clinical application. Thus, for example, it can lead the psychiatrist to be careful about suggesting to depressed patients, who show strong guilt feelings and a pattern of reacting which corresponds to the negative therapeutic reaction, that they should 'take a holiday'. The patient may react by experiencing severe pain and depression, even to the extent of committing suicide.

The published literature has developed the concept of the negative therapeutic reaction in two main ways. The first of these is the blurring of the specificity of the reaction in the direction of linking it with more general types of resistance and 'negativistic' attitudes or with masochism in its various forms. While such contributions have increased our understanding of *resistance*, the specificity of the negative therapeutic reaction lies in the fact that it is a process involving a 'step forward' of one sort or another, followed by a retreat. In our view it is extremely important to differentiate the reaction from the general concept of resistance, and to retain the designation 'negative therapeutic reaction' for the phenomenon as originally described by Freud as a two-step process. However, Roussillon (1985) has made a convincing case that there are three stages rather than two in the negative therapeutic reaction. These are the amelioration of the patient's condition, leading to satisfaction expressed by the analyst, followed by a worsening of the patient's condition. Here the reaction is seen as a transference phenomenon. We might speculate that the separate phases in the negative therapeutic reaction may, quite apart from any other pathology, reflect experiences in infancy of encouragement, expectation, or optimism which have regularly been followed by disappointment.

The second major direction of development of the concept has been to extend the understanding of its dynamics and pathology factors to other than an unconscious sense of guilt. As we have shown in this chapter, there are many possible sources of a negative therapeutic reaction. So, while 'negative therapeutic reaction' should be retained as a *description* of a particular reaction, as we have indicated, the restriction of the *explanation* of the phenomenon to the operation of an unconscious sense of guilt is certainly far too narrow.

CHAPTER NINE

Acting out

O f all the clinical concepts considered in this book, *acting out* has probably suffered the greatest extension and change of meaning since it was first introduced by Freud (Atkins, 1970; Boesky, 1982; Erard, 1983; Freud, 1905e [1901]; Holder, 1970; Infante, 1976; Langs, 1976; Thomä & Kächele, 1987). Blos (1966) has commented in regard to the resulting confusion that

> the concept of acting out is overburdened with references and meanings. The rather clear-cut definition . . . when acting out during analysis was considered a legitimate and analysable form of resistance has by now been expanded to accommodate delinquent behaviour and all kinds of . . . pathology and impulsive actions. This expansion of the concept has reached a conceptual breaking point. I feel . . . [as if I am] groping my way through the underbrush of an overgrown concept eager to find a clearing which would permit a wider view.

The term now tends to be considered, by psychoanalysts and others, to include a whole range of impulsive, anti-social or dangerous actions, often without regard to the contexts in which such actions arise. It is sometimes used in a pejorative sense to denote disapproval of actions of patients or even colleagues. Examination of the relevant recent literature shows the great variety of current usages, the only common denominator appearing to be the assumption that the particular action referred to as 'acting out' has unconscious determinants.

Part of the present confusion surrounding the concept derives from the translation of Freud's original term. In 1901, in *The Psychopathology of Everyday Life,* he had made use of the colloquial German term *handeln* [to act] in his description of 'faulty' acts or parapraxes which could be understood to have an unconscious significance. In 1905, however, in his description of the 'Dora' case, he made use of the word *agieren* (also meaning 'to act', but with a slightly more emphatic connotation) in a particular technical sense. *Agieren* was translated as 'acting out', and it is probable that the choice of this latter term, and in particular the inclusion of the preposition 'out', has contributed to some of the changes in meaning of the concept in the English and American literature. Bellak (1965), for example, remarks that Freud first mentioned *acting out* in *The Psychopathology of Everyday Life,* but Bellak confuses *handeln* and *agieren* and goes on to describe practically every type of clinically significant action as one or other variety of 'acting out'. The implicit equation of acting [*handeln*] and acting out [*agieren*] is also made by Greenacre (1950) and Rexford (1966).

Freud's patient 'Dora' broke off treatment after some three months, and he subsequently attributed this abrupt termination to his failure to notice the patient's transference on to him of feelings towards an important figure of the past. Freud wrote, 'In this way the transference took me unawares, and, because of the unknown quality in me which reminded Dora of Herr K., she took her revenge on me as she wanted to take her revenge on him, and deserted me as she believed herself to have been deceived and deserted by him. Thus she *acted out* an essential part of her recollections and phantasies instead of producing it in the treatment' (1905e [1901]). Here acting out was related to transference and resistance, and it was also seen as a substitute for remembering. She did not recollect the past and report it in her free associations but, instead, enacted the memory.

Freud's most extensive discussion of the concept is to be found in his technical paper on 'Remembering, Repeating and Working Through' (1914g). Here acting out is related quite strictly to the clinical psychoanalytic treatment situation. As in the 'Dora' case, it is used to refer to actions the patient produces as substitutes for memories. He says, 'The patient does not *remember* anything of what he has forgotten and repressed, but *acts* it out. He reproduces it not as a memory but as an action; he *repeats* it, without, of course, knowing that he is repeating it. For instance, the patient does not say that he remembers that he used to be defiant and critical towards his parents' authority; instead, he behaves that way to the doctor.'

Freud goes on to refer to acting out as a *way of remembering* which makes its appearance in the analysis. He draws attention to the fact that transference, too, can be regarded as a 'piece of repetition', and that transference and acting out are at one when the patient repeats the past in a way that involves the person of the physician (as when the patient falls in love with the analyst). However, he also relates acting out to resistance. 'The greater the resistance, the more extensively will acting out (repetition) replace remembering . . . if, as the analysis proceeds, the transference becomes hostile or unduly intense and therefore in need of repression, remembering at once gives way to acting out.'

Freud distinguishes between acting out *within* the analytic situation and acting out *outside* the analysis. Both forms are regarded as a consequence of the analytic work and the treatment situation. Within analysis the transference provides the vehicle for acting out, and this may be the only way in which repressed memories initially find their way to the surface. Acting out outside the analysis carries with it potential dangers to the treatment and to the patient, but it is often impossible to prevent such acting out—nor, indeed, is such intervention always desirable. Freud comments that one tries to protect the patient from injuries consequent on his carrying out his impulses by obtaining a promise that he take no important decisions affecting his life during treatment. He adds, however:

at the same time one willingly leaves untouched as much of the patient's personal freedom as is compatible with these restrictions, nor does one hinder him from carrying out unimportant intentions, even if they are foolish; one does not forget that it is in fact only through his own experience and mishaps that a person learns sense. There are also people whom one cannot restrain from plunging into some quite undesirable project during the treatment, and who only afterwards become ready for, and accessible to, analysis. Occasionally, too, it is bound to happen that the untamed instincts assert themselves before there is time to put the reins of the transference on them, or that the bonds which attach the patient to the treatment are broken by him in a repetitive action. [1914g]

However, as analyses now take longer than in the past, the request to patients to refrain from making major decisions (e.g. marriage) during the course of the analysis has tended to be modified or abandoned.

Freud's views on acting out remained essentially unaltered in his subsequent discussions of the subject (1920g, 1939a, 1940a [1938]), and it is clear that he consistently regarded acting out as a *clinical* psychoanalytic concept related quite specifically to psychoanalytic treatment (see also A. Freud, 1936). Departures from Freud's original usage began to occur fairly early in the psychoanalytic literature, and a number of factors appear to be responsible for this. Some of these are listed below.

(1) A comment made by Freud, but often taken out of context, has been used to broaden the concept substantially. In considering what it is that the patient repeats under conditions of resistance, Freud remarked, 'We may now ask what it is that he in fact repeats or acts out. The answer is that he repeats everything that has already made its way from the sources of the repressed into his manifest personality—his inhibitions and unserviceable attitudes and his pathological character traits. He also repeats all his symptoms in the course of the treatment' (1914g). This should not be taken to imply that repetition and acting out are synonymous, even though acting out is a form of repetition. Nor does Freud's statement remove acting out from its *clinical* context.

(2) The choice of acting *out* as the translation of *agieren* has resulted in certain authors restricting the concept to acting out *outside* the analytic treatment situation. This has led to the coining of the term 'acting in' for some aspects of what Freud referred to as acting out within the analysis (Eidelberg, 1968; Rosen, 1965; Zeligs, 1957), although the term 'acting in' is now used less frequently.

(3) The tendency to broaden psychoanalytic theory into a general psychology (Hartmann, 1939, 1944, 1964) has led to the reformulation of a number of *clinical* concepts in more general psychological terms. This tendency was, of course, encouraged by Freud's repeated references to the fact that the phenomena that can be observed in psychoanalytic treatment can also be observed outside it. A consequence of attempts to generalize clinical concepts is that they may lose something of their clinical precision. This has been discussed in relation to transference (chapter four), and the same considerations apply to acting out.

(4) The concept of acting out was derived in the context of the psychoanalytic method applied to adult patients who were predominantly neurotic, and who were regarded as being capable of adhering to the basic technical rule of free association. With the application of psychoanalysis to the treatment of patients with severe personality disorders, to psychotics, adolescents, and children, new technical problems arose, and this resulted in a widening of the concept. Because of similarities between the impulsive aspects of the behaviour of patients in the above-mentioned groups and the acting out of the neurotic patient under the pressure of the analysis, the temptation to label all impulsive behaviour as 'acting out' was very strong (A. Freud, 1968).

(5) Acting out was regarded by Freud as a particular manifestation of resistance which could have undesirable consequences for the patient or for the progress of his analysis. Because of this it appears to have been a natural step for his colleagues and followers to apply it more to behaviour that was 'undesirable' in a general sense than to other forms of behaviour. Carried to its extreme, socially or morally undesirable behaviour, in patients and others, tended by some to be labelled 'acting out'.

Acting out has been discussed by Fenichel (1945b) with reference both to treatment-related phenomena and to impulsive tendencies lodged in the personality and pathology of the individual. He links the tendency to impulsive action with difficulties in the first year of life, giving rise to a tendency to react to frustration with violence. He also suggests that traumatic experiences in childhood may lead to repeated attempts to master, through activity, what was once passively and traumatically experienced. Fenichel distinguishes more sharply than Freud had done between transference and acting out, suggesting that the tendency to act out was a function of the particular individual concerned and can consequently be considered in a wider context than that of psychoanalytic treatment. Individuals who show a proclivity for acting out will tend to act out whether or not they are in analysis. They have

> in common an insufficient differentiation between the present and the past, an unwillingness to learn, a readiness to substitute certain rigid reactive patterns for adequate responses to certain stimuli. But these reactive patterns . . . are not necessarily real actions—sometimes they consist in mere emotional attitudes; and we rather call it 'transference' if the attitude concerns definite persons, and 'acting out' if something has to be done regardless towards whom.

Fenichel's main point, that certain persons show a greater tendency to express their unconscious impulses in action than others, is an interesting one, but his retention of the term 'acting out' for such impulsive actions weakens the link that previously existed between acting out and transference resistance. In considering acting out in this way, he is in fact discussing a different topic, i.e. the character of those individuals who tend to *enact* in an impulsive fashion.

Greenacre (1950) also sees acting out as a habitual phenomenon which creates special problems of therapeutic management. She defines acting out as 'a special form of remembering, in which the old memory is re-enacted in a more or less organized and often only slightly disguised form. It is not a clearly conscious visual or verbal recollection, nor is there any awareness that the special activity is motivated by memory. His behaviour seems to the subject to be plausible and appropriate'. This last characteristic of acting out, its 'ego syntonic' quality, has been emphasized in much of the subsequent literature (e.g. Blum, 1976; Greenson, 1966, 1967).

The developmental determinants of habitual forms of acting out are also considered by Greenacre, and to those enumerated by Fenichel (1945b) she adds 'a special emphasis on visual sensitization producing a bent for dramatization ... and a largely unconscious belief in the magic of action'. Greenacre's formulations suggest that the tendency to habitual acting out is chiefly the result of certain disturbances in the first two years of life. The link between acting out and preverbal experiences has been emphasized in much of the subsequent psychoanalytic literature, especially by the followers of Melanie Klein (e.g. Bion, 1962; Grinberg, 1968, 1987; Meltzer, 1967; Rosenfeld, 1965b), although others have also stressed this point. Blum (1976) emphasizes that 'very early childhood trauma fosters and fixates the process of acting out. Preoedipal and preverbal traumata interfere with emerging cognitive and impulse controls and may lead to obligatory "living out". . . . The developmental disturbance of separation–individuation (Mahler, 1968; Greenacre, 1968) predisposes to later acting out associated with ego fragility'. Anastasopoulos (1988) has suggested that acting out, particularly in adolescence, can be an expression of a regression in the ability to symbolize, resulting in a slowing down of abstract thinking. He also considers acting out to be an expression of primitive symbolic communication.

The tendency to use the term to refer more or less indiscriminately to actions of all sorts has increased in recent years, and we find two editions of *Acting Out* (Abt & Weissman, 1965, 1976) devoted to a discussion of such diverse behavioural disturbances as drug addiction, alcoholism, psychosomatic illness, obesity, homosexuality, learning inhibitions, and the like, all regarded as special forms of acting out. In the foreword to this book, Bellak (1965) remarks:

> Even in its narrower definition, acting out is of great social importance. The character disorder, be it as a carrier of emotional contagion within a small family group, or as a

demagogue of national scale, is a serious problem. The delinquent, the adult criminal, the drug addict, the ordinary psychotic, as well as the political lunatic, are problems of great social import which demand solutions. We need to know how to prevent the development of such bad actors, understand them well enough to control them therapeutically or socially, and we need to know right now most urgently how to predict who is likely to act out and when.

Similarly, Deutsch (1966) has widened the concept from a clinical one to one of general psychology:

> To some extent, we are all actors-out, because nobody is free of regressive trends, repressed strivings, burdens of more or less conscious fantasies, etc. Artists are able to create in acting out their work of art; neurotics of every type and degree are using their symptoms to act out; hysterics in conversion symptoms, and often very dramatic twilight states; obsessionals in their ceremonies; psychotics in hallucinations and delusions; delinquents in their asocial behaviour.

But such extension of the concept would appear to rob it entirely of its original meaning, and it is perhaps unfortunate that a term such as 'enactment' was not used systematically in the literature to distinguish the general tendency to impulsive or irrational action from acting out linked with the treatment process. Moreover, the extension of the term appears to add to its pejorative connotation.

Fenichel once commented (1941) that 'we must think of so-called "acting out" from the therapeutic point of view. In individuals who do not indulge in it generally, acting out is a welcome sign that in the analysis something has happened which we can and must utilize in finding out the unconscious processes behind it.' However, in the more recent literature, a reaction to the indiscriminate use of the term can be discerned, and some psychoanalytic writers have advocated a restriction of 'acting out' to the enactment of unconsciously determined urges during the course of treatment (e.g. Bilger, 1986; Blum, 1976; Erard, 1983; A. Freud, 1968; Greenson, 1967; Limentani, 1966; Rangell, 1968). With this development, there has also been a move away from looking upon acting out as undesirable, as simply a manifestation of resistance to the analytic process (chapter seven), and towards its evaluation as a source of information and significant as a special form of communication or expression. In this respect, the assessment of the concept of acting out as a clinical phenomenon has undergone a similar change to that which occurred in the case of transference (chapter four) and countertransference (chapter six), both of which were initially regarded as obstacles to treatment, but were later seen as valuable sources of information. With this there has also been a move away from regarding acting out exclusively as a form of resistance, particularly against transference (Blum, 1976; Erard, 1983; Greenson, 1967; Khan, 1963; Mitscherlich-Nielsen, 1968; Rangell, 1968; Rosenfeld, 1965b; Winnicott, 1949).

The broadening of the clinical concept to include forms of action which are not a simple reflection of resistance has raised further problems of definition. Thus Laplanche and Pontalis (1973) have remarked, 'One of the outstanding tasks of psychoanalysis is to ground the distinction between transference and acting out on criteria other than purely technical ones. ... This task presupposes a reformulation of the concepts of *action* and *actualization* and a fresh definition of the different modalities of *communication.*' In line with this are the attempts to distinguish between various forms of action. Greenson (1966) suggests that differentiations should be made between re-living, symptomatic acts, and acting out. Rangell (1968, 1981) argues for a distinction between acting out, normal action, and neurotic action.

Thomä and Kächele (1987) comment that any such reconsideration of the concept would have to take into account the following topics:

affective and impulsive abreactions and controls; blind acting out and goal-directed action; motor discharge and highly organized acts such as play and scenic representation, structuring of relationships, creative achievement, and other ways of resolving tensions and conflicts by means of differentiated and complex courses of movement and action; acting out as the result and resolution of defence and adaptation potentials in the repertoire of an individual in relationship to his environment.

These authors go on to list a number of unconscious conditions that may increase the tendency to act out. These include:

> early traumas with a deficient capacity for the formation of symbols, since memory and remembering are connected with the acquisition of word symbols, which themselves lead to a state in which the memory apparatus has a useful structure. . . . Disturbances of the sense of reality, visual sensibilization, fixations at the level of the 'magic of action' are different kinds of conditions which may put emphasis on action language in contrast to verbal language. At the same time, fantasies and action are possible preverbal means of problem solving and communicating.

It is fairly widely accepted that actions that may be characterized as acting out occur in every analysis (Boesky, 1982). It has been stressed that even when acting out is regarded as a product of resistance, it can also serve the function of communication (e.g. Erard, 1983; Greenson, 1966; Langs, 1976). Indeed, emphasis in recent years has been placed on the relation of acting out in the analysis to the analyst's countertransference.

The analyst assesses the patient in terms of his own value system and personality (Klauber, 1981). So while one analyst may see a piece of behaviour as acting out, another might regard the same activity as appropriate and adaptive. The analyst's flexibility and capacity to tolerate and understand the unconscious meaning of the patient's action must influence the judgement of whether the activity is acting out or not (Bilger, 1986; Thomä & Kächele, 1987). His countertransference response to the patient's acting out has the potential to be a valuable source of information about the role-interaction which the patient is attempting to impose on the situation (Sandler, 1976). Kluewer (1983) comments that the seduction of the therapist into acting out in concert with the patient, that is, 'entering into an action dialogue' [in German *agieren und mitagieren*], can become an organ for new insights just as much as countertransference more generally. In line with this, Bilger (1986) has suggested that the designation of behaviour as acting out is based less on the behaviour itself than on the experience of pressure this imposes on the analyst and the feeling that boundaries have been transgressed: the diagnosis of acting out therefore becomes dependent on the nature of the counter-transference. He points out that the increasing emphasis on the positive, creative, and dialogue-centred aspects of acting out should not lead to a denial by the analyst of its negative features, i.e. those that the analyst experiences as indications of resistance. The understanding of the resistance aspects of acting out may allow for greater access to the negative transference in the analysis (see chapter four).

There is now a tendency to evaluate it as a possible first indication of new material emerging from unconscious sources (Bilger, 1986). Limentani (1966), for instance, quotes the example of the patient who calls at the analyst's consulting room at the usual time, having overlooked the fact that there was no session because of a national holiday. He suggests that there may be little evidence of resistance in such behaviour, and it can be taken as a useful source of analytic material. Balint (1968) makes a similar point in regard to the analysis of patients who have a 'basic fault' in their personalities.

The 'positive' aspects of acting out as a form of *adaptation* have been underlined by several authors. Blos (1963) and Anastasopoulos (1988) have written of the protective and adaptive functions of acting out in the adolescent, a reflection of the need to preserve the integrity of the self. Others (e.g. Mitscherlich-Nielsen, 1968) have stressed the value of acting out as 'trial' behaviour following interpretation and insight.

To sum up, it can be said that the concept of acting out has been used in psychoanalysis in two main senses:

(1) To describe certain behavioural phenomena that arise during the course of an analysis and which are a consequence of that treatment. The concept refers to mental contents (wishes, memories, etc.) which are pushing their way towards the surface as a result of their revival in the analytic situation, particularly as an aspect of the transference, these contents being enacted rather than remembered. In this regard acting out can be viewed as a result of resistance to the development of the transference. Such enactment has been referred to as 'acting out in the transference', but acting out includes other treatment-related and treatment-inspired forms of enactment. In its original sense, acting out can

occur either within the treatment setting or outside it. The term 'acting in' would refer simply to acting out within the treatment situation. Acting out has been regarded as having a communicative function within the analysis, a function which can coexist with resistance, for the resistance may itself be meaningful and significant.

(2) To describe habitual modes of action and behaviour that are a consequence of existing personality and pathology, and which are related to the type of individual rather than to the treatment process. Perhaps the most lucid statement regarding such individuals is still that given by Hartmann (1944):

> There is . . . a large number of people in whom active social conduct represents not a rational action but an 'acting out', which is more or less neurotic, in relation to social reality. In this 'acting out' they repeat infantile situations and seek to utilize their social conduct to resolve intrapsychic conflicts. A strong reliance on reality can also be used to overcome fear. It can, but it does not need to, have the character of a symptom. It also depends on the peculiarities of the social milieu, what conflicts and anxiety tensions are overcome by the social behaviour. On the other hand, sometimes a modification of the social structure which limits this activity . . . leads to a reappearance of those conflicts which were temporarily overcome and serves to precipitate a neurosis.

The application of the concept of acting out to behaviour in contexts other than that of psychoanalytic treatment poses certain difficulties. These difficulties do not arise if we use the concept in its widest sense, i.e. as relating to individual personality tendencies, for these exist apart from the treatment situation. In the narrower and technical sense, however, a problem does arise if we adhere to the view that acting out is a substitute for remembering, as other forms of treatment, with different goals and using different methods, may not involve or stimulate the recall of the patient's childhood past. Nevertheless the concept of acting out, if used in its extended sense, is capable of application in such forms of treatment. Enactments of earlier states can occur, and can usefully be referred to as acting out. An example of such acting out might be the case of a patient receiving behaviour therapy who develops unconscious hostile feelings towards his therapist as a consequence of his dependence on him, and who may enact these towards someone else. Similarly, an inpatient may deal with irrational guilt feelings towards his doctor which have developed, in the regression fostered by the hospital situation, by provoking reproval or 'punishment' from the hospital authorities. The awareness and understanding by the doctor of acting out tendencies occurring within a treatment situation of any sort can be of value, it would seem, not only in the handling of the patient, but also in gaining clues in regard to his psychopathology. Acting out is, of course, not only confined to the patient group. Irrational actions towards patients resulting from the doctor's countertransference could probably also be designated as acting out on the part of the doctor. And, insofar as intra-staff relationships may foster infantile attitudes, the irrational behaviour that may arise in response, for example, to the death or retirement of a key figure in the institution may lead to behaviour which could be designated as acting out. There is no doubt, however, that such an extension of the concept to other treatment modalities does imply the acceptance of a change in meaning from the original psychoanalytic usage.

CHAPTER TEN

Interpretations
and other interventions

Previous chapters have concentrated on concepts that relate to the communications brought by the patient and to the factors in both patient and therapist that either facilitate or hinder the free flow and understanding of these communications. In the chapter on *working through* (chapter twelve), we shall discuss, among other things, those interventions of the analyst that aim at bringing about enduring changes in the patient and also the need for continual elaboration and reinforcement of these interventions. The term 'interpretation' is often used in a general sense to refer to such interventions. In the *Standard Edition* of Freud's works the term 'interpretation' is used to translate the German *Deutung*. However, as Laplanche and Pontalis (1973) point out, the two words do not correspond exactly: *Deutung* appears to be closer to 'explanation' or 'clarification', and Freud writes that the *Deutung* of the dream 'consists in ascertaining its *Bedeutung* or meaning'.

Interpretation occupies a special place in the literature on psychoanalytic technique. Bibring (1954) remarks that *'Interpreta-*

tion is the supreme agent in the hierarchy of therapeutic principles characteristic of analysis'. The central role of interpretation is equally stressed by Gill (1954), who asserts that 'Psychoanalysis is that technique which, employed by a neutral analyst, results in the development of a regressive transference neurosis and the ultimate resolution of this neurosis by techniques of interpretation alone'. Loewald (1979) remarks that 'psychoanalytic interpretations are based on self-understanding, and self-understanding is reactivated in the act of interpretation to the patient', and Arlow (reported by Rothstein, 1983) states that 'from the very beginning of its history, psychoanalysis represented a science of the mind, a discipline of interpretation, first of psychopathology and later of mental functioning in general. . . . [Interpretation] is . . . generally considered as the essential element in effecting therapeutic results through psychoanalysis . . . giving interpretation is the most characteristic feature of the analyst's activity'.

Because the psychoanalytic technique is predominantly a *verbal* one, and because the psychoanalytic training has become so specialized, it is perhaps natural that a certain mystique has become attached to the analyst's 'interpretations'. Some analysts even adopt a special tone of voice when delivering interpretations. Menninger (1958) points out that

> interpretation is a rather presumptuous term, loosely applied by (some) analysts to every voluntary verbal participation made by the analyst in the psychoanalytic treatment process. I dislike the word because it gives young analysts the wrong idea about their main function. They need to be reminded that they are not oracles, not wizards, not linguists, not detectives, not great wise men who, like Joseph and Daniel, 'interpret' dreams—but quiet observers, listeners, and occasionally commentators. Their participation in a two-party process is predominantly passive . . . their *occasional* active participation is better called intervention. It may or may not 'interpret' something. It may or may not be an interruption. But whenever the analyst speaks he contributes to a process.

As we have described, Freud, in his early writings (1895d), wrote of the recovery of 'forgotten' memories by his patients. At

that time he restricted his own verbal interventions in the therapeutic situation to those required to induce the necessary free
expression of the patient's thoughts. He attempted to avoid direct
suggestion of the sort that had characterized the hypnotic method
from which the psychoanalytic technique derived. His comments
and suggestions were directed only towards *facilitating* the
patient's production of verbal material in the belief that the
stream of associations would eventually lead to the recall, more or
less spontaneously, of emotionally charged memories surrounding important and significant events of the patient's past. In this
first phase of psychoanalysis the emotional abreaction that
accompanied such recall was regarded as the essential therapeutic agent, for the patient's symptoms were thought to be brought
about by the persistence of 'dammed-up' affects. Freud gradually
formed the view that the hysterical patient's symptoms also sym-
bolized, unbeknown to the patient, aspects of the assumed traumatic event and the thoughts and feelings connected with that
forgotten event. By 1897 Freud had given up the traumatogenic
theory of hysteria and was devoting himself to a searching examination of processes of symbolic representation, especially as they
occurred in dreams. Indeed, Freud's first references to interpretation are to dream interpretation (1900a). The concept referred, in
this connection, to the analyst's understanding and reconstruction of the hidden sources and meaning of the dream ('latent
content'). This was arrived at by an examination of the free associations of the patient to the conscious memory of the dream itself
('manifest content'). In the early years of psychoanalysis the analyst conveyed and explained his interpretation to the patient, but
this was a relatively didactic communication of the interpretation
arrived at by the analyst.

By the time Freud came to write his papers on psychoanalytic
technique (1911e, 1912b, 1912e, 1913c, 1914g, 1915a) he commented that there had been changes in the manner of presentation of the analyst's understanding of the patient's productions.
The analyst's interpretations of the patient's dreams and free
associations were not to be freely imparted but might be withheld
until resistances appeared. Freud (1913c) now expressed his 'con-
demnation of any line of behaviour which would lead us to give
the patient a translation of his symptoms as soon as we have

guessed it ourselves'. From this time onwards Freud more or less consistently distinguished between the interpretation and the *communication* of the interpretation. Thus he wrote (1926e), 'When you have found the right interpretation, another task lies ahead. You must wait for the right moment at which you can communicate your interpretation to the patient with some prospect of success. . . . You will be making a bad mistake if . . . you throw your interpretations at the patient's head as soon as you have found them.'

In 1937 Freud differentiated between interpretations and 'constructions' in analysis. '"Interpretation" applies to something that one does to some single element of the material, such as an association or a parapraxis. But it is a "construction" when one lays before the subject of the analysis a piece of his early history that he has forgotten' (1937d). A construction (now usually called a 'reconstruction') represents a 'preliminary labour' which facilitates the emergence of memories of the past or their repetition in the transference. The definition of interpretation referred to here has a strange ring, coming relatively late in Freud's writings, and has not been maintained in the subsequent literature. No emphasis is placed now on the 'single' element as the subject of interpretation.

While, early on, interpretation was regarded as a process occurring in the mind of the analyst, no great confusion could arise if the term was also applied to what the analyst said to the patient, for (apart from restrictions imposed by the need for 'analytic tact') the content of the two was the same. With the increasing realization that resistances and defences had also to be pointed out to the patient, more emphasis began to be placed on the *form* in which the analyst gave his comments and explanations to the patient. This has led to a use of the term 'interpretation' in the psychoanalytic literature after Freud which emphasizes what the analyst says to the patient rather than its being restricted to the analyst's understanding of the patient's productions. The term is now regularly employed to describe one or other aspect of the analyst's comments. The 'art of interpretation' demanded of the analyst has come to mean the art of making a successful verbal intervention of a particular sort rather than the art of understanding the unconscious meaning of the patient's material. Thus Fenichel (1945a) refers to interpretation as 'helping something unconscious to become conscious by naming it at the moment it is striving to break through'.

It would seem that the change in the concept was an inevitable result of the introduction of the structural theory by Freud (1923b, 1926d) and the move away from the previous 'topographical' conception (see chapter one). In the area of psychoanalytic technique more and more stress came to be laid on formulating interpretations which were acceptable to the patient or which would be particularly effective at a given time. Greater importance was attributed to *what* the analyst chose to relay to the patient, *when* he chose to do it, and the *form* in which he did it (Fenichel, 1941, 1945a; A. Freud, 1936; Greenson, 1967; Hartmann, 1939, 1951; Kris, 1951; Loewenstein, 1951; W. Reich, 1928). In addition, emphasis has come to be placed on the non-verbal factors that enter into effective interpretation. Brenner (quoted by Rothstein, 1983) made it clear that 'for him the tone and affect of a communication are important aspects of a therapeutic intervention insofar as they contribute to the meaning intended by the analyst and therefore facilitate insight'. Other writers (e.g. Gedo, 1979; Klauber, 1972, 1980; Rosenfeld, 1972) emphasize the context of the relationship between analyst and patient for the production of a creative and insight-producing interpretation. Blum (reported by Halpert, 1984) refers to 'the importance of the realities of the analytic situation such as the real attributes, style, and function (as well as possible malfunction) of the analyst as extratransference factors that tend to activate or lend reality to transference fantasy and gratifications'. Clearly, the conviction with which the analyst makes the interpretation and the tolerance he shows towards the patient's unconscious wishes and fantasies will play an important role in determining the effect of the interpretation.

From 1897 to 1923 the patient's free associations were regarded as being surface derivatives of unconscious wishes and impulses 'forcing their way to the surface from the depths'. The problem of interpretation was seen as being predominantly one of understanding 'deeper' unconscious material derived from conscious productions. After 1923 the structural viewpoint emphasized the role of the organized part of the personality (the ego) in finding compromises between instinctual urges (the id), the dictates of conscience and of ideals (the superego), and external reality. Interpretations were seen as being addressed to the ego of the patient, and the ego's strengths and weaknesses had to be taken into account. The analyst was forced to consider the *effect* of what he wanted to say. This is exemplified by Fenichel's (1941) anecdote of the analyst who unsuccessfully interpreted, for weeks on end, the patient's wish to kill him. While the analyst's understanding of the patient's unconscious wish appeared to be correct, what the analyst said to the patient did not appear to be so. According to Fenichel, 'Such an interpretation in that sort of situation *augments* the anxiety and with it the ego's defence, instead of diminishing it. The correct interpretation would have been: "You cannot talk because you are afraid that thoughts and impulses might come to you which would be directed against me".' There are analysts (fortunately, a decreasing number) who still regard their task as that of continuously interpreting deeply unconscious material to the patient and who apparently take the view, 'the deeper the better'.

The situation at present appears to be that the term 'interpretation' is used both as a synonym for nearly all the analyst's verbal (and even occasionally non-verbal) interventions on the one hand, and as *a particular variety* of verbal intervention on the other. There have been occasional attempts in the literature to distinguish, at a descriptive level, between the various components of the analyst's verbal interventions. Loewenstein (1951) considers that those comments of the analyst which 'create conditions without which the analytic procedure would be impossible' are not interpretations but, rather, comments that aim at freeing the patient's associations (e.g. 'those which induce the patient to follow the fundamental rule, the purpose of which is to loosen the barrier or censorship existing normally between conscious and preconscious processes'). Interpretations proper are, for Loewenstein, verbal interventions that produce 'those dynamic changes which we call insight'. He thus excludes instructions and explanations from the concept of interpretation, considering the latter to be a term 'applied to those explanations, given to patients by the analyst, which add to their knowledge about themselves. Such knowledge is drawn by the analyst from elements contained and expressed in the patient's own thoughts, feelings, words and behaviour.' Loewenstein introduces a certain problem here in defining an interpretation on the basis of the effect it produces, i.e. dynamic changes leading to insight. We can readily conceive of interpretations that are correct but not effective, and conversely of interpretations that are incorrect but effective (Glover, 1931). Defining an interpretation by its aim rather than by its effect could produce greater conceptual clarity. Loewenstein also draws attention to interventions that could be called 'preparations for interpretation', as, for example, the pointing out of similar patterns in experiences thought by the patient to be quite unconnected.

Some interventions (e.g. commands to phobic patients) are not part of the 'basic model of psychoanalytic technique', according to Eissler (1953). They constitute what he calls 'parameters of technique'. In the same paper, Eissler adds that certain verbal interventions other than interpretations are also essential to the 'basic model'. These include those instructions thought to be appropriate for the particular patient (e.g. about the basic rule of free association), as well as questions aimed at elucidating the material. He takes the view that 'the question as a type of communication is a basic and therefore indispensable tool of analysis, and one essentially different from interpretation'. Olinick (1954) provides a useful discussion of the role of questioning in psychoanalytic technique.

The verbal components of analytic techniques have been dissected by Greenson (1967). He considers that 'The term analysing is a shorthand expression which refers to ... [certain] ... insight furthering techniques'. Among these he includes:

Confrontation. This is regarded as a process of drawing the patient's attention to a particular phenomenon, making it explicit, and getting him to recognize something which he has been avoiding and which will have to be further understood.

Clarification. While this may follow confrontation, and blend with it, it represents more the process of bringing the psychological phenomena with which the patient has been confronted (and which he is now more willing to consider) into sharp focus. It involves the 'digging out' of significant details, which have to be separated from extraneous matter. Essentially the same distinction between clarification and interpretation, as described by Greenson, was made in an interesting paper on the topic by Bibring (1954).

Interpretation. This means 'to make conscious the unconscious meaning, source, history, mode or cause of a given psychic event. This usually requires more than a single intervention.'

In addition to these three, often interwoven, procedures, *working through* is added by Greenson as the fourth component of the procedure of analysis.

To sum up at this point, the term 'interpretation' has been used in the psychoanalytic literature to mean the following:

1. the analyst's inferences and conclusions regarding the unconscious meaning and significance of the patient's communications and behaviour;
2. the communication by the analyst of his inferences and conclusions to the patient;
3. all comments made by the analyst—this is the common colloquial usage of the term;
4. verbal interventions, which are specifically aimed at bringing about 'dynamic change' through the medium of insight.

Some authors have differentiated the following from interpretation, but the degree of arbitrariness in some of these distinctions is striking.

1. instructions given to the patient about analytic procedure in order to create and maintain the analytic setting;
2. constructions (or reconstructions) of aspects of the patient's early life and experiences derived from material brought or enacted during the analysis;
3. questions aimed at eliciting and elucidating material;
4. preparations for interpretation (for example, the demonstration of recurring patterns in the patient's life);

5. confrontations, as described by Greenson (1967);

6. clarifications, as described by Greenson (1967).

It is now fairly generally accepted that no interpretation can ever be complete, and the majority of psychoanalytic authors (e.g. Bibring, 1954; Klauber, 1972; Loewald, 1979; Schafer, 1983) agree with Greenson's view that the process of interpretation occurs in a series of steps. Arlow (1987) writes,

> Interpretation is not a one-shot experience. It is a process that unfolds in logical sequence. . . . The analyst interprets the dynamic effect of each contributor to the patient's unconscious conflicts. He demonstrates how, at different times, considerations of guilt, fear of punishment, of loss of love, of realistic consequences, opposed or even took sides with the fantastic wishes of childhood. The analyst makes the patient aware of how the dynamic shifts in the patient's associations bear testimony to the influence of the many forces in conflict in the patient's mind. The process of interpretation, therefore, may extend over a considerable period of time, as the analyst proceeds in a measured fashion, responsive to the dynamic interplay between wish, defence, and guilt at each level of interpretation.

For Arlow the significance of the analyst's intervention 'goes far beyond elucidation, clarification, confrontation, affirmation, or whatever term may be used to describe the content of the intervention. Attention shifts to the process. The real significance lies in the dynamic potential of the intervention, in the way in which the equilibrium between impulse and defence is altered.'

Perhaps the most practical use of the concept of interpretation would be to include within it all comments and other verbal interventions that have the aim of immediately making the patient aware of some aspect of his psychological functioning of which he was not previously conscious. Indeed, Brenner (in Rothstein, 1983), in line with Menninger (1958), employs the term 'therapeutic intervention' to include the terms 'interpretation' and 'reconstruction'. We would suggest that the general term 'interpretation' can be taken to refer to much of what have been called 'preparations for interpretation', i.e. to confrontations, clarifications, reconstructions, and so forth. It would *exclude* the normal and inevitable verbal social interchanges and instructions as to analytic procedure. While these may nonetheless have an effect on the patient (e.g. the reassurance gained through the arrangement of regular appointments), we would suggest that an interpretation should be seen from the viewpoint of the analyst's intention to provide insight rather than on the basis of the effect of his remarks on the patient. Rycroft (1958) has elegantly described what could, from this point of view, be considered as the central element in interpretation:

> The analyst invites the patient to talk to him, listens, and from time to time talks himself. When he talks, he talks neither to himself nor about himself *qua* himself, but to the patient about the patient. His purpose in doing so is to enlarge the patient's self-awareness by drawing his attention to certain ideas and feelings which the patient has not explicitly communicated but which are nonetheless part of and relevant to his present psychological state. These ideas, which the analyst is able to observe and formulate because they are implicit in what the patient has said or in the way in which he has said it, have either been unconscious, or, if they have been conscious, it has been without any awareness of their present and immediate relevance. . . . In other words, the analyst seeks to widen the patient's endopsychic perceptual field by informing him of details and relations within the total configuration of his present mental activity which for defensive reasons he is unable to perceive or communicate himself.

Attempts to narrow the concept of interpretation have a secondary effect on interpretative technique, particularly if certain interpretations are thought to be the only 'good' interventions. Such an effect has been evident in regard to the value put on transference interpretations which, because they have been regarded by some analysts as the 'proper' form of interpretation, have become the only ones given by them. Consequently, there is a danger of all interpretations being forced into a 'transference' mould (see chapters four and five, and the comment on 'mutative' interpretations made below).

Quite apart from the form of interpretations, their content has received a considerable amount of attention in the literature, particularly with regard to the relative effectiveness of different types of interpretation. In what follows we shall comment on some of these varieties of interpretation.

Content interpretation is an expression used to denote the 'translation' of the manifest or surface material into what the psychoanalyst understands to be its deeper meaning, usually with particular emphasis on childhood sexual and aggressive wishes and fantasies. This was the predominant type of interpretation given in the first decades of psychoanalysis. Such interpretations are concerned only with the meaning (unconscious content) of what was thought to have been repressed rather than with the conflict and struggle that have kept the memories and fantasies unconscious. Together with *symbolic* interpretations, which are the translation of symbolic meanings as they appear in dreams, in slips of the tongue, and so forth, content interpretations are popularly regarded as constituting the bulk of the psychoanalyst's activity, a misconception that dates from Freud's early work.

Defence interpretation is a particular form of the analysis of resistances (chapter seven). Such interpretations are aimed at showing the patient the mechanisms and manoeuvres which he uses to deal with the painful feelings involved in a particular conflict and, if possible, the origins of these operations. Defence interpretation is thought to be an indispensable complement to content interpretation, which is thought to be insufficient unless the patient is also shown the methods he unconsciously uses to cope with infantile impulses in himself. Anna Freud (1936) remarks that 'a technique which confined itself too exclusively to translating symbols would be in danger of bringing to light material which consisted, also too exclusively, of id-contents. . . . One might seek to justify such a technique by saying that there was really no need for it to take the circuitous route by way of the ego. . . . Nevertheless, its results would still be incomplete.' Defence interpretations are believed to be of special importance in bringing about a modification of psychic organization in the neurotic patient, as his psychopathology is considered to be rooted, in part, in his particular defensive organization, i.e. in his particular methods of coping with conflict. Changes in this organization are considered to be an essential part of the therapeutic process (chapter seven).

The idea that some interpretations are more effective than others is embodied in the concept of the *mutative* interpretation. Strachey (1934) suggested that the crucial changes in the patient brought about by interpretation are those that affect his superego. Interpretations that have this effect are considered to be 'mutative', and in order to be effective they must be concerned with processes occurring in the immediate 'here-and-now' of the analytic situation (in Strachey's view, only interpretations of such immediate processes, especially transference processes, have sufficient urgency and impact to bring about fundamental change). This idea has contributed, as has been mentioned earlier, to the view that only *transference* interpretations (chapters four and five) should be given by the analyst, as these are the only interpretations that can be effective (mutative). In fact this does not appear to have been Strachey's belief and does not accord with the practice of the majority of analysts, who make use of *extratransference* interpretations as well (Halpert, 1984; Rosenfeld, 1972).

There has been since Strachey, particularly because of the work of Melanie Klein, an increasing tendency to concentrate more or less exclusively on transference interpretations in the analytic work (Gill, 1982; Joseph, 1985). But more recently there has been a revival of interest in *extratransference interpretations*. In a comprehensive review of the topic, Blum (1983) has commented:

> Extratransference interpretation refers to interpretation that is relatively outside the analytic transference relationship. Although interpretive resolution of the transference neurosis is the central area of analytic work, transference is not the sole or whole focus of interpretation, or the only effective 'mutative' interpretation, or always the most significant interpretation. . . . Extratransference interpretation has a position and value which is not simply ancillary, preparatory, and supplementary to transference interpretation. Transference analysis is essential, but extratransference interpretation, including genetic interpretation and reconstruction, is also necessary. . . . Analytic understanding should encompass the overlapping

transference and extratransference spheres, fantasy and reality, past and present. A 'transference only' position is theoretically untenable and could lead to an artificial reduction of all associations and interpretations into a transference mould and to an idealized *folie à deux*.

In a Panel on 'The Value of Extratransference Interpretation' (reported by Halpert, 1984), Stone remarks that 'there are situations in which transferences themselves may spontaneously occur in the patient's immediate life without evident processing through the analytic situation, and interpretation of these transferences can provide a significant contribution to the psychoanalytic process beyond their immediate therapeutic effects'. Leites points out that 'everything the patient says is not always latently concerned with the analyst . . . feelings toward the primary persons of the past, reactivated by the analysis, may be directly transferred to other persons in his life, and these transferences are not always displacements of transference to the analyst'. Nevertheless, there is substantial general agreement today on the centrality of transference interpretation, and, as Gray puts it, 'the more the analysis can be focused on the analytic data as it occurs inside the analytic situation, the more effective interpretation becomes'.

Kohut and the school of psychoanalytic self psychology have paid particular attention to a specific technique devised for the analysis of narcissistic and borderline patients. Ornstein and Ornstein (1980) say:

> Psychoanalytic self psychology has led to a clinical and theoretical expansion of our central concepts of transference and resistance and along with these it has also led to a decisive dual shift in the manner in which we formulate and focus our clinical interpretations. This dual shift is (a) away from single interpretive statements to more comprehensive reconstructions or, as we would now say, reconstructive interpretations: and (b) away from a predominantly inferential to a predominantly empathic mode of observations and communication.

While it is difficult to see that psychoanalytic self psychologists can be more empathic than other analysts, it is clear that they regard the analyst's empathy as an important quality to be conveyed in the interpretation given to the patient. Moreover, because great stress is laid on the importance of deficits in early experience (as distinct from conflict), empathic, reconstructive interpretations are 'the essential method of analysis, regardless of the conflict-based or deficiency- based nature of the patient's psychopathology' (Ornstein & Ornstein, 1980). In spite of the emphasis on the role of the analyst's empathy, Kohut (1984) does indeed maintain that the self psychologist's empathy is no different from the empathy employed by those analysts who are not self psychologists. However, he adds, 'I know that a number of my self psychological colleagues will not agree with my negative answer'.

Clearly the structure and content of interpretations are to a large degree dependent on the particular psychoanalytic frame of reference of the analyst. As psychoanalytic theory has developed and changed on the basis of clinical experience, leading to new emphases, so has the nature of the psychoanalytic interpretation changed. Thus interpretations may nowadays be directed more, and in some circles even exclusively, towards the transference, and to the way in which early pre-oedipal developmental processes and conflicts manifest themselves in the present. Moreover, the analyst's views on the centrality of 'deficit' versus conflict will affect interpretation (Wallerstein, 1983).

The relation of therapeutic success to the making of 'correct' interpretations has occupied a number of authors. For example, Glover (1931) suggests that inexact, inaccurate, and incomplete interpretations may still result, in certain circumstances, in therapeutic progress. He regards this effect as coming about through the provision for the patient of an alternative system or organization which can act as a 'new substitute product' (in place of the previous symptom), which 'is now accepted by the patient's ego'. Isaacs (1939), in discussing the process of interpretation, takes the view that the good analyst, by virtue of his training, uses interpretations as scientific hypotheses concerning the patient's functioning. She says that

> this becoming aware of the deeper meaning of the patient's material is sometimes described as an intuition. I prefer to avoid this term because of its mystical connotation. The process of understanding may be largely unconscious but it is not

mystical. It is better described as a *perception*. We perceive the unconscious meaning of the patient's words and conduct as an objective process. Our ability to see it depends . . . on a wealth of processes in ourselves, partly conscious and partly unconscious. But it is an objective perception of what is in the patient, and it is based upon actual data.

The emphasis on the 'objective perception of objective data' is disputed by Rycroft (1958), who suggests that what Freud did was not to explain a phenomenon

> causally, but to understand it and give it meaning, and the procedure he engaged in was not the scientific one of elucidating causes but the semantic one of making sense of it. It can indeed be argued that much of Freud's work was really semantic and that he made a revolutionary discovery in semantics, viz. that neurotic symptoms are meaningful disguised communications, but that, owing to his scientific training and allegiance, he formulated his findings in the conceptual framework of the physical sciences.

Certainly, Isaacs' contention that the analyst's perception of unconscious meaning is an objective process is highly disputable, to say the least. But, on the other hand, the contrast between 'scientific' and 'semantic' as made by Rycroft is also open to question. An intermediate view appears to be that of Kris (1956a), who refers to

> the well-known fact that the reconstruction of childhood events may well be, and I believe regularly is, concerned with some thought processes and feelings which did not necessarily 'exist' at the time the 'event' took place. They may either never have reached consciousness or may have emerged at a later time, during the 'chain of events' to which the original experience became attached. Through reconstructive interpretations they tend to become part of the selected set of experiences constituting the biographical picture which in favourable cases emerges in the course of analytic therapy.

Balint (1968) pointed out that the particular analytic language and frame of reference of a psychoanalyst must inevitably determine the way a patient comes to understand himself. From this point of view it would appear that therapeutic change as a consequence of analysis depends, to a large degree, on the provision of a structured and organized conceptual and affective framework within which the patient can effectively place himself and his subjective experience of himself and others (see Novey, 1968). The view of analysis as a sort of archeological expedition into the patient's past, with the aim of recovering repressed memories in order to gain insight into the unconscious psychological roots of the patient's character and pathology, has been increasingly challenged in recent years. The idea of discovering the so-called 'historical truth' has been questioned, and somewhat radical views of psychoanalytic reconstruction have been put forward by, for example, Michels (reported by Compton, 1977), Schafer (1979, 1980, 1983), and Spence (1982, 1986). Michels suggests that

> any interpretation is a myth, that is, an interpretation offers an organizing principle for comprehending one's experience, integrating one's past in a context of meaning previously unavailable. Every interpretation is a myth in the sense that every history is a myth. Interpretations are not true or false. There are many myths consistent with any set of 'facts' about the past. Historical truth is not discovered, but, rather, meaning is created, though not without regard for constraints.

Schafer (1983) proposes the idea of analysis as a *narrative transaction*. He says that 'the analyst is in effect regarding both the analysand's talking and his or her disruptions of talking as a species of narrative performance, that is, as a way of telling or giving an account of life events in the past and present'. He continues:

> When the analysand is viewed as being engaged in narrative performance, he or she will be understood to be giving only one of a great number of possible accounts that could be given of these life events. Indeed, on this view, one can never have unmediated access to these events, for the events can exist only in narrative accounts that have been or may be developed by the analysand or analyst for different purposes and in different contexts . . . the analyst may be said to be engaged in acts of retelling or narrative revision . . . the analyst follows certain storylines of personal development, conflictual situations, and subjective experience that are the distinguishing features of

his or her analytic theory and approach ... one may, therefore, say of analytic interpretation that, far from unearthing
and resurrecting old and archaic experiences as such, it constitutes and it develops new, vivid, verbalizable, and verbalized
versions of those experiences. Only then can these new versions
be given a secure place in a continuous, coherent, convincing
and up-to-date psychoanalytic life history.

Spence (1982) points out that the truth of an interpretation
or reconstruction can never really be known. The analyst con-
structs a 'history' which satisfies certain aesthetic and pragmatic
criteria, and interprets within a narrative tradition in which
what counts is coherence, consistency, and the persuasive power
of the narrative. In place of historical truth, narrative truth
creates a way of explaining and understanding the facts of the
past and provides apparent certainty in place of knowledge which
is unreachable. There can be little doubt that the formulations of
Spence and Schafer emphasize an important aspect of reconstruction. Their approach fits with that of Balint, as well as that of
Wallerstein (1988) who comments that 'all our theoretical perspectives, Kleinian, but also ego psychological, and all the others
are but our chosen explanatory *metaphors*, heuristically useful
to us, in terms of our varying intellectual value commitments,
in explaining, i.e. making sense of the primary clinical data
of our consulting rooms'. He adds: 'Put most simply this conceptualization makes all our grand general theory (and all of our
pluralism of general theory) nothing but our chosen array of
metaphor.' However, Wallerstein's approach may carry the ques-
tionable implication that all interpretative systems are, if they
fulfil particular criteria, of equal value.

The concept of interpretation is obviously not limited to the
psychoanalytic treatment setting or to various forms of psychodynamic psychotherapy. The verbalization by a general practitioner of a patient's unformulated fears about his health can be
conceptualized as an interpretation, as it has the intention of
conveying new insight by presenting to the patient some aspect of
his feelings and behaviour of which he was not previously aware.
It does not always follow, of course, that the type of interpretation
appropriate in one setting is appropriate in others.

CHAPTER ELEVEN

Insight

T he concept of 'insight' is one that is widely used in psychoanalysis, in the systems of psychotherapy derived from it, and in dynamic psychiatry in general. The term is often quoted as if its meaning is readily apparent, but close study soon reveals that it is anything but clear. As Zilboorg (1952) has put it, 'Among the unclarities which are of utmost clinical importance and which cause utmost confusion is the term insight. It came from nowhere, so to speak. No one knows who employed it first, and in what sense.' And Poland (1988) remarks, 'Insight . . . has never found a comfortable place in analytic conceptualizations'. This view echoes that of Barnett (1978), who complains that 'our concepts of insight have become so diffuse and expanded, that a sense of futility and frustration often attends our attempts to encompass all into the design of effective insight therapies'.

There appears to be a complex relationship between the psychoanalytic and psychiatric meanings of the term. In psychiatry, 'insight' was introduced to indicate the patient's 'knowledge that the symptoms of his illness are abnormalities or morbid phenomena' (Hinsie & Campbell, 1970). This is the sense in which the term has been used in psychiatry since the early years of this century, and remains in use with this particular meaning. Jung, speaking of psychotic patients who have severe intellectual and emotional impairment, remarks that they can have 'signs of more or less extensive insight into the illness' (1907). Following Kraepelin (1906), Bleuler (1911), and Jaspers (1913), the 'absence of insight' is principally associated with psychotic mental states. However, although the word 'insight' has been extended from psychiatry to psychoanalysis, the specific psychiatric meaning has been lost in this extension. It is worth noting that the *early* use of the term in psychoanalysis was not a specialized technical one. It does not appear in the index of the *Standard Edition of the Complete Psychological Works of Freud,* although it is used in a non-technical sense at various points in the text. It would seem that a relatively colloquial word in both German [*Einsicht*] and English was elevated, at some point in the history of psychoanalysis, to the status of a technical concept. The *Oxford English Dictionary* points out that the 'original notion appears to have been "internal sight", i.e. with the eyes of the mind or understanding'. Among the definitions given are: 'internal sight; mental vision or perception; discernment, the fact of penetrating with the eyes of the understanding, into the inner character or nature of things; a glimpse or view beneath the surface.' The present, more or less colloquial, usage seems to have been affected by the psychoanalytical technical concept, so that its meaning at times corresponds to that which the *Oxford English Dictionary* describes as obsolete, i.e. 'understanding, intelligence, wisdom'.

Nonetheless, the concept, in the more technical forms in which it is now used in psychoanalysis, appears to be firmly rooted in Freud's formulations regarding the processes of change that lead to 'cure'.

In *Studies on Hysteria*, Freud (1895d) had written:

> We found, to our great surprise, at first, that *each individual hysterical symptom immediately and permanently disappeared when we had succeeded in bringing clearly to light the memory of the event by which it was provoked and in arousing its accompanying affect, and when the patient had described that event in*

the greatest possible detail and had put the affect into words.
Recollection without affect almost invariably produces no
results.

A similar point was made by Freud (1895d) when he commented of the patient that

> if we can succeed in eliciting a really vivid memory in him, and
> if he sees things before him with all their original actuality, we
> shall observe that he is completely dominated by some affect.
> And if we then compel him to put this affect into words, we
> shall find that, at the same time as he is producing this violent
> affect, the phenomenon of his pains emerges very markedly
> once again and that thenceforward the symptom, in its chronic
> character, disappears.

The element of 'cognitive' knowledge—'the memory of the
event'—was stressed by Freud in the first phase of psychoanalysis
in the context of emotional release. The idea of recovery through
affect discharge in the form of abreaction was related to the
notion of a specific traumatic event being the pathogenic agent in
such conditions as hysteria. The emotional accompaniment to the
recovery of repressed memories is close to what many psychoanalysts today regard as 'emotional insight'.

With the change in Freud's view of pathogenesis (in 1897) as a
result of the shift of emphasis from an external traumatic event to
the vicissitudes of the instinctual drives, and his increasing interest in the interpretation of dreams (1900a), the importance of
the emotional element seemed to recede. The analyst's insight
was now more or less equated with his understanding of the
meaning of the patient's productions, and it was this understanding which he communicated to the patient, often making use of
explanations and intellectual arguments. However, the gradual
realization of the importance of the need to analyse the transference and transference resistance led to an awareness once more of
the relevance of the emotional context in which the patient's understanding was embedded. As Freud (1913c) put it: 'It is true
that in the earliest days of analytic technique we took an intellec-
tualist view of the situation. We set a high value on the patient's
knowledge of what he had forgotten, and in this we made hardly

any distinction between our knowledge of it and his. . . . It was a severe disappointment when the expected success was not forthcoming.'

The term 'insight' does not appear to have been used in the title of a psychoanalytic paper until that by French on 'Insight and Distortion in Dreams' in 1939. French quite explicitly took over the term from the Gestalt psychologist W. Koehler (1925), who described how the perception by an experimental animal of the way to solve a problem may occur suddenly as an 'insight'. French regarded insight in psychoanalysis as a similar phenomenon, i.e. as 'a "practical grasp" of the conflict situation'. Such insight was not regarded by French as a therapeutic agent *per se*, but as a precondition for the further 'problem-solving' that could lead to cure.

The major problem in the psychoanalytic literature following Freud appears to lie in the need to define the qualities that distinguish 'true' or 'emotional' insight on the one hand and purely 'intellectual' insight on the other. It is generally believed by psychoanalysts that the distinction can in fact be made and that the differentiation is of crucial importance from the point of view of analytic technique. The bare intellectual knowledge of the psychoanalytic view of the sources of disturbance is manifestly ineffective (otherwise a patient might be cured by giving him a textbook of psychoanalysis to read). It would seem that, from the point of view of psychoanalytic therapy, some form of emotional experience is an essential accompaniment of what is regarded as effective insight. However, the precise definition of what constitutes 'true', 'emotional', or 'effective' insight has posed problems of definition with which many writers have struggled (e.g. Barnett, 1978; Blacker, 1981; Bush, 1978; A. Freud, 1981; Hatcher, 1973; Horowitz, 1987; Kerz-Ruehling, 1986; Kris, 1956a; Kubie, 1950; Martin, 1952; Michels, 1986; Myerson, 1960, 1963, 1965; Poland, 1988; Pressman, 1969a, 1969b; ; Rangell, 1981; Reid & Finesinger, 1952; Richfield, 1954; Segal, 1962; Silverberg, 1955; Valenstein, 1962; Zilboorg, 1952).

One of the difficulties inherent in the problem of finding a suitable definition of effective psychoanalytic insight has been the temptation to succumb to a tautology, viz. if insight is ineffective in producing change, it is not 'true' insight. *Ergo*, insight which brings about change is effective. If we are to avoid these difficulties, it would appear to be necessary to divorce the concept of emotional insight from the concept of 'cure', for it does not follow that such insight is necessarily followed by progressive and therapeutic changes in the patient. Richfield (1954) and Reid and Finesinger (1952) have attempted to apply philosophical analysis in their efforts to clarify the problem. The latter authors make use of the term 'dynamic insight' as the efficacious variety, quoting Kubie's (1950) statement that 'insight begins to have therapeutic effect only when it leads to an appreciation of the relationship between varied experiences and the unconscious conflicts, out of which arise both the neurotic components of the personality and the neurotic symptoms themselves'. Reid and Finesinger themselves attempt to distinguish between 'neutral' and 'emotional' insight, 'neutral insight' implying that 'neither of the terms in the relation whose significance is grasped by the act of insight is an emotion, nor does the act of insight mediate or release at the time an emotional response in the person who has the insight'. In 'emotional' insight 'the emotion is a part of the subject matter into which the patient has insight, or, more precisely, it is a term in the relation whose significance is grasped through insight'. Alternatively, insight may be regarded as 'emotional' or 'dynamically effective' if 'it makes the patient conscious of a fact, which itself may or may not be an emotion, that *releases* or *sets off* an emotional response'. This is a definition of insight that is not necessarily tied to the criteria of 'correctness' or therapeutic change.

In spite of the acceptance of the fact that the 'intellectual' elements in insight are ineffective on their own, there has been an increasing awareness of the role of the cognitive processes entering into the creation of insight (Barnett, 1978; Bush, 1978). Barnett comments that 'knowledge truly becomes insight only when accompanied by significant change in the patient's mental functioning and methods of ordering experience. The thrust of our concern with insight must shift towards the re-patterning and re-forming of our patient's ways of knowing as the bridge between insight and therapeutic change'.

Parallel with a renewed concern with cognitive aspects of insight has been the attention paid by child analysts to the development of the capacity for insight. Kennedy (1979) speaks of a developmental line of insight, emphasizing changes in this capacity from the pre-school child through to the adolescent and adult. The capacity develops 'from the infant's transitory awareness of pleasurable and painful feeling states to the adult's detached and objective self-observation with an intrapsychic focus which, together with the ego's integrative functions, bring insight into useful psychic contexts'. Kennedy adds that

> we do not aim, in child analysis, to reconstruct for the child a true and 'objective' picture of his past, but focus on dissecting his adaptations to the pressures he feels operate on him now. . . . The analyst's interventions organize and articulate what the child is experiencing. Whenever the analyst interprets and expresses his 'insights' in terms that the child is capable of understanding, some new integration will take place. . . . We must assume that their 'analytic understanding' becomes absorbed into the general experiential matrix.

Another child analyst, Neubauer (1979), stresses that

> child analysis has to address itself to the phases of cognitive organisation. . . . This brings into focus the role of self-observation as one of the major components of insight. Another requirement of insight is the ability to distinguish object and self-representations in the context of stable organisation of time and space. These different components of insight are all significant to the understanding of the role of insight in psychoanalysis.

Anna Freud (1981) reviews the development of the capacity for insight in childhood and discusses its presence and absence as a factor in normal development. She considers that adolescence provides the child who has not developed adequate insight with a 'second chance' in this regard.

The attaining of insight is a normal developmental phenomenon. Michels (1986) remarks that a psychoanalytic theory of insight

> would recognize that psychological development is not only a story of organismic cravings, fears, relationships, patterns of mental functioning, perceptions of self and others, and understanding of the world, but also of shifting, evolving, and impor-

tant understandings and awarenesses of the self. Psychological development proceeds throughout the life cycle, and different perspectives may be most helpful in organising our understanding of different developmental epochs. A period that is relatively 'latent' from the point of view of drives may be crucial from the perspective of insight.

Gray (1990) takes the view that each new piece of insight gained by the patient 'is accompanied by the important, *experientially acquired insight* into the reality that . . . [the] adult ego is in fact capable of consciously, willingly managing the restraint or discharge of . . . instinctual life. . . . This aspect of therapeutic action is a form of *learning* of his capacity for ego strength *through the experience* of gradually, autonomously exercising his control over the impulses being reclaimed.' Gray remarks that 'at appropriate moments and with acceptable words, I invite the patient to share in observing what has taken place.'

The role of the re-establishment of an early affective tie to the mother and the reinstatement of the sense of infantile omnipotence in regard to the gaining of insight is emphasized by Mangham (1981). In this he amplifies the comment of Kris (1956b) who stated, in a classic paper on the topic, that in 'insight "the cognitive elements" are merged with a particular kind of assurance'. Kris's paper has been discussed by Abend (1988) in the light of later developments.

The importance of the formation in the analysand of an 'ideal of insight' is stressed by Blum (1981). He comments, 'Psychoanalytic insight into unconscious processes and contents involves a gradual transformation of inner interdictions and ideals through the tolerance of previously forbidden curiosity and knowledge. The analytic process depends upon relaxation of censorship and analysis of the motives and modes of self-criticism and self-punishment.'

The role of insight in the interaction between patient and analyst in the analytic situation has been commented on (e.g. Joseph, 1987; Mangham, 1981; Neubauer, 1979; Segal & Britton, 1981). Thus Shengold (in a Panel reported by Blacker, 1981) considers that the process of insight is stimulated by the analytic situation and the way patient and analyst interact. Similarly,

Anthony (in the same Panel) underlines the relevance of the analyst's insight into his own counter-reactions to the patient and his growing knowledge of the patient's inner life. Consequently analysis is punctuated by an interplay between the analyst's and the patient's insights. Anthony (like Blacker, 1981; Hatcher, 1973; Horowitz, 1987; Poland, 1988; Rangell, 1981) emphasizes the point that analytic insight has to be considered as a *process*.

That this process of discovery and insight may continue and expand after the analysis is ended is pointed out by Horowitz (1987). He says, 'It would seem, from certain successful analyses, that responses to interpretation leading to useful insight undergo continuous revision both during the analysis and following termination. Continuous revision allows for the patient's own discoveries and is linked to the patient's own memories and reconstructions of his or her biography.'

In a Panel on 'Psychic Change' (Naiman, 1976), Sandler indicates that 'The gaining of insight through the analyst's interventions brings about a reintegration with the creation of new aspects of psychic organization. As a consequence of working through, this insight can become "automatic", i.e. can lead to the preconscious inhibition of previous modes of functioning and the utilisation of more appropriate ones.' In this context the attainment of insight leads to 'structures of insight', i.e. enduring sets of internal relationships that can be used to modify and control previously acquired ways of functioning. This would include changes in internal object relationships.

Finally, Poland (1988) makes a valuable comment on analytic insight when he says,

> Insight connects past and present, content and process, into a mental unity not well represented by logical reasoning and theory. Clinical analysis brings to life inner forces within a unique dyadic context that makes implicit meaning meaningful with immediacy and thus permits historical facts to grow into personal truths . . . an analyst cannot 'give' an insight. His interpretations can offer new knowledge, his interactions can provide new emotional experience, but the patient must digest the knowledge or experience to turn these into insights.

It appears to us that the notion of 'correct' insight leads to a great many difficulties (see the discussion of historical truth and narrative truth in the previous chapter). At the same time, the concept of 'effective' insight may result in a tautological argument. Perhaps the most useful approach to the problem is to differentiate 'intellectual' aspects of insight from those aspects which either release emotions or involve some aspect of a 'feeling-state' as part of the content of the insight itself. This would be consistent with the view we expressed earlier in chapter ten that 'it would appear that therapeutic change as a consequence of analysis depends, to a large degree, on the provision of a structured and organized conceptual and affective framework within which the patient can effectively place himself and his subjective experience of himself and others'. This would permit us to understand how different psychoanalytic and psychotherapeutic points of view, as mirrored in the interpretations given to the patient, may at times prove equally effective in their therapeutic results.

CHAPTER TWELVE

Working through

P sychoanalytic treatment shares with other forms of psychotherapy the aim of bringing about lasting changes within the patient. In common with other 'insight' therapies it makes use of interpretations and other verbal interventions (chapter ten). While these are aimed partly at making unconscious content and processes conscious, it has been maintained since the early days of psychoanalytic treatment that 'making what is unconscious conscious' and the gaining of insight are not sufficient, in the ordinary course of events, to bring about a fundamental change in the patient. In contrast to procedures involving hypnosis and massive abreaction (catharsis), the psychoanalytic method depends for its success on a number of additional elements. Some of these, particularly the elements of treatment alliance (chapter three), transference (chapters four and five), and the analysis of resistance (chapter seven) have been discussed in previous chapters. It is the purpose of the present chapter to examine those further factors in the psychoanalytic treatment situation which have been encompassed under the heading of *working through*.

Freud had used such terms as 'wearing away' and 'working over' in his earliest psychoanalytic writings (1895). He had, in fact, also used the phrase 'working through' once in *Studies on Hysteria* [1895d], but in a sense that is quite different from the way in which he used the concept later. The clinical concept of working through, however, was introduced in the paper, 'Remembering, Repeating and Working Through' (1914g). There Freud pointed out that the aim of treatment during the first phase of psychoanalysis had been the recall of the pathogenic traumatic event thought to lie behind the neurosis and the abreaction of the dammed-up affect associated with that event. With the giving-up of hypnosis, the therapeutic task became that of recovering significant forgotten mental content and associated affects through the patient's free associations, and this called for an 'expenditure of work' on the part of the patient because of his resistances to uncovering what was repressed. The recall of significant memories gave way, in prime importance, to the unconscious *repetition* of these memories in the form of transference and acting out (chapter nine). The analytic work was now regarded as being in large part directed towards the interpretation of the patient's resistances as well as being concerned with showing the patient how the past repeats itself in the present. However, even if the analyst has uncovered a resistance and shown it to the patient, this in itself will not cause the treatment to progress.

Freud remarked (1914g):

> One must allow the patient time to become more conversant with this resistance with which he has now become acquainted, to *work through* it, to overcome it, by continuing, in defiance of it, the analytic work according to the fundamental rule of analysis. Only when the resistance is at its height can the analyst, working in common with his patient, discover the repressed instinctual impulses which are feeding the resistance. . . . This working through of the resistances may in practice turn out to be an arduous task for the subject of the analysis and a trial of patience for the analyst. Nevertheless it is a part of the work which effects the greatest changes in the patient

and which distinguishes analytic treatment from any kind of treatment by suggestion.

Although Freud later differentiated a number of different sources of resistance (chapter seven), he came to link the need for working through with the particular form of resistance that follows from the 'compulsion to repeat' (1920g), and the so-called 'id resistance' (1926d). This can be regarded as a reflection of the 'opposition' of the instinctual impulses to detachment from their previous objects and modes of discharge (1915a, 1915f). Freud also wrote, borrowing a term from Jung, of 'psychical inertia' (1918b [1914]), of 'adhesiveness' (1916-17), and 'sluggishness' (1940a [1938]) of the libido as forces operating against recovery. These terms reflect Freud's concept of instinctual impulses as energy that can be attached to particular mental representations, in particular those of childhood love objects. This concept-ualization of instinctual drives as energy that can be invested in an object has increasingly and convincingly come under attack. In 1937 he related 'psychical inertia' to inherent constitutional factors and to ageing (1937c). Ageing was thought at this time to make the psychoanalytic process less effective, so that old age was regarded as a contraindication for psychoanalytic treatment, a view that is no longer widely held. For Freud, 'working through' represented the work entailed, for both analyst and patient, in overcoming resistances to change due primarily to the tendency for the instinctual drives to cling to accustomed patterns of discharge. Working through represented analytic work that was *additional* to that involved in uncovering conflicts and resist-ances. Intellectual insight without working through was not re-garded as sufficient for the therapeutic task, as the tendency for the previous modes of functioning to repeat themselves in accus-tomed ways would remain.

It is of historical interest that Fenichel, in commenting on Ferenczi's and Rank's book *The Development of Psycho-Analysis* (1925), draws attention to their emphasis on the reliving of emotional experiences in the transference and says (1941) of the authors that 'in their emphasis on experiencing they became ad-mirers of abreaction, of acting out, and thus working through was the loser'. Fenichel (1937, 1941) regards working through as an activity of the analyst rather than of both analyst and patient, and refers to it as 'a special type of interpretation'. He points out that the patient will show repeated resistance to the awareness of unconscious material that had previously been interpreted and that the work of interpretation has itself to be repeated, even though the process may now go more quickly and easily than before. While at times exactly the same picture may reappear in the patient, at other times *variants* will occur in different contexts. 'The process that requires demonstrating to patients the same thing again and again at different times or in various connections, is called, following Freud, "working through".'

Although Fenichel narrows Freud's concept in restricting working through to a type of interpretation, he widens it by relating it to the resistance of the ego and superego to change. Further, he likens working through to the process of mourning, a point also made by a number of later authors (e.g. Parkin, 1981). Fenichel says (1941), 'A person who has lost a friend must in all situations which remind him of this lost friend make clear to himself anew that he has this friend no longer and that a renunciation is necessary. The conception of this friend *has representation* in many complexes of memories and wishes, and the detachment from the friend must take place separately in each complex.' Fenichel saw working through as resulting in the freeing of small quantities of the 'energy' attached to the representation, being in this way similar to abreaction, although quite the opposite of the single massive abreaction. At the same time, he spoke of interpretation as having the effect of 'educating the patient to produce steadily less distorted derivatives' (1937). Since Fenichel, what one might call the 'micro-abreaction' aspect of working through has received relatively little consideration. In contrast, the 'learning' and 'unlearning' aspects have moved more into the foreground (Ekstein, 1966; Schmale, 1966; Thomä & Kächele, 1987).

Fundamental to working through is the—at times laborious— tracing of the ramifications of a conflict in different areas of the patient's life. As Fromm-Reichmann (1950) put it: 'Any understanding, any new piece of awareness which has been gained by interpretive clarification, has to be reconquered and tested time and again in new connections and contacts with other interlocking experiences, which may or may not have to be approached interpretively in their own right.'

In 1956 Greenacre stressed the importance of working through in those cases where a childhood traumatic event has had extensive effects in different areas of the personality. She pointed out that:

It was early recognized that if the infantile memories were recovered too quickly, or were *acted out* in the transference and not adequately interpreted, the abreaction at the time might be appreciable, but had no lasting effect. In such instances, the working through had not seemed necessary for the recovery of the memory, but now became essential to sustain any therapeutic effect—not to diminish the resistance and *reach* the memory, but to demonstrate again and again to the patient the working of instinctual trends in various situations in life.

Greenacre comments further that 'the defensive conflict remained somewhat structured unless worked with repetitively and in connection with its effect in various situations'. She also suggests that increased emphasis on the analysis of the mechanisms of defence has led to 'the recognition of the need for consistent work with the patterns of defence. . . . This has taken over much of what would previously have been referred to as *working through*'.

In the same year Kris (1956a) pointed out that the work of interpretation leads eventually to reconstruction of the patient's past, and that an aspect of working through is the need to apply these reconstructions to many different areas and levels of the patient's material. Related to this is a more general point made by Loewald (1960), who sees analysis as a process leading to structural changes in the patient. (The term 'structure' is used in the psychoanalytic literature to refer specifically to the trio of id, ego, and superego, but is nowadays used more generally to denote psychological organizations with a slow rate of change.) He says that

the analyst structures and articulates . . . the material and the productions offered by the patient. If an interpretation of unconscious meaning is timely, the words by which this meaning is expressed are recognizable to the patient as expressions of what he experiences. They organize for him what was previously less organized and thus give him the 'distance' from himself which enables him to understand, to see, to put into words and to 'handle' what was previously not visible, understandable, speakable, tangible. ... The analyst functions as a representative of a higher stage of organization and mediates this to the patient, insofar as the analyst's understanding is attuned to what is, and the way in which it is, in need of organization.

Loewald's formulation of this aspect of the analyst's function allows us to consider the theoretical framework and techniques of the analyst not from the point of view of whether it is 'right' or 'wrong', but whether they are *useful* in the sense described.

In a cogent discussion of working through, Novey (1962) considers the difficulties surrounding the concept and suggests that there are factors involved between analyst and patient which psychoanalysis has in common with other therapies, and which promote working through. These factors (supportive techniques, etc.) appear to be necessary and operate over and above the giving of correct interpretations. Working through also occurs outside the analytic session. 'Much of what we would consider working through in its proper sense is the time involved in actually experiencing and re-experiencing in intellectual as well as affective terms, so as to bring about constructive change.' A similar point is made by Valenstein (1962) in regard to the 'work' which may go on after an analysis has ended. 'As working-through goes on apace during that unending phase of self-analytic work which follows the conclusion of the analysis in its formal form, these new action patterns, as well as new thought and affect patterns, develop an increasing degree of structuralization.' Both Stewart (1963) and Greenson (1965b) adhere to Freud's view that working through is primarily directed against 'id resistance'. However, Greenson arrives at a definition of working through centred around insight and change, i.e.:

We do not regard the analytic work as working through before the patient has insight, only after. It is the goal of working through to make insight effective, i.e. to make significant and lasting changes in the patient. ... The analysis of those resistances which keep insight from leading to change is the work of working through. The analyst and the patient each contributes to this work . . . working through is essentially the repetition, deepening, and extension of the analysis of the resistances.

Greenson (1965b, 1966) adds that 'the analytic work leading to insight may be designated as the analytic work proper. The analytic work which leads from insight to change in behaviour, attitude and structure is the work of working through.' He goes on to list the elements in this work:

1. the repetition of interpretations, particularly the analysis of the transference resistances;

2. the breaking down of the isolation of affects and impulses from experiences and memories;

3. the extension, deepening, and broadening of interpretations, the uncovering of the multiple functions and determinants of the various antecedents and derivatives of a piece of behaviour;

4. reconstructions of the past which place the patient and other important figures of the environment in a living perspective; this includes reconstructions of the self-image at different periods of the past;

5. facilitating changes in reactions and behaviour which enable the previously inhibited patient to risk new modes of reaction and behaviour in regard to the impulses and objects he had considered dangerous until then. Usually the patient will first test out the new behaviour in the analytic situation and then in the outside world. The new behaviour will be some less distorted derivative of the infantile past.

A developmental approach to working through has been advocated by Shane (1979), who emphasizes that the process is similar to that which occurs in normal childhood development. He says that 'interpretation is a necessary but insufficient construct to account for therapeutic change. . . . the working through process consists not only of repeated interpretation of resistance and content in the many and varied experiences of the analysand, but also of an equally important process of development'. This development is seen as promoting structural change, which is the result of a number of steps that follow each correct interpretation. These steps constitute working through:

1. receiving and understanding the new insight (including the overcoming of resistances to insight);

2. applying the new insight to attain new capacities (beginning structural development);

3. conceiving of oneself differently because of the new capacities (continuing structural development);

4. mourning and overcoming the loss of the old self and, often, old object attachments (with consolidation of structural development).

As we have shown previously, some relatively early authors (e.g. Fenichel, 1941, 1945a; Glover, 1955) took the view that working through is predominantly work undertaken by the analyst rather than by the patient. This is also the position of some of the followers of Melanie Klein. So Pick (1985) writes:

Constant projecting by the patient into the analyst is the essence of analysis: every interpretation aims at a move from the paranoid/schizoid to the depressive position. This is true not only for the patient, but for the analyst who needs again and again to regress and work through. I wonder whether the real issue of truly deep versus superficial interpretation resides not so much in terms of which level has been addressed, but to what extent the analyst has worked the process through internally in the act of giving the interpretation. . . . it is the issue of how the analyst allows himself to have the experience, digest it, formulate it and communicate it as an interpretation.

This is in line with Bion's concepts (1962) of maternal 'reverie' and the function of the mother (and analyst) as a 'container' of the patient's anxieties and distress. Barande has commented (1982) that the Kleinian approach would seem to involve very hard and dramatic work as well as unceasing vigilance on the part of the analyst.

In contrast, O'Shaughnessy (1983), also a Kleinian analyst, stresses the work that needs to be done by the patient:

> ... as the patient feels understood by the analyst's words (the mutative interpretations) he may slowly become more aware of his primitive modes of relating, until, ultimately ... he is himself able to express his understanding of himself in his own words. This brings structural change and a resumption of ego development, and is a mutative moment. In brief: mutative interpretations are not by themselves the agency of change. They put the patient in a position to change. He himself must do the active, mutative working through in his own words.

Other writers (e.g. Stewart, 1963; Valenstein, 1983) also see working through as work for the patient. For example Sedler (1983), in a comprehensive discussion of the concept, says,

> Psychoanalysis has clearly defined the problem of neurosis, but it cannot resolve it; that, each individual must do for himself. The analytic situation is specially structured to facilitate this resolution and ... the analyst, his technical skill, and the transference events are indispensable factors in the overall process. ... working through names that aspect of the process which the analysand shall ultimately hold most dear for it signifies his own triumph—and 'not ours—over the clandestine operations of neurotic life.

The development of self psychology by Kohut has led to a re-evaluation of the concept. Kohut sees the goal of working through as the resumption of the individual's development, in terms of a readiness of the self for empathic interaction. Kohut speaks of interaction between the person's self and its 'selfobject' (see chapter four). In analysis, says Kohut (1984), 'the flow of empathy between analyst and analysand that had been opened through the originally established selfobject transference is remobilized. The patient's self is then sustained once more by a selfobject matrix that is empathically in tune with him.'

Working through is thus seen by the self psychologists as the overcoming of resistances against the establishment of archaic narcissistic transferences. Muslin (1986) comments, 'Working through is best conceptualized, from a self psychological perspective, as the analytic work performed in dissolving the patient's resistances to entering a new self-selfobject relationship. These resistances represent attempts to preserve archaic childhood bonds that, however stifling to growth, have heretofore provided the primary type of security known to these individuals.' In essence, the self psychological view of working through is in many respects no different from the more traditional one. The difference would appear to lie in what is worked through rather than in the nature of the process. Thus Kohut (1984) says: 'Whereas self psychology relies on the same tools as traditional analysis (interpretation followed by working through in an atmosphere of abstinence) to bring about the analytic cure, self psychology sees in a different light not only the results that are achieved, but also the very role that interpretation and working through play in the analytic process.'

From a very different psychoanalytic perspective, Brenner (1987) reviews the various meanings given to working through and its relation to the work of analysis. He concludes that,

in short, what each of the authors who has written on the subject saw analysis to be in its very essence was what each said must be worked through if analysis is to be successful: the will to remember, actions as well as words, the real relationship between patient and analyst, maturation and development, and so on. Thus everyone has said the same thing, to wit, 'When I analyse a patient it takes a long time. Analysis is slow work. Patients are not cured by a single interpretation, however profound and correct it may be'.

He adds,

Working through is not a regrettable delay in the process of analytic cure. It is analysis. It is the interpretative work which, as Freud wrote in 1914, leads to truly valuable insight and to dependable, lasting therapeutic change. . . . The analysis of psychic conflict in all of its aspects is what should properly be called working through.

Some of the confusion surrounding the concept appears to be a consequence of the failure of many psychoanalytic writers to maintain a clear differentiation between working through as a

description of an important part of the psychoanalytic therapeutic work, and the *psychological processes* that bring about the
need for, and which accompany and follow on, working through.
The 'arduous task' for the subject and the 'trial of patience' for the
analyst (Freud, 1914g) in covering the same ground over and over
again, in tracing the ramifications of unconscious impulses, conflicts, fantasies, and defences as these appear and reappear in the
patient's material, seems to be the essence of working through.
Such a description of working through would probably be acceptable to most psychoanalysts, but disagreement arises as soon as
the concept is broadened. These disagreements reflect different
theoretical orientations within psychoanalysis, as well as the
emphasis on different aspects of mental functioning at various
times in the history of psychoanalytic theory. Freud was careful
to distinguish between working through, the factors that were
thought to make it necessary (in particular, the id resistance),
and the results which working through was considered to bring
about, i.e. changes more permanent than those obtained by suggestion or abreaction only.

It is clear that developments in psychoanalytic theory after
Freud have affected the concept in various ways, so that some of
its original descriptive simplicity has been lost. Indeed, Novey
(1962) writes of 'our failure to understand the process of working
through', a view echoed by Sedler (1983). Bird (in Schmale, 1966)
expresses the view that there is no need for the term. However, it
continues to be widely used and is fairly generally regarded as a
basic psychoanalytic clinical or technical concept. In spite of its
shortcomings it is advisable to retain it as an essentially descriptive clinical concept. It involves work by both analyst and patient
and is related to the need to overcome resistances from all
sources. Of course, the failure of the patient to change following
interpretation or insight may be due to factors other than resistance. The concept of resistance is another instance of a descriptive
concept that has been given explanatory power. We have previously emphasized the need to distinguish between *forms* and
sources of resistance, and in regard to the latter we have
suggested that so-called 'id resistance' is a special instance of the
more general resistance to the giving up of past adaptive solutions (including neurotic symptoms) because of the need for

'unlearning' or extinction. The need for reinforcement and reward in order to accomplish learning (including learning through 'insight') and to bring about the formation of new structures and the inhibition or extinction of old ones is relevant in this connection. Such modification of structure by learning would not be part of working through, but a consequence of it.

It is worth emphasizing, in conclusion, that psychoanalytic writers uniformly maintain that, although working through is an essential part of the psychoanalytic process, the interpretation of unconscious mental content and of transference repetitions, together with the gaining of insight, are equally vital to the success of the analytic work. Any technique that does not make use of all of these elements cannot be regarded as truly psychoanalytic. This is not to say, however, that working through cannot play a role in other forms of therapy, especially in those that involve an element of 'retraining' or 're-education'.

REFERENCES

Abend, S. M. (1982). Serious illness in the analyst: counter-transference considerations. *Journal of the American Psychoanalytic Association*, 30: 365–379.

Abend, S. M. (1986). Countertransference, empathy, and the analytic ideal: the impact of life stresses on analytic capability. *Psychoanalytic Quarterly*, 55: 563–575.

Abend, S. M. (1988). Neglected classics: Ernst Kris's 'On some vicissitudes of insight in psycho-analysis'. *Psychoanalytic Quarterly*, 57: 224–228.

Abend, S. M., Porder, M., & Willick, M. S. (1983). *Borderline Patients: Psychoanalytic Perspectives*. New York: International Universities Press.

Abraham, K. (1908). The psycho-sexual differences between hysteria and dementia praecox. In: *Selected Papers on Psycho-Analysis*. London: Hogarth Press, 1927. [Reprinted London: Karnac Books, 1979.]

Abraham, K. (1919). A particular form of neurotic resistance against the psychoanalytic method. In: *Selected Papers on Psycho-*

Analysis. London: Hogarth Press, 1927. [Reprinted London: Karnac Books, 1979.]

Abt, L., & Weissman, S. (Eds.) (1965). *Acting Out: Theoretical and Clinical Aspects*. New York: Grune & Stratton.

Abt, L., & Weissman, S. (Eds.) (1976). *Acting Out: Theoretical and Clinical Aspects* (second edition). New York: Grune & Stratton.

Adler, G. (1980). Transference, real relationship and alliance. *International Journal of Psycho-Analysis*, 61: 547–558.

Adler, G. (1981). The borderline-narcissistic personality disorder continuum. *American Journal of Psychiatry*, 138: 46–50.

Adler, G. (1984). Issues in the treatment of the borderline patient. In: P. E. Stepansky & A. Goldberg (Eds.), *Kohut's Legacy : Contributions to Self Psychology*. Hillsdale, NJ: Analytic Press.

Adler, G. (1985). *Borderline Psychopathology and its Treatment*. New York: Jason Aronson.

Adler, G. (1989). Transitional phenomena, projective identification and the essential ambiguity of the psychoanalytic situation. *Psychoanalytic Quarterly*, 58: 81–104.

Adler, G., & Buie, D. H. (1979). Aloneness and borderline psychopathology: the possible relevance of child development issues. *International Journal of Psycho-Analysis*, 60: 83–96.

Alexander, F. (1925). A metapsychological description of the process of cure. *International Journal of Psycho-Analysis*, 6: 13–34.

Alexander, F. (1948). *Fundamentals of Psychoanalysis*. New York: Norton.

Alexander, F. (1950). Analysis of the therapeutic factors in psycho-analytic treatment. *Psychoanalytic Quarterly*, 19: 482–500.

Alexander, F., & French, T. M. (1946). *Psychoanalytic Therapy*. New York: Ronald Press.

Anastasopoulos, D. (1988). Acting out during adolescence in terms of regression in symbol formation. *International Review of Psychoanalysis*, 15: 177–185.

Arkin, F. S. (1960). Discussion of Salzman, L., The negative therapeutic reaction. In: J. H. Masserman (Ed.), *Science and Psychoanalysis, Vol. 3* (pp. 314–317). New York: Grune & Stratton.

Arlow, J. A. (1985). Some technical problems of countertransference. *Psychoanalytic Quarterly*, 54: 164–174.

Arlow, J. A. (1987). The dynamics of interpretation. *Psychoanalytic Quarterly*, 56: 68–87.

Arlow, J. A., & Brenner, C. (1964). *Psychoanalytic Concepts and the Structural Theory*. New York: International Universities Press.

Arlow, J. A., & Brenner, C. (1969). The psychopathology of the psychoses: a proposed revision. *International Journal of Psycho-Analysis*, 50: 5–14.

Asch, S. (1976). Varieties of negative therapeutic reaction and problems of technique. *Journal of the American Psychoanalytic Association*, 24: 383–407.

Atkins, N. B. (1967). Comments on severe and psychotic regression in analysis. *Journal of the American Psychoanalytic Association*, 15: 584–605.

Atkins, N. B. (1970). Action, acting out and the symptomatic act. *Journal of the American Psychoanalytic Association*, 18: 631–643.

Auchincloss, E. L. (reporter) (1989). Panel: The opening phase of psycho-analysis. *Journal of the American Psycho-analytic Association*, 37: 199–214.

Balint, M. (1933). On transference of emotions. In: *Primary Love and Psycho-Analytic Technique*. London: Tavistock, 1965. [Reprinted London: Karnac Books, 1985.]

Balint, M. (1934). Charakteranalyse und Neubeginn. *Internationale Zeitschrift für Psycho-analyse*, 20: 54–65.

Balint, M. (1949). Changing therapeutical aims and techniques in psycho-analysis. In: *Primary Love and Psycho-Analytic Technique*. London: Tavistock, 1965. [Reprinted London: Karnac Books, 1985.]

Balint, M. (1965). The benign and malignant forms of regression. In: G. E. Daniel (Ed.), *New Perspectives in Psychoanalysis*. New York: Grune & Stratton.

Balint, M. (1968). *The Basic Fault, Therapeutic Aspects of Regression*. London: Tavistock.

Balint, M., & Balint, A. (1939). On transference and counter-transference. In: *Primary Love and Psycho-Analytic Technique*. London: Tavistock, 1965. [Reprinted London: Karnac Books, 1985.]

Barande, R. (1982). 'Hard work' or 'working through'. *Revue Française de Psychanalyse*, 46: 301–305.

Baranger, W. (1974). A discussion of the paper by Helena Besserman Vianna on 'A peculiar form of resistance to psychoanalytical treatment'. *International Journal of Psycho-Analysis*, 55: 445–447.

Barnett, J. (1978). Insight and therapeutic change. *Contemporary Psychoanalysis*, 14: 534–544.

Bateson, G., Jackson, D. D., Haley, J., & Wearland, J. (1956). Towards a theory of schizophrenia. *Behavioral Science*, 1: 251–264.

Bégoin, J., & Bégoin, F. (1979). Negative therapeutic reaction: envy and catastrophic anxiety. *Paper to 3rd Conference of the European Psycho-Analytical Federation. London.*

Bellak, L. (1965). The concept of acting out: theoretical considerations. In: L. Abt & S. Weissman (Eds.), *Acting Out: Theoretical and Clinical Aspects*. New York: Grune & Stratton.

Beres, D., & Arlow, J. A. (1974). Fantasy and identification in empathy. *Psychoanalytic Quarterly*, 43: 26–50.

Berg, M. D. (1977). The externalizing transference. *International Journal of Psycho-Analysis*, 58: 235–244.

Bernstein, I., & Glenn, J. (1988). The child and adolescent analyst's reaction to his patients and their parents. *International Review of Psycho-Analysis*, 15: 225–241.

Bibring, E. (1954). Psychoanalysis and the dynamic psychotherapies. *Journal of the American Psychoanalytic Association*, 2: 745–770.

Bibring-Lehner, G. (1936). A contribution to the subject of transference-resistance. *International Journal of Psycho-Analysis*, 17: 181–189.

Bilger, A. (1986). Agieren: Problem und Chance. *Forum der Psychoanalyse*, 2: 294–308.

Bion, W. R. (1959). Attacks on linking. *International Journal of Psycho-Analysis*, 40: 308–315.

Bion, W. R. (1961). *Experiences in Groups*. London: Tavistock.

Bion, W. R. (1962). *Learning from Experience*. London: Heinemann. [Reprinted London: Karnac Books, 1984.]

Blacker, K. H. (reporter) (1981). Panel: Insight: clinical conceptualizations. *Journal of the American Psychoanalytic Association*, 29: 659–671.

Bleger, J. (1967). Psychoanalysis of the psychoanalytic frame. *International Journal of Psycho-Analysis*, 48: 511–519.

Bleger, J. (1981). *Symbiose et Ambiguité*. Paris: Presses Universitaires de France.

Bleuler, E. (1911). *Dementia Praecox or the Group of Schizophrenias.* New York: International Universities Press, 1950.

Blos, P. (1963). The concept of acting out in relation to the adolescent process. *Journal of the American Academy of Child Psychiatry*, 2: 118–143.

Blos, P. (1966). Discussion remarks. In: E. Rexford (Ed.), *Developmental Approach to Problems of Acting Out.* Monographs of the American Academy of Child Psychiatry, No. 1.

Blum, H. P. (1971). On the conception and development of the transference neurosis. *Journal of the American Psychoanalytic Association*, 19: 41–53.

Blum, H. P. (1973). The concept of erotized transference. *Journal of the American Psychoanalytic Association*, 21: 61–76.

Blum, H. P. (1976). Acting out, the psychoanalytic process, and interpretation. *The Annual of Psychoanalysis*, 4: 163–184.

Blum, H. P. (1981). The forbidden quest and the analytical ideal: the superego and insight. *Psychoanalytic Quarterly*, 50: 535–556.

Blum, H. P. (1983). The position and value of extratransference interpretation. *Journal of the American Psychoanalytic Association*, 33: 587–617.

Blum, H. P. (1985). Foreword. In: H. P. Blum (Ed.), *Defense and Resistance.* New York: International Universities Press.

Blum, H. P. (1986). Countertransference and the theory of technique: discussion. *Journal of the American Psychoanalytical Association*, 34: 309–328.

Boesky, D. (1982). Acting out: a reconsideration of the concept. *International Journal of Psycho-Analysis*, 63: 39–55.

Boesky, D. (1985). Resistance and character theory. In: H. P. Blum (Ed.), *Defense and Resistance.* New York: International Universities Press.

Bollas, C. (1987). *The Shadow of the Object.* London: Free Association Books.

Boschán, P. J. (1987). Dependence and narcissistic resistances in the psychoanalytic process. *International Journal of Psycho-Analysis*, 68: 109–118.

Brandschaft, B. (1983). The negativism of the negative therapeutic reaction and the psychology of the self. In: A. Goldberg (Ed.), *The Future of Psychoanalysis.* New York: Guilford Press.

Brenner, C. (1959). The masochistic character: genesis and treatment. *Journal of the American Psychoanalytic Association*, 7: 197–226.

Brenner, C. (1976). *Psychoanalytic Technique and Psychic Conflict*. New York: International Universities Press.

Brenner, C. (1979). Working alliance, therapeutic alliance, and transference. *Journal of the American Psychoanalytic Association*, 27 (supplement): 137–157.

Brenner, C. (1981). Defense and defense mechanisms. *Psychoanalytic Quarterly*, 50: 557–569.

Brenner, C. (1982). *The Mind in Conflict*. New York: International Universities Press.

Brenner, C. (1985). Countertransference as compromise formation. *Psychoanalytic Quarterly*, 54: 155–163.

Brenner, C. (1987). Working through: 1914–1984. *Psychoanalytic Quarterly*, 56: 88–108.

Brown, G. W., Bone, M., Dalison, B., & Wing, J. R. (1966). *Schizophrenia and Social Care: A Comparative Follow-up Study of 339 Schizophrenic Patients*. London: Oxford University Press.

Buie, D. H., & Adler, G. (1982–3). Definitive treatment of the borderline personality. *International Journal of Psychoanalytic Psychotherapy*, 9: 51–87.

Bush, M. (1978). Preliminary considerations for a psychoanalytic theory of insight: historical perspective. *International Review of Psycho-Analysis*, 5: 1–13.

Calogeras, R., & Alston, T. (1985). Family pathology and the infantile neurosis. *International Journal of Psycho-Analysis*, 66: 359–374.

Cesio, F. R. (1956). Un caso de reacción terapeutica negativa. *Revista de psicoanalisis*, 13: 522–526.

Cesio, F. R. (1958). La reacción terapeutica negativa. *Revista de psicoanalisis*, 15: 293–299.

Cesio, F. R. (1960a). El letargo, un contribución al estudio de la reacción terapeutica negativa. *Revista de psicoanalisis*, 17: 10–26.

Cesio, F. R. (1960b). Contribución al estudio de la reacción terapeutica negativa. *Revista de psicoanalisis*, 17: 289–298.

Chediak, C. (1979). Counter-reactions and countertransference. *International Journal of Psycho-Analysis*, 60: 117–129.

Coen, S. J. (1981). Sexualization as a predominant mode of defense. *Journal of the American Psychoanalytic Association*, 29: 893–920.

Cohen, M. B. (1952). Counter-transference and anxiety. *Psychiatry*, 15: 231–243.

Colarusso, C. A., & Nemiroff, R. A. (1979). Some observations and hypotheses about the psycho-analytic theory of adult development. *International Journal of Psycho-Analysis*, 60: 59–71.

Compton, A. (reporter) (1977). Panel: Psychic change in psychoanalysis. *Journal of the American Psychoanalytic Association*, 25: 669–678.

Cooper, A. M. (1987a). Changes in psychoanalytic ideas: transference interpretation. *Journal of the American Psychoanalytic Association*, 35: 77–98.

Cooper, A. M. (1987b). The transference neurosis: a concept ready for retirement. *Psychoanalytic Inquiry*, 7: 569–585.

Curtis, H. C. (1979). The concept of therapeutic alliance: implications for the 'widening scope'. *Journal of the American Psychoanalytic Association*, 27, Supplement: 159–192.

Davies, S. (1990). Whose treatment alliance is it anyhow? *Paper to Weekend Conference for English-speaking Members of European Societies. London.*

Deutsch, H. (1939). A discussion of certain forms of resistance. *International Journal of Psycho-Analysis*, 20: 72–83.

Deutsch, H. (1966). Discussion remarks. In: E. Rexford (Ed.), *Developmental Approach to Problems of Acting Out*. Monographs of the American Academy of Child Psychiatry, No. 1.

Dewald, P. A. (1980). The handling of resistances in adult psychoanalysis. *International Journal of Psycho-Analysis*, 61: 61–69.

Dewald, P. A. (1982). Serious illness in the analyst: transference, countertransference, and reality responses. *Journal of the American Psychoanalytic Association*, 30: 347–364.

Dickes, R. (1967). Severe regressive disruptions of the therapeutic alliance. *Journal of the American Psychoanalytic Association*, 15: 508–533.

Dickes, R. (1975). Technical considerations of the therapeutic and working alliances. *International Journal of Psychoanalytic Psychotherapy*, 4: 1–24.

Eagle, M. N., & Wolitzky, D. L. (1989). The idea of progress in psychoanalysis. *Psychoanalysis and Contemporary Thought*, 12: 27–72.

Eidelberg, L. (1948). A contribution to the study of masochism. In: *Studies in Psychoanalysis*. New York: International Universities Press.

Eidelberg, L. (Ed.) (1968). *Encyclopedia of Psychoanalysis*. New York: The Free Press.

Eissler, K. R. (1953). The effect of the structure of the ego on psychoanalytic technique. *Journal of the American Psychoanalytic Association*, 1: 104–143.

Ekstein, R. (1966). Termination of analysis and working through. In: R. E. Litman (Ed.), *Psychoanalysis in the Americas: Original Contributions from the First Pan-American Congress for Psychoanalysis*. New York: International Universities Press.

English, O. S., & Pearson, G. H. (1937). *Common Neuroses of Children and Adults*. New York: W. W. Norton.

Erard, R. E. (1983). New wine in old skins: a reappraisal of the concept 'acting out'. *International Review of Psycho-Analysis*, 10: 63–73.

Erikson, E. H. (1950). *Childhood and Society*. New York: W. W. Norton.

Erikson, E. H. (1956). The problem of ego identity. *Journal of the American Psychoanalytic Association*, 4: 56–121.

Erikson, E. H. (1968). *Identity, Youth and Crisis*. New York: Norton.

Escoll, P. J. (reporter) (1983). Panel: The changing vistas of transference: the effect of developmental concepts on the understanding of transference. *Journal of the American Psychoanalytic Association*, 31: 699–711.

Evans, R. (1976). Development of the treatment alliance in the analysis of an adolescent boy. *The Psychoanalytic Study of the Child*, 31: 193–224.

Fairbairn, W. R. D. (1958). On the nature and aims of psychoanalytical treatment. *International Journal of Psycho-Analysis*, 39: 374–385.

Federn, P. (1943). Psychoanalysis of psychoses. *Psychiatric Quarterly*, 17: 3–19, 246–257, 470–487.

Feigenbaum, D. (1934). Clinical fragments. *Psychoanalytic Quarterly*, 3: 363–390.

Fenichel, O. (1937). On the theory of the therapeutic results of psycho-analysis. *International Journal of Psycho-Analysis*, 18: 133–138.

Fenichel, O. (1941). *Problems of Psychoanalytic Technique*. New York: Psychoanalytic Quarterly, Inc.

Fenichel, O. (1945a). *The Psychoanalytic Theory of Neurosis*. London: Routledge & Kegan Paul.

Fenichel, O. (1945b). Neurotic acting out. *Psychoanalytic Review*, 32: 197–206.

Fenichel, O. (1954). Symposium on the therapeutic results of psychoanalysis. In: *Collected Papers, Vol. 2*. London: Routledge & Kegan Paul.

Ferenczi, S. (1912). Transitory symptom-constructions during the analysis (transitory conversion, substitution, illusion, hallucination, character-regression, and expression-displacement). In *Sex in Psycho-Analysis*. New York: Basic Books, 1950.

Ferenczi, S. (1914). Falling asleep during the analysis. In *Further Contributions to the Theory and Technique of Psycho-Analysis*. London: Hogarth Press, 1926. [Reprinted London: Karnac Books, 1980.]

Ferenczi, S., & Rank, O. (1925). *The Development of Psycho-Analysis*. New York/Washington: Nervous and Mental Diseases Publishing Company.

Fischer, N. (1971). An interracial analysis: transference and counter-transference significance. *Journal of the American Psychoanalytic Association*, 19: 736–745.

Fliess, R. (1942). The metapsychology of the analyst. *Psychoanalytic Quarterly*, 11: 211–227.

Fliess, R. (1953). Counter-transference and counter-identification. *Journal of the American Psychoanalytic Association*, 1: 268–284.

Fonagy, P. (1990). Discussion of Kit Bollas's paper, 'The origins of the therapeutic alliance'. *Paper to Weekend Conference for English-speaking Members of European Societies. London*.

Frank, A. (1985). Id resistance and the strength of the instincts. In: H. P. Blum (Ed.), *Defense and Resistance*. New York: International Universities Press.

French, T. M. (1939). Insight and distortion in dreams. *International Journal of Psycho-Analysis*, 20: 287–298.

Freud, A. (1928). *Introduction to the Technique of Child Analysis*. New York/Washington: Nervous & Mental Disease Publishing Company.

Freud, A. (1936). *The Ego and the Mechanisms of Defence*. London: Hogarth Press.

Freud, A. (1954). The widening scope of indications for psychoanalysis: discussion. *Journal of the American Psychoanalytic Association*, 2: 607–620.

Freud, A. (1965). *Normality and Pathology in Childhood*. London: Hogarth Press. [Reprinted London: Karnac Books, 1989.]

Freud, A. (1968). Acting out. *International Journal of Psycho-Analysis*, 49: 165–170.

Freud, A. (1969). *Difficulties in the Path of Psychoanalysis*. New York: International Universities Press.

Freud, A. (1971). The infantile neurosis. *The Psychoanalytic Study of the Child*, 26: 79–90.

Freud, A. (1981). Insight, its presence and absence as a factor in normal development. *The Psychoanalytic Study of the Child*, 36: 241–249.

Freud, S. (1895d). *Studies on Hysteria. Standard Edition*, 2. London: Hogarth Press.

Freud, S. (1896b). Further remarks on the neuro-psychoses of defence. *Standard Edition*, 3. London: Hogarth Press.

Freud, S. (1897). Letter to Wilhelm Fliess of 21 September 1897. In: *The Origins of Psycho-Analysis: Letters to Wilhelm Fliess, Drafts and Notes*. London: Imago, 1954.

Freud, S. (1900a). *The Interpretation of Dreams. Standard Edition*, 4–5. London: Hogarth Press.

Freud, S. (1901b). *The Psychopathology of Everyday Life. Standard Edition*, 6. London: Hogarth Press.

Freud, S. (1904a). Freud's psycho-analytic procedure. *Standard Edition*, 7. London: Hogarth Press.

Freud, S. (1905d). Three essays on the theory of sexuality. *Standard Edition*, 7. London: Hogarth Press.

Freud, S. (1905e [1901]). Fragment of an analysis of a case of hysteria. *Standard Edition*, 7. London: Hogarth Press.

Freud, S. (1910a [1909]). Five lectures on psycho-analysis. *Standard Edition*, 11. London: Hogarth Press.

Freud, S. (1909b). Analysis of a phobia in a five-year-old boy. *Standard Edition*, 10. London: Hogarth Press.

Freud, S. (1909d). Notes upon a case of obsessional neurosis. *Standard Edition*, 10. London: Hogarth Press.

Freud, S. (1910d). The future prospects of psycho-analytic therapy. *Standard Edition*, 11. London: Hogarth Press.

Freud, S. (1911c). Psycho-analytic notes on an autobiographical account of a case of paranoia (Dementia Paranoides). *Standard Edition*, 12. London: Hogarth Press.

Freud, S. (1911e). The handling of dream-interpretation in psycho-analysis. *Standard Edition*, 12. London: Hogarth Press.

Freud, S. (1912b). The dynamics of transference. *Standard Edition*, 12. London: Hogarth Press.

Freud, S. (1912e). Recommendations to physicians practising psycho-analysis. *Standard Edition*, 12. London: Hogarth Press.

Freud, S. (1913c). On beginning the treatment (Further recommendations on the technique of psycho-analysis, I). *Standard Edition*, 12. London: Hogarth Press.

Freud, S. (1913i). The disposition to obsessional neurosis. *Standard Edition*, 12. London: Hogarth Press.

Freud, S. (1914c). On narcissism: an introduction. *Standard Edition*, 14. London: Hogarth Press.

Freud, S. (1914g). Remembering, repeating and working-through (Further recommendations on the technique of psycho-analysis, II.) *Standard Edition*, 12. London: Hogarth Press.

Freud, S. (1915a). Observations on transference-love (Further recommendations on the treatment of psycho-analysis, III). *Standard Edition*, 12. London: Hogarth Press.

Freud, S. (1915c). Instincts and their vicissitudes. *Standard Edition*, 14. London: Hogarth Press.

Freud, S. (1915f). A case of paranoia running counter to the psycho-analytic theory of the disease. *Standard Edition*, 14. London: Hogarth Press.

Freud, S. (1916d). Some character-types met with in psycho-analytic work. *Standard Edition*, 14. London: Hogarth Press.

Freud, S. (1916–17). *Introductory Lectures on Psycho-Analysis*. *Standard Edition*, 15–16. London: Hogarth Press.

Freud, S. (1918b [1914]). From the history of an infantile neurosis. *Standard Edition*, 17. London: Hogarth Press.

Freud, S. (1920g). *Beyond the Pleasure Principle. Standard Edition*, 18. London: Hogarth Press.

Freud, S. (1921c). *Group Psychology and the Analysis of the Ego*. *Standard Edition*, 18. London: Hogarth Press.

Freud, S. (1923b). *The Ego and the Id*. *Standard Edition*, 19. London: Hogarth Press.

Freud, S. (1924c). The economic problem of masochism. *Standard Edition*, 19. London: Hogarth Press.

Freud, S. (1925d). *An Autobiographical Study*. *Standard Edition*, 20. London: Hogarth Press.

Freud, S. (1926d). *Inhibitions, Symptoms and Anxiety*. *Standard Edition*, 20. London: Hogarth Press.

Freud, S. (1926e). *The Question of Lay Analysis*. *Standard Edition*, 20. London: Hogarth Press.

Freud, S. (1931b). Female sexuality. *Standard Edition*, 21. London: Hogarth Press.

Freud, S. (1933a). *New Introductory Lectures on Psycho-Analysis*. *Standard Edition*, 22. London: Hogarth Press.

Freud, S. (1937c). Analysis terminable and interminable. *Standard Edition*, 23. London: Hogarth Press.

Freud, S. (1937d). Constructions in analysis. *Standard Edition*, 23. London: Hogarth Press.

Freud, S. (1939a). *Moses and Monotheism*. *Standard Edition*, 23. London: Hogarth Press.

Freud, S. (1940a [1938]). *An Outline of Psycho-Analysis*. *Standard Edition*, 23. London: Hogarth Press.

Freud, S. (1950a [1887–1902]). *The Origins of Psycho-Analysis*. *Standard Edition*, 1. London: Hogarth Press.

Friedman, L. (1969). The therapeutic alliance. *International Journal of Psycho-Analysis*, 50: 139–153.

Fromm-Reichmann, F. (1950). *Principles of Intensive Psychotherapy*. Chicago: Chicago University Press.

Frosch, J. (1967). Severe regressive states during analysis. *Journal of the American Psychoanalytic Association*, 15: 491–507, 606–625.

Frosch, J. (1983). *The Psychotic Process*. New York: International Universities Press.

Gabbard, G. O., Horwitz, L., Frieswyk, S., Allen, J. G., Colson, D. B., Newsom, G., & Coyne, L. (1988). The effect of therapist interventions on the therapeutic alliance with borderline patients. *Journal of the American Psychoanalytic Association*, 36: 657–727.

Gedo, J. E. (1979). *Beyond Interpretation*. New York: International Universities Press.

Gero, G. (1936). The construction of depression. *International Journal of Psycho-Analysis*, 17: 423–461.

Gero, G. (1951). The concept of defense. *Psychoanalytic Quarterly*, 17: 565–578.

Gerstley, L., McLellan, A. T., Alterman, A. I., Woody, G. E., Luborsky, L., & Prout, M. (1989). Ability to form an alliance with the therapist: a possible marker of prognosis for patients with antisocial personality disorder. *American Journal of Psychiatry*, 146: 508–512.

Gill, H. S. (1988). Working through resistances of intrapsychic and environmental origins. *International Journal of Psycho-Analysis*, 69: 535–550.

Gill, M. M. (1954). Psychoanalysis and exploratory psychotherapy. *Journal of the American Psychoanalytic Association*, 2: 771–797.

Gill, M. M. (1982). *Analysis of Transference: Vol. 1. Theory and Technique*. New York: International Universities Press.

Gillman, R. D. (1987). A child analyzes a dream. *The Psychoanalytic Study of the Child*, 42: 263–273.

Giovacchini, P. (1987a). Treatment, holding environment and transitional space. *Modern Psychoanalysis*, 12: 151–162.

Gitelson, M. (1952). The emotional position of the analyst in the psychoanalytic situation. *International Journal of Psycho-Analysis*, 33: 1–10.

Gitelson, M. (1954). Therapeutic problems in the analysis of the 'normal' candidate. *International Journal of Psycho-Analysis*, 35: 174–183.

Gitelson, M. (1962). The curative factors in psychoanalysis. *International Journal of Psycho-Analysis*, 43: 194–205.

Glover, E. (1931). The therapeutic effect of inexact interpretation. *International Journal of Psycho-Analysis*, 12: 397–411.

Glover, E. (1937). The theory of the therapeutic results of psychoanalysis. *International Journal of Psycho-Analysis*, 18: 125.

Glover, E. (1955). *The Technique of Psycho-Analysis*. London: Bailliere, Tindall & Cox.

Gray, P. (1990). The nature of therapeutic action in psychoanalysis. *Journal of the American Psychoanalytic Association*, 38: 1083–1097.

Greenacre, P. (1950). General problems of acting out. *Psychoanalytic Quarterly*, 19: 455–467.

Greenacre, P. (1956). Re-evaluation of the process of working through. *International Journal of Psycho-Analysis*, 37: 439–444.

Greenacre, P. (1968). The psychoanalytic process, transference and acting out. In: *Emotional Growth*. New York: International Universities Press, 1971.

Greenbaum, H. (1956). Combined psychoanalytic therapy with negative therapeutic reactions. In: A. H. Rifkin (Ed.), *Schizophrenia in Psychoanalytic Office Practice*. New York: Grune & Stratton.

Greenson, R. R. (1965a). The working alliance and the transference neurosis. *Psychoanalytic Quarterly*, 34: 155–181.

Greenson, R. R. (1965b). The problem of working through. In: M. Schur (Ed.), *Drives, Affects, Behavior*. New York: International Universities Press.

Greenson, R. R. (1966). Comment on Dr. Limentani's paper. *International Journal of Psycho-Analysis*, 47: 282–285.

Greenson, R. R. (1967). *The Technique and Practice of Psychoanalysis, Vol. 1*. New York: International Universities Press.

Greenson, R. R., & Wexler, M. (1969). The non-transference relationship in the psychoanalytic situation. *International Journal of Psycho-Analysis*, 50: 27–39.

Grinberg, L. (1962). On a specific aspect of countertransference due to the patient's projective identification. *International Journal of Psycho-Analysis*, 43: 436–440.

Grinberg, L. (1968). On acting out and its role in the psychoanalytic process. *International Journal of Psycho-Analysis*, 49: 171–178.

Grinberg, L. (1987). Dreams and acting out. *Psychoanalytic Quarterly*, 56: 155–176.

Grunert, U. (1979). Die negative therapeutische Reaktion als Ausdruck einer Störung im Loslösungs-und Individuationsprozess. *Psyche*, 33: 1–29.

Gunderson, J. G. (1977). Characteristics of borderlines. In: P. Hartocollis (Ed.), *Borderline Personality Disorders: The Concept, the Symptom, the Patient*. New York: International Universities Press.

Gunderson, J. G. (1984). *Borderline Personality Disorder*. Washington, DC: American Psychiatric Press.

Gutheil, T. G., & Havens, L. L. (1979). The therapeutic alliance: contemporary meanings and confusions. *International Review of Psycho-Analysis*, 6: 467–481.

Halpert, E. (reporter) (1984). Panel: The value of extratransference interpretation. *Journal of the American Psychoanalytic Association*, 32: 137–146.

Hammett, V. B. O. (1961). Delusional transference. *American Journal of Psychotherapy*, 15: 574–581.

Hanly, C. (1982). Narcissism, defence and the positive transference. *International Journal of Psycho-Analysis*, 63: 427–444.

Harley, M. (1971). The current status of transference neurosis in children. *Journal of the American Psychoanalytic Association*, 19: 26–40.

Hartmann, H. (1939). *Ego Psychology and the Problem of Adaptation*. London: Imago, 1958.

Hartmann, H. (1944). Psychoanalysis and sociology. In: *Essays on Ego and Psychology*. London: Hogarth Press, 1964.

Hartmann, H. (1951). Technical implications of ego psychology. *Psychoanalytic Quarterly*, 20: 31–43.

Hartmann, H. (1956). The development of the ego concept in Freud's work. *International Journal of Psycho-Analysis*, 37: 425–438.

Hartmann, H. (1964). *Essays on Ego Psychology*. London: Hogarth Press.

Hatcher, R. L. (1973). Insight and self-observation. *Journal of the American Psychoanalytic Association*, 21: 377–398.

Heimann, P. (1950). On counter-transference. *International Journal of Psycho-Analysis*, 31: 81–84.

Heimann, P. (1960). Counter-transference. *British Journal of Medical Psychology*, 33: 9–15.

Hill, D. (1968). Depression: disease, reaction or posture? *American Journal of Psychiatry*, 125: 445–457.

Hinshelwood, R. D. (1989). *A Dictionary of Kleinian Thought*. London: Free Association Books.

Hinsie, L. E., & Campbell, R. J. (1970). *Psychiatric Dictionary* (4th edition). London: Oxford University Press.

Hoffer, W. (1956). Transference and transference neurosis. *International Journal of Psycho-Analysis*, 37: 377–379.

Holder, A. (1970). Conceptual problems of acting out in children. *Journal of Child Psychotherapy*, 2: 5–22.

Horney, K. (1936). The problem of the negative therapeutic reaction. *Psychoanalytic Quarterly*, 5: 29–44.

Horowitz, M. H. (1987). Some notes on insight and its failures. *Psychoanalytic Quarterly*, 56: 177–198.

Infante, J. A. (1976). Acting out: a clinical reappraisal. *Bulletin of the Menninger Clinic*, 40: 315–324.

Isaacs, S. (1939). Criteria for interpretation. *International Journal of Psycho-Analysis*, 20: 148–160.

Ivimey, M. (1948). Negative therapeutic reaction. *American Journal of Psychoanalysis*, 8: 24–33.

Jacobs, T. J. (1973). Posture, gesture and movement in the analysis: cues to interpretation and countertransference. *Journal of the American Psychoanalytic Association*, 21: 77–92.

Jacobs, T. J. (1983). The analyst and the patient's object world: notes on an aspect of countertransference. *Journal of the American Psychoanalytic Association*, 31: 619–642.

Jacobs, T. J. (1986). On countertransference enactments. *Journal of the American Psychoanalytic Association*, 34: 289–307.

Jacobs, T. J. (1987). Notes on the unknowable: analytic secrets and the transference neurosis. *Psychoanalytic Inquiry*, 7: 485–509.

Jaspers, K. (1913). *Allgemeine Psychopathologie*. Berlin: Springer Verlag.

Joffe, W. G., & Sandler, J. (1965). Notes on pain, depression and individuation. *Psychoanalytic Study of the Child*, 20: 394–424.

Joffe, W. G., & Sandler, J. (1967). On the concept of pain, with special reference to depression and psychogenic pain. *Journal of Psychosomatic Research*, 11: 69–75.

Jones, E. (1955). *Sigmund Freud: Life and Work, Vol. 2*. New York: Basic Books.

Joseph, B. (1985). Transference: the total situation. *International Journal of Psycho-Analysis*, 66: 447–454.

Joseph, B. (1987). Projective identification: clinical aspects. In: J. Sandler (Ed.), *Projection, Identification, Projective Identification*. Madison CT: International Universities Press.

Jung, C. G. (1907). Ueber die Psychologie der Dementia Praecox: Ein Versuch, Halle A. S. In: *Collected Works, 3*. London: Routledge & Kegan Paul, 1960.

Kanzer, M. (1981). Freud's 'analytic pact': the standard therapeutic alliance. *Journal of the American Psychoanalytic Association*, 29: 69–87.

Kaplan, A. (1964). *The Conduct of Inquiry*. San Francisco: Chandler Publishing Co.

Kemper, W. W. (1966). Transference and countertransference as a functional unit. *Official Report on Pan-American Congress for Psycho-analysis*.

Kennedy, H. (1979). The role of insight in child analysis: a developmental viewpoint. *Journal of the American Psychoanalytic Association*, 27 (supplement): 9–28.

Kepecs, J. G. (1966). Theories of transference neurosis. *Psychoanalytic Quarterly*, 35: 497–521.

Kernberg, O. F. (1965). Notes on countertransference. *Journal of the American Psychoanalytic Association*, 13: 38–56.

Kernberg, O. F. (1967). Borderline personality organisation. *Journal of the American Psychoanalytic Association*, 15: 641–685.

Kernberg, O. F. (1975). *Borderline Conditions and Pathological Narcissism*. New York: Jason Aronson.

Kernberg, O. F. (1976a). *Object Relations Theory and Clinical Psychoanalysis*. New York: Jason Aronson.

Kernberg, O. F. (1976b). Technical considerations in the treatment of borderline personality organisation. *Journal of the American Psychoanalytic Association*, 24: 795–829.

Kernberg, O. F. (1980a). Character structure and analyzability. *Bulletin of the Association of Psychoanalytic Medicine*, 19: 87–96.

Kernberg, O. F. (1980b). *Internal World and External Reality*. New York: Jason Aronson.

Kernberg, O. F. (1985). Object relations theory and character analysis. In: H. P. Blum (Ed.), *Defense and Resistance*. New York: International Universities Press.

Kernberg, O. F. (1987). An ego psychology-object relations theory approach to the transference. *Psychoanalytic Quarterly*, 56: 197–221.

Kernberg, O. F. (1988). Object relations theory in clinical practice. *Psychoanalytic Quarterly*, 57: 481–504.

Kerz-Ruehling, I. (1986). Freuds Theorie der Einsicht. *Psyche*, 40: 97–123.

Khan, M. M. R. (1960). Regression and integration in the analytic setting. *International Journal of Psycho-Analysis*, 41: 130–146.

Khan, M. M. R. (1963). Silence as communication. *Bulletin of the Menninger Clinic*, 27: 300–317.

Khan, M. M. R. (1972). Dread of surrender to resourceless dependence in the analytic situation. *International Journal of Psycho-
Analysis*, 53: 225–230.

King, P. (1974). Notes on the psychoanalysis of older patients. Reappraisal of the potentialities for change during the second half of
life. *Journal of Analytical Psychology*, 19: 22–37.

Klauber, J. (1972). On the relationship of transference and interpretation in psychoanalytic therapy. *International Journal of Psycho-
Analysis*, 53: 385–391.

Klauber, J. (1980). Formulating interpretations in clinical psycho-
analysis. *International Journal of Psycho-Analysis*, 61: 195–202.

Klauber, J. (1981). *Difficulties in the Analytic Encounter*. New York:
Jason Aronson. [Reprinted London: Karnac Books, 1986.]

Klein, M. (1932). *The Psycho-Analysis of Children*. London: Hogarth
Press.

Klein, M. (1946). Notes on some schizoid mechanisms. In: M. Klein,
P. Heimann, S. Isaacs, & J. Riviere (Eds.), *Developments in
Psycho-Analysis*. London: Hogarth Press, 1952. [Reprinted Lon-
don: Karnac Books, 1989.]

Klein, M. (1948). *Contributions to Psycho-Analysis*. London: Hogarth
Press.

Klein, M. (1957). Envy and gratitude. In: *Envy and Gratitude and
Other Works, 1946–1963*. London: Hogarth Press, 1975.

Kluewer, R. (1983). Agieren und Mitagieren. *Psyche*, 37: 828–840.

Knight, R. P. (1940). Introjection, projection and identification.
Psychoanalytic Quarterly, 9: 334–341.

Knight, R. P. (1953). Borderline states. *Bulletin of the Menninger
Clinic*, 17: 1–12.

Koehler, W. (1925). *The Mentality of Apes*. New York: Harcourt Brace
& World Inc.

Kohut, H. (1966). Forms and transformations of narcissism. In: P.
Ornstein (Ed.), *The Search For the Self*. New York: International
Universities Press, 1978.

Kohut, H. (1968). The psychoanalytic treatment of narcissistic
personality disorders. Outline of a systematic approach. *The
Psychoanalytic Study of the Child*, 23: 86–113.

Kohut, H. (1971). *The Analysis of the Self*. New York: International
Universities Press.

Kohut, H. (1977). *The Restoration of the Self*. New York: International Universities Press.

Kohut, H. (1984). *How Does Analysis Cure?* Chicago: University of Chicago Press.

Kraepelin, E. (1906). *Lectures on Clinical Psychiatry*. New York: Hafner, 1969.

Kramer, M. K. (1959). On the continuation of the analytic process after psychoanalysis. *International Journal of Psycho-Analysis*, 40: 17–25.

Kris, E. (1951). Ego psychology and interpretation in psychoanalytic therapy. *Psychoanalytic Quarterly*, 20: 15–29.

Kris, E. (1952). *Explorations in Art*. New York: International Universities Press.

Kris, E. (1956a). The recovery of childhood memories in psychoanalysis. *The Psychoanalytic Study of the Child*, 11: 54–88.

Kris, E. (1956b). On some vicissitudes of insight in psychoanalysis. *International Journal of Psycho-Analysis*, 37: 445–455.

Kubie, L. S. (1950). *Practical and Theoretical Aspects of Psychoanalysis*. New York: International Universities Press.

Lampl-De Groot, J. (1967). On obstacles standing in the way of psycho-analytic cure. *The Psychoanalytic Study of the Child*, 22: 20–35.

Langs, R. J. (1975). The therapeutic relationship and deviations in technique. *International Journal of Psychoanalytic Psychotherapy*, 4: 106–141.

Langs, R. J. (1976). *The Therapeutic Interaction, Vols. 1 and 2*. New York: Jason Aronson.

Langs, R. J. (1978). The adaptational-interactional dimension of counter-transference. *Contemporary Psychoanalysis*, 14: 502–533.

Laplanche, J., & Pontalis, J. B. (1973). *The Language of Psychoanalysis*. London: Hogarth Press. [Reprinted London: Karnac Books, 1988.]

Lasky, R. (1989). Some determinants of the male analyst's capacity to identify with female patients. *International Journal of Psycho-Analysis*, 70: 405–418.

Leider, R. J. (reporter) (1984). Panel: The neutrality of the analyst in the analytic situation. *Journal of the American Psychoanalytic Association*, 32: 573–585.

Leites, N. (1977). Transference interpretations only? *International Journal of Psycho-Analysis*, 58: 275–287.

Lester, E. P. (1985). The female analyst and the erotized transference. *International Journal of Psycho-Analysis*, 66: 283–293.

Levy, J. (1982). A particular kind of negative therapeutic reaction based on Freud's 'borrowed guilt'. *International Journal of Psycho-Analysis*, 63: 361–368.

Lewin, B. (1950). *The Psychoanalysis of Elation*. New York: W. W. Norton.

Lewin, B. (1961). Reflections on depression. *Psychoanalytic Study of the Child*, 16: 321–331.

Lidz, T., Fleck, S., & Cornelison, A. (Eds.) (1965). *Schizophrenia and the Family*. New York: International Universities Press.

Limentani, A. (1966). A re-evaluation of acting out in relation to working through. *International Journal of Psycho-Analysis*, 47: 274–282.

Limentani, A. (1981). On some positive aspects of the negative therapeutic reaction. *International Journal of Psycho-Analysis*, 62: 379–390.

Lipton, S. D. (1977). Clinical observations on resistance to the transference. *International Journal of Psycho-Analysis*, 58: 463–472.

Little, M. (1951). Countertransference and the patients response to it. *International Journal of Psycho-Analysis*, 32: 32–40.

Little, M. (1958). On delusional transference (transference psychosis). *International Journal of Psycho-Analysis*, 39: 134–138.

Little, M. (1960a). On basic unity. *International Journal of Psycho-Analysis*, 41: 377–384.

Little, M. (1960b). Countertransference. *British Journal of Medical Psychology*, 33: 39–31.

Little, M. (1966). Transference in borderline states. *International Journal of Psycho-Analysis*, 47: 476–485.

Loewald, H. W. (1960). On the therapeutic action of psychoanalysis. *International Journal of Psycho-Analysis*, 41: 16–33.

Loewald, H. W. (1972). Freud's conception of the negative therapeutic reaction with comments on instinct theory. *Journal of the American Psychoanalytic Association*, 20: 235–245.

Loewald, H. W. (1974). Current status of the concept of infantile neurosis: discussion. *The Psychoanalytic Study of the Child*, 29: 183–190.

Loewald, H. W. (1979). Reflections of the psychoanalytic process and its therapeutic potential. *The Psychoanalytic Study of the Child*, 34: 155–168.

Loewald, H. W. (1986). Transference-countertransference. *Journal of the American Psychoanalytic Association*, 34: 275–287.

Loewenstein, R. M. (1951). The problem of interpretation. *Psychoanalytic Quarterly*, 20: 1–14.

Loewenstein, R. M. (1954). Some remarks on defences, autonomous ego and psychoanalytic technique. *International Journal of Psycho-Analysis*, 35: 188–193.

Loewenstein, R. M. (1969). Developments in the theory of transference in the last fifty years. *International Journal of Psycho-Analysis*, 50: 583–588.

London, N. J. (1987). Discussion: in defence of the transference neurosis concept: a process and interactional definition. *Psychoanalytic Inquiry*, 7: 587–598.

Lorand, S. (1958). Resistance. *Psychoanalytic Quarterly*, 27: 462–464.

Mahler, M. S. (1968). *On Human Symbiosis and the Vicissitudes of Individuation, Vol. 1.* New York: International Universities Press.

Mahler, M. S., Pine, F., & Bergman, A. (1975). *The Psychological Birth of the Human Infant: Symbiosis and Individuation.* New York: Basic Books. [Reprinted London: Karnac Books, 1985.]

Main, T. F. (1957). The ailment. *British Journal of Medical Psychology*, 30: 129–145.

Main, T. F. (1989). *The Ailment and Other Psychoanalytic Essays.* London: Free Association Books.

Mangham, C. A. (1981). Insight: pleasurable affects associated with insight and their origins in infancy. *The Psychoanalytic Study of the Child*, 36: 271–277.

Martin, A. R. (1952). The dynamics of insight. *American Journal of Psychoanalysis*, 12: 24–38.

Masterson, J. (1972). *Treatment of the Borderline Adolescent. A Developmental Approach.* New York: Wiley-Interscience.

Masterson, J. (1976). *Psychotherapy of the Borderline Adult. A Developmental Approach.* New York: Brunner/Mazel.

Masterson, J. (1978). *New Perspectives on Psychotherapy of the Borderline Adult.* New York: Brunner/Mazel.

McDougall, J. (1978). Primitive communication and the use of countertransference. *Contemporary Psychoanalysis*, 14: 173–209.

McLaughlin, J. T. (1981). Transference, psychic reality and countertransference. *Psychoanalytic Quarterly*, 50: 639–664.

McLaughlin, J. T. (1983). Some observations on the application of frame theory to the psychoanalytic situation and process. *Psychoanalytic Quarterly*, 52: 167–179.

Meissner, W. W. (1978). Theoretical assumptions of concepts of the borderline personality. *Journal of the American Psychoanalytic Association*, 26: 559–598.

Meltzer, D. (1967). *The Psychoanalytical Process*. London: Heinemann.

Menninger, R. (1958). *Theory of Psychoanalytic Technique*. New York: Basic Books.

Michels, R. (1986). Oedipus and insight. *Psychoanalytic Quarterly*, 55: 599–617.

Mishler, E. G., & Waxler, N. E. (1966). Family interaction patterns and schizophrenia: a review of current theories. *International Journal of Psychiatry*, 2: 375–413.

Mitscherlich-Nielsen, M. (1968). Contribution to symposium on acting out. *International Journal of Psycho-Analysis*, 49: 188–192.

Modell, A. H. (1984). *Psychoanalysis in a New Context*. New York: International Universities Press.

Modell, A. H. (1988). The centrality of the psychoanalytic setting and the changing aims of treatment. *Psychoanalytic Quarterly*, 57: 577–596.

Modell, A. H. (1989). The psychoanalytic setting as a container of multiple levels of reality: a perspective of the theory of psychoanalytic treatment. *Psychoanalytic Inquiry*, 9: 67–87.

Moeller, M. L. (1977a). Zur Theorie der Gegenübertragung. *Psyche*, 31: 142–166.

Moeller, M. L. (1977b). Self and object in countertransference. *International Journal of Psycho-Analysis*, 58: 365–374.

Money-Ryrle, R. E. (1956). Normal counter-transference and some of its deviations. *International Journal of Psycho-Analysis*, 37: 360–366.

Moore, B. E., & Fine, B. D. (1967). *A Glossary of Psychoanalytic Terms and Concepts*. New York: American Psychoanalytic Association.

Moore, B. E., & Fine, B. D. (1990). *Psychoanalytic Terms and Concepts*. New Haven, CT: The American Psychoanalytic Association and Yale University Press.

Morgenthaler, F. (1978). *Technik. Zur Dialektik der psychoanalytischen Praxis*. Frankfurt: Syndikat.

Muslin, H. (1986). On working through in self psychology. In: A. Goldberg, *Progress in Self Psychology, Vol. 2*. New York: International Universities Press.

Myerson, P. A. (1960). Awareness and stress: post-psychoanalytic utilization of insight. *International Journal of Psycho-Analysis*, 41: 147–156.

Myerson, P. A. (1963). Assimilation of unconscious material. *International Journal of Psycho-Analysis*, 44: 317–327.

Myerson, P. A. (1965). Modes of insight. *Journal of the American Psychoanalytic Association*, 13: 771–792.

Naiman, J. (reporter) (1976). Panel: The fundamentals of psychic change in clinical practice. *International Journal of Psycho-Analysis*, 57: 411–418.

Neubauer, P. B. (1979). The role of insight in psychoanalysis. *Journal of the American Psychoanalytic Association*, 27 (supplement): 29–40.

Novey, S. (1962). The principle of 'working through' in psychoanalysis. *Journal of the American Psychoanalytic Association*, 10: 658–676.

Novey, S. (1968). *The Second Look*. Baltimore, MD: Johns Hopkins Press.

Novick, J. (1970). The vicissitudes of the 'working alliance' in the analysis of a latency girl. *The Psychoanalytic Study of the Child*, 25: 231–256.

Novick, J. (1980). Negative therapeutic motivation and negative therapeutic alliance. *The Psychoanalytic Study of the Child*, 35: 299–320.

Nunberg, H. (1920). The course of the libidinal conflict in a case of schizophrenia. In: *Practice and Theory of Psycho-Analysis*. New York: International Universities Press, 1948.

Nunberg, H. (1951). Transference and reality. *International Journal of Psycho-Analysis*, 32: 1–9.

Offenkrantz, W., & Tobin, A. (1978). Problems of the therapeutic alliance: analysis with simultaneous therapeutic and research goals. *International Review of Psychoanalysis*, 5: 217–230.

Ogden, T. H. (1983). The concept of internal object relations. *International Journal of Psycho-Analysis*, 64: 227–241.

Olinick, S. L. (1954). Some considerations of the use of questioning as a psychoanalytic technique. *Journal of the American Psychoanalytic Association*, 2: 57–66.

Olinick, S. L. (1964). The negative therapeutic reaction. *International Journal of Psycho-Analysis*, 45: 540–548.

Olinick, S. L. (reporter) (1970). Panel: Negative therapeutic reaction. *Journal of the American Psychoanalytic Association*, 18: 655–672.

Olinick, S. L. (1978). The negative therapeutic reaction: a retrospective fifteen years later. *Journal of the Philadelphia Association for Psychoanalysis*, 5: 165–176.

Olinick, S. L., Poland, W. S., Grigg, K. A., & Granatir, W. L. (1973). The psychoanalytic work ego: process and interpretation. *International Journal of Psycho-Analysis*, 54: 143–151.

Ornstein, P., & Ornstein, A. (1980). Formulating interpretations in clinical psychoanalysis. *International Journal of Psycho-Analysis*, 61: 203–211.

Orr, D. W. (1954). Transference and countertransference: a historical survey. *Journal of the American Psychoanalytic Association*, 2: 621–670.

O'Shaughnessy, E. (1983). Words and working through. *International Journal of Psycho-Analysis*, 64: 281–289.

Parkin, A. (1981). Repetition, mourning and working through. *International Journal of Psycho-Analysis*, 62: 271–281.

Person, E. (1983). Women in therapy: therapist gender as a variable. *International Review of Psychoanalysis*, 10: 193–204.

Person, E. (1985). The erotic transference in women and men: differences and consequences. *Journal of the American Academy of Psychoanalysis*, 13: 159–180.

Pick, I. B. (1985). Working through in the countertransference. *International Journal of Psycho-Analysis*, 66: 157–166.

Poland, W. S. (1988). Insight and the analytic dyad. *Psychoanalytic Quarterly*, 57: 341–369.

Pressman, M. (1969a). The cognitive function of the ego in psychoanalysis: I. The search for insight. *International Journal of Psycho-Analysis*, 50: 187–196.

Pressman, M. (1969b). The cognitive function of the ego in psychoanalysis: II. Repression, incognizance and insight formation. *International Journal of Psycho-Analysis*, 50: 343–351.

Racker, H. (1953). A contribution to the problem of countertransference. *International Journal of Psycho-Analysis*, 34: 313–324.

Racker, H. (1957). The meanings and uses of countertransference. *Psychoanalytic Quarterly*, 26: 303–357.

Racker, H. (1968). *Transference and Countertransference*. New York: International Universities Press. [Reprinted London: Karnac Books, 1985.]

Rangell, L. (1955). On the psychoanalytic theory of anxiety. *Journal of the American Psychoanalytic Association*, 3: 389–414

Rangell, L. (1968). A point of view on acting out. *International Journal of Psycho-Analysis*, 49: 195–201.

Rangell, L. (1981). From insight to change. *Journal of the American Psychoanalytic Association*, 29: 119–141.

Rangell, L. (1985). Defense and resistance in psychoanalysis and life. In: H. P. Blum (Ed.), *Defense and Resistance*. New York: International Universities Press.

Rapaport, D. (1959). A historical survey of ego psychology. In: E. Erikson, *Identity and the Life Cycle*. New York: International Universities Press.

Rappaport, E. A. (1956). The management of an erotized transference. *Psychoanalytic Quarterly*, 25: 515–529.

Reed, G. S. (1987). Scientific and polemical aspects of the term 'transference neurosis' in psychoanalysis. *Psychoanalytic Inquiry*, 7: 465–483.

Reed, G. S. (1990). A reconsideration of the concept of transference neurosis. *International Journal of Psycho-Analysis*, 71: 205–217.

Reich, A. (1951). On countertransference. *International Journal of Psycho-Analysis*, 32: 25–31.

Reich, A. (1960). Further remarks on countertransference. *International Journal of Psycho-Analysis*, 41: 389–395.

Reich, W. (1928). On character analysis. In: R. Fliess (Ed.), *The Psycho-Analytic Reader*. London: Hogarth Press, 1950.

Reich, W. (1929). The genital character and the neurotic character. In: R. Fliess (Ed.), *The Psycho-Analytic Reader*. London: Hogarth Press, 1950.

Reich, W. (1933). *Charakteranalyse*. Vienna: private publication.

Reich, W. (1934). *Psychischer Kontakt und vegetative Strömung*. Copenhagen: Sexpol Verlag.

Reid, J. R., & Finesinger, J. E. (1952). The role of insight in psychotherapy. *American Journal of Psychiatry*, 108: 726–734.

Reider, N. (1957). Transference Psychosis. *Journal of the Hillside Hospital*, 6: 131–149.

Rexford, E. (1966). A survey of the literature. In: E. Rexford (Ed.), *Developmental Approach to Problems of Acting Out*. Monographs of the American Academy of Child Psychiatry, No. 1.

Richfield, J. (1954). An analysis of the concept of insight. *Psychoanalytic Quarterly*, 23: 390–408.

Rinsley, D. B. (1977). An object relations view of borderline personality. In: P. Hartocollis (Ed.), *Borderline Personality Disorders: The Concept, the Syndrome, the Patient*. New York: International Universities Press.

Rinsley, D. B. (1978). Borderline psychopathology: a review of aetiology, dynamics and treatment. *International Review of Psychoanalysis*, 5: 45–54.

Riviere, J. (1936). A contribution to the analysis of the negative therapeutic reaction. *International Journal of Psycho-Analysis*, 17: 304–320.

Romm, M. (1957). Transient psychotic episodes during psychoanalysis. *Journal of the American Psychoanalytic Association*, 5: 325–341.

Rosen, J. (1946). A method of resolving acute catatonic excitement. *Psychiatric Quarterly*, 20: 183–198.

Rosen, J. (1965). The concept of 'acting-in'. In: L. Abt & S. Weissman (Eds.), *Acting Out*. New York: Grune & Stratton.

Rosenfeld, H. A. (1952). Transference phenomena and transference analysis in an acute catatonic schizophrenic patient. *International Journal of Psycho-Analysis*, 33: 457–464.

Rosenfeld, H. A. (1954). Considerations regarding the psychoanalytic approach to acute and chronic schizophrenia. *International Journal of Psycho-Analysis*, 35: 135–140.

Rosenfeld, H. A. (1965a). *Psychotic States: A Psychoanalytic Approach*. London: Hogarth Press.

Rosenfeld, H. A. (1965b). An investigation into the need of neurotic and psychotic patients to act out during analysis. In: *Psychotic States: A Psychoanalytic Approach*. London: Hogarth Press. [Reprinted London: Karnac Books, 1985.]

Rosenfeld, H. A. (1968). Negative therapeutic reaction. Unpublished paper.

Rosenfeld, H. A. (1969). On the treatment of psychotic states by psychoanalysis: an historical approach. *International Journal of Psycho-Analysis*, 50: 615–631.

Rosenfeld, H. A. (1971). A clinical approach to the psychoanalytic theory of the life and death instincts: an investigation into the aggressive aspects of narcissism. *International Journal of Psycho-Analysis*, 52: 169–178.

Rosenfeld, H. A. (1972). A critical appreciation of James Strachey's paper on the nature of the therapeutic action of psychoanalysis. *International Journal of Psycho-Analysis*, 53: 455–461.

Rosenfeld, H. A. (1975). Negative therapeutic reaction. In: P. Giovacchini (Ed.), *Tactics and Technique in Psychoanalytic Therapy, Vol. 2*. New York: Jason Aronson.

Rothstein, A. (reporter) (1983). Panel: Interpretation: Toward a contemporary understanding of the term. *Journal of the American Psychoanalytic Association*, 31: 237–245.

Roussillon, R. (1985). La réaction thérapeutique négative du protiste au jeu de construction. *Revue française de psychanalyse*, 49: 597–621.

Rycroft, C. (1958). An enquiry into the function of words in the psychoanalytical situation. *International Journal of Psycho-Analysis*, 39: 408–415.

Rycroft, C. (1968). *A Critical Dictionary of Psychoanalysis*. London: Thomas Nelson.

Rycroft, C. (1985). *Psychoanalysis and Beyond*. London: Chatto & Windus.

Salzman, L. (1960). The negative therapeutic reaction. In: J. H. Masserman (Ed.), *Science and Psychoanalysis, Vol. 3* (pp. 303–313). New York: Grune & Stratton.

Sandler, J. (1959). On the repetition of early childhood relationships. In: J. Sandler (Ed.), *From Safety to Superego*. New York: Guilford, 1987. London: Karnac Books, 1987.

Sandler, J. (1960a). The background of safety. In: J. Sandler (Ed.), *From Safety to Superego*. New York: Guilford, 1987. London: Karnac Books, 1987.

Sandler, J. (1960b). On the concept of superego. In: Sandler (Ed.), *From Safety to Superego*. New York: Guilford, 1987. London: Karnac Books, 1987.

Sandler, J. (1968). Psychoanalysis: an introductory survey. In: W. G. Joffe (Ed.), *What Is Psychoanalysis?* London: Bailliere, Tindall & Cassell.

Sandler, J. (1969). *On the Communication of Psychoanalytic Thought*. Leiden: University Press.

Sandler, J. (1976). Countertransference and role-responsiveness. *International Review of Psycho-Analysis*, 3: 43–47.

Sandler, J. (1983). Reflections on some relations between psychoanalytic concepts and psychoanalytic practice. *International Journal of Psycho-Analysis*, 64: 35–45.

Sandler, J. (Ed.) (1987). *Projection, Identification, Projective Identification*. Madison CT: International Universities Press. London: Karnac Books.

Sandler, J. (1988). Psychoanalytic technique and 'Analysis terminable and interminable'. *International Journal of Psycho-Analysis*, 69: 335–345.

Sandler, J. (1990a). Internal objects and internal object relationships. *Psychoanalytic Inquiry*, 10: 163–181.

Sandler, J. (1990b). Internal object relations. *Journal of the American Psychoanalytic Association*, 38: 859–880.

Sandler, J., Dare, C., & Holder, A. (1970a). Basic psychoanalytic concepts: I. The extension of clinical concepts outside the psychoanalytic situation. *British Journal of Psychiatry*, 116: 551–554.

Sandler, J., Dare, C., & Holder, A. (1970b). Basic psychoanalytic concepts: III. Transference. *British Journal of Psychiatry*, 116: 667–672.

Sandler, J., Dare, C., & Holder, A. (1970c). Basic psychoanalytic concepts: VIII. Special forms of transference. *British Journal of Psychiatry*, 117: 561–568.

Sandler, J., Dare, C., & Holder, A. (1970d). Basic psychoanalytic concepts: IX. Working through. *British Journal of Psychiatry*, 117: 617–621.

Sandler, J., Dare, C., & Holder, A. (1971). Basic psychoanalytic concepts: X. Interpretations and other interventions. *British Journal of Psychiatry*, 118: 53–59.

Sandler, J., Dare, C., & Holder, A. (1973). *The Patient and the Analyst* (first edition). New York: International Universities Press. [Reprinted London: Karnac Books, 1979.]

Sandler, J., & Freud, A. (1985). *The Analysis of Defense*. New York: International Universities Press.

Sandler, J., Holder, A., & Dare, C. (1970a). Basic psychoanalytic concepts: II. The treatment alliance. *British Journal of Psychiatry*, 11: 555–558.

Sandler, J., Holder, A., & Dare, C. (1970b). Basic psychoanalytic concepts: IV. Counter-transference. *British Journal of Psychiatry*, 117: 83–88.

Sandler, J., Holder, A., & Dare, C. (1970c). Basic psychoanalytic concepts: V. Resistance. *British Journal of Psychiatry*, 117: 215–221.

Sandler, J., Holder, A., & Dare, C. (1970d). Basic psychoanalytic concepts: VI. Acting out. *British Journal of Psychiatry*, 117: 329–334.

Sandler, J., Holder A., & Dare, C. (1970e). Basic psychoanalytic concepts: VII. The negative therapeutic reaction. *British Journal of Psychiatry*, 117: 431–435.

Sandler, J., Holder A., & Meers, D. (1963). The ego ideal and the ideal self. *The Psychoanalytic Study of the Child*, 18: 139–158.

Sandler, J., Holder A., Kawenoka, M., Kennedy, H. E., & Neurath, L. (1969). Notes on some theoretical and clinical aspects of transference. *International Journal of Psycho-Analysis*, 50: 633–645.

Sandler, J., & Joffe, W. G. (1968). Psychoanalytic psychology and learning theory. In: J. Sandler (Ed.), *From Safety to Superego*. New York: Guilford, 1987. London: Karnac Books, 1987.

Sandler, J., & Joffe, W. G. (1969). Toward a basic psychoanalytic model. In: J. Sandler (Ed.), *From Safety to Superego*. New York: Guilford, 1987. London: Karnac Books, 1987.

Sandler, J., & Joffe, W. G. (1970). Discussion of towards a basic psychoanalytic model. *International Journal of Psycho-Analysis*, 51: 183–193.

Sandler, J., Kennedy, H., & Tyson, R. L. (1980). *The Technique of Child Analysis: Discussions with Anna Freud*. Cambridge, MA: Harvard University Press. [Reprinted London: Karnac Books, 1990.]

Sandler, J., & Sandler, A.-.M. (1984). The past unconscious, the present unconscious, and interpretation of the transference. *Psychoanalytic Inquiry*, 4: 367–399.

Saul, L. J. (1962). The erotic transference. *Psychoanalytic Quarterly*, 31: 54–61.

Saussure, J. de (1979). Narcissistic elements in the negative therapeutic reaction. *Paper to 3rd Conference of the European Psycho-Analytical Federation, London*.

Schafer, R. (1976). *A New Language for Psychoanalysis*. New Haven, CT/London: Yale University Press.

Schafer, R. (1977). The interpretation of transference and the conditions for loving. *Journal of the American Psychoanalytic Association*, 25: 335–362.

Schafer, R. (1979). The appreciative analytic attitude and the construction of multiple histories. *Psychoanalysis and Contemporary Thought*, 2: 13–24.

Schafer, R. (1980). Narration in psychoanalytic dialogue. *Critical Inquiry*, 7: 29–53.

Schafer, R. (1983). *The Analytic Attitude*. New York: Basic Books.

Schmale, H. T. (1966). Working through [panel report]. *Journal of the American Psychoanalytic Association*, 14: 172–182.

Schon, D. A. (1963). *The Displacement of Concepts*. London: Tavistock.

Schowalter, J. E. (1976). Therapeutic alliance and the role of speech in child analysis. *The Psychoanalytic Study of the Child*, 31: 415–436.

Searles, H. F. (1961). Phases of patient-therapist interaction in the psychotherapy of chronic schizophrenia. *British Journal of Medical Psychology*, 34: 160–193.

Searles, H. F. (1963). Transference psychosis in the psychotherapy of chronic schizophrenia. *International Journal of Psycho-Analysis*, 44: 249–281.

Sedler, M. J. (1983). Freud's concept of working through. *Psychoanalytic Quarterly*, 52: 73–98.

Segal, H. (1962). The curative factors in psychoanalysis. *International Journal of Psycho-Analysis*, 43: 212–217.

Segal, H. (1964). *Introduction to the Work of Melanie Klein*. London: Heinemann. [Reprinted London: Karnac Books, 1988.]

Segal, H. (1981). Melanie Klein's technique. In: *The Work of Hanna Segal. A Kleinian Approach to Clinical Practice*. New York: Jason Aronson. [Reprinted London: Karnac Books, 1986.]

Segal, H. (1977). Countertransference. *International Journal of Psychoanalytic Psychotherapy*, 6: 31–37.

Segal, H. (1983). Some clinical implications of Melanie Klein's work. *International Journal of Psycho-Analysis*, 64: 269–280.

Segal, H., & Britton, R. (1981). Interpretation and primitive psychic processes: a Kleinian view. *Psychoanalytic Inquiry*, 1: 267–277.

Shane, M. (1979). The developmental approach to 'working through' in the analytic process. *International Journal of Psycho-Analysis*, 60: 375–382.

Shapiro, E. R., Shapiro, R. L., Zinner, J., & Berkowitz, D. A. (1977). The borderline ego and the working alliance: indications for family and individual treatment in adolescence. *International Journal of Psycho-Analysis*, 58: 77–87.

Sharpe, E. F. (1947). The psycho-analyst. *International Journal of Psycho-Analysis*, 28: 1–6.

Silverberg, W. V. (1955). Acting out versus insight: a problem in psychoanalytic technique. *Psychoanalytic Quarterly*, 24: 527–544.

Silverman, M. A. (1985). Countertransference and the myth of the perfectly analyzed analyst. *Psychoanalytic Quarterly*, 54: 175–199.

Sodré, I. (1990). Treatment alliances: therapeutic and anti-therapeutic. *Paper to Weekend Conference for English-speaking Members of European Societies, London.*

Spence, D. P. (1982). *Narrative Truth and Historical Truth*. New York: Norton.

Spence, D. P. (1986). When interpretation masquerades as explanation. *Journal of the American Psychoanalytic Association*, 34: 3–22.

Spillius, E. (1979). Clinical reflections on the negative therapeutic reaction. *Paper to 3rd Conference of the European Psycho-Analytical Federation, London.*

Spillius, E. (1983). Some developments from the work of Melanie Klein. *International Journal of Psycho-Analysis*, 64: 321–332.

Spillius, E. B. (Ed.) (1988). *Melanie Klein Today: Vol. 2, Mainly Practice*. London: Routledge.

Spitz, R. (1956). Countertransference: comments on its varying role in the analytic situation. *Journal of the American Psychoanalytic Association*, 4: 256–265.

Spruiell, V. (1983). The rules and frames of the psychoanalytic situation. *Psychoanalytic Quarterly*, 52: 1–33.

Sterba, R. (1934). The fate of the ego in analytic therapy. *International Journal of Psycho-Analysis*, 15: 117–126.

Sterba, R. (1940). The dynamics of the dissolution of the transference resistance. *Psychoanalytic Quarterly*, 9: 363–379.

Sterba, R. F. (1953). Clinical and therapeutic aspects of character resistance. *Psychoanalytic Quarterly*, 22: 1–20.

Stern, A. (1924). On the countertransference in psychoanalysis. *Psychoanalytic Review*, 11: 166–174.

Stern, D. (1985). *The Interpersonal World of the Infant*. New York: Basic Books.

Stewart, W. A. (1963). An inquiry into the concept of working through. *Journal of the American Psychoanalytic Association*, 11: 474–499.

Stone, L. (1961). *The Psychoanalytic Situation*. New York: International Universities Press.

Stone, L. (1967). The psychoanalytic situation and transference: postscript to an earlier communication. *Journal of the American Psychoanalytic Association*, 15: 3–58.

Stone, L. (1973). On resistance to the psychoanalytic process; some thoughts on its nature and motivations. In: B. B. Rubenstein (Ed.), *Psychoanalysis and Contemporary Science, Vol. 2*. New York: Macmillan.

Stone, M. (1980). *The Borderline Syndromes*. New York: McGraw-Hill.

Strachey, J. (1934). The nature of the therapeutic action of psychoanalysis. *International Journal of Psycho-Analysis*, 15: 127–159.

Strupp, H. H. (1960). *Psychotherapists in Action*. New York: Grune & Stratton.

Sullivan, H. S. (1931). The modified psycho-analytic treatment of schizophrenia. *American Journal of Psychiatry*, 11: 519–540.

Swartz, J. (1967). The erotized transference and other transference problems. *Psychoanalytic Forum*, 3: 307–318.

Szasz, T. S. (1963). The concept of transference. *International Journal of Psycho-Analysis*, 44: 432–443.

Tarachow, S. (1963). *An Introduction to Psychotherapy*. New York: International Universities Press.

Tartakoff, H. H. (1956). Recent books on psychoanalytic technique: a comparative study. *Journal of the American Psychoanalytic Association*, 4: 318–343.

Thomä, H. (1984). Der Beitrag des Psychoanalytikers zur Uebertragung. *Psyche*, 38: 29–62.

Thomä, H., & Kächele, H. (1987). *Psychoanalytic Practice*. New York: Springer.

Tower, L. E. (1956). Countertransference. *Journal of the American Psychoanalytic Association*, 4: 224–255.

Tylim, I. (1978). Narcissistic transference and countertransference in adolescent treatment. *The Psychoanalytic Study of the Child*, 33: 279–292.

Tyson, P. (1980). The gender of the analyst in relation to transference and countertransference manifestations in prelatency children. *The Psychoanalytic Study of the Child*, 35: 321–338.

Tyson, R. L. (1986). Countertransference evolution in theory and practice. *Journal of the American Psychoanalytic Association*, 34: 251–274.

Valenstein, A. F. (1962). The psychoanalytic situation: affects, emotional reliving and insight in the psycho-analytic process. *International Journal of Psycho-Analysis*, 43: 315–324.

Valenstein, A. F. (1973). On attachment to painful feelings and the negative therapeutic reaction. *The Psychoanalytic Study of the Child*, 28: 365–392.

Valenstein, A. F. (reporter) (1974). Panel: Transference. *International Journal of Psycho-Analysis*, 55: 311–321.

Valenstein, A. F. (1983). Working through and resistance to change: insight and the action system. *Journal of the American Psychoanalytic Association*, 31 (supplement 3): 353–373.

Van Dam, H. (1987). Countertransference during an analyst's brief illness. *Journal of the American Psychoanalytic Association*, 35: 647–655.

Van Der Leeuw, P. J. (1979). Some additional remarks on problems of transference. *Journal of the American Psychoanalytic Association*, 27: 315–326.

Vianna, H. B. (1974). A peculiar form of resistance to psychoanalytical treatment. *International Journal of Psycho-Analysis*, 55: 439–444.

Vianna, H. B. (1975). A peculiar form of resistance to psychoanalytical treatment: a reply to the discussion by Willy Baranger. *International Journal of Psycho-Analysis*, 56: 263.

Waelder, R. (1956). Introduction to the discussion on problems of transference. *International Journal of Psycho-Analysis*, 37: 367–368.

Wallerstein, R. S. (1967). Reconstruction and mastery in the transference psychosis. *Journal of the American Psychoanalytic Association*, 15: 551–583.

Wallerstein, R. S. (1983). Self psychology and 'classical' psychoanalytic psychology: the nature of their relationship. *Psychoanalysis and Contemporary Thought*, 6: 553–595.

Wallerstein, R. S. (1988). One psychoanalysis or many? *International Journal of Psycho-Analysis*, 69: 5–21.

Wexler, M. (1960). Hypotheses concerning ego deficiency in schizophrenia. In: *The Out-Patient Treatment of Schizophrenia*. New York: Grune & Stratton.

Winnicott, D. W. (1949). Hate in the countertransference. *International Journal of Psycho-Analysis*, 30: 69–74.

Winnicott, D. W. (1951). Transitional objects and transitional phenomena. In: *Collected Papers: Through Paediatrics to Psycho-Analysis*. London: Tavistock Publications, 1958. [Reprinted London: Karnac Books, 1991.]

Winnicott, D. W. (1954). Metapsychological and clinical aspects of regression within the psychoanalytical set-up. In: *Collected Papers: Through Paediatrics to Psycho-Analysis*. London: Tavistock Publications, 1958. [Reprinted London: Karnac Books, 1991.]

Winnicott, D. W. (1955). Clinical varieties of transference. In: *Collected Papers: Through Paediatrics to Psycho-Analysis*. London: Tavistock Publications, 1958. [Reprinted London: Karnac Books, 1991.]

Winnicott, D. W. (1960). Countertransference. *British Journal of Medical Psychology*, 33: 17–21.

Winnicott, D. W. (1965). *The Maturational Processes and the Facilitating Environment*. London: Hogarth Press. [Reprinted London: Karnac Books, 1990.]

Winnicott, D. W. (1971). *Playing and Reality*. London: Tavistock Publications.

Wolf, E. (1979). Countertransference in disorders of the self. In: L. Epstein & A. Feiner (Eds.), *Countertransference*. New York: Jason Aronson.

Wrye, H. K., & Welles, J. K. (1989). The maternal erotic transference. *International Journal of Psycho-Analysis*, 70: 673–684.

Wylie, H. W., & Wylie, M. L. (1987). The older analysand: countertransference issues in psychoanalysis. *International Journal of Psycho-Analysis*, 68: 343–352.

Wynne, L., & Singer, M. (1963). Thought disorder and family relations of schizophrenics. *Archives of General Psychiatry*, 9: 191–198, 199–206.

Zeligs, M. (1957). Acting in. *Journal of the American Psychoanalytic Association*, 5: 685–706.

Zetzel, E. R. (1956). Current concepts of transference. *International Journal of Psycho-Analysis*, 37: 369–376.

Zetzel, E. R. (1958). Therapeutic alliance in the analysis of hysteria. In: *The Capacity For Emotional Growth*. London: Hogarth Press, 1970. [Reprinted London: Karnac Books, 1987.]

Zilboorg, G. (1952). The emotional problem and the therapeutic role of insight. *Psychoanalytic Quarterly, 21:* 1–24.

INDEX